D0464141

Also by Dave Itzkoff

Cocaine's Son: A Memoir

Lads: A Memoir of Manhood

MAD AS HELL

MAD AS HELL

THE MAKING OF *NETWORK* AND THE FATEFUL VISION OF THE ANGRIEST MAN IN MOVIES

DAVE ITZKOFF

TIMES BOOKS

HENRY HOLT AND COMPANY

NEW YORK

Times Books
Henry Holt and Company, LLC
Publishers since 1866
175 Fifth Avenue
New York, New York 10010

Henry Holt® is a registered trademark of Henry Holt and Company, LLC.

Copyright © 2014 by Dave Itzkoff
All rights reserved.
Distributed in Canada by Raincoast Book Distribution Limited

Grateful acknowledgment is made to Dan Chayefsky for permission to reprint excerpts of material from the Paddy Chayefsky papers at the Billy Rose Theatre Division of the New York Public Library for the Performing Arts.

Excerpts from *The Hospital* and *Network* by Paddy Chayefsky. Reprinted by permission of Hal Leonard/Applause Theatre Books and Dan Chayefsky.

Network. By Paddy Chayefsky. Copyright © 1976 Metro-Goldwyn-Mayer Inc. and United Artists Corporation. All rights reserved. Reprinted with permission of Applause Theatre and Cinema Books, LLC.

The Hospital. By Paddy Chayefsky. Copyright © 1971 Simcha Productions. Reprinted with permission of Applause Theatre and Cinema Books, LLC.

Library of Congress Cataloging-in-Publication Data

Itzkoff, Dave.
    Mad as hell : the making of Network and the fateful vision of the angriest man in movies / David Itzkoff.
        pages   cm
    Includes index.
    ISBN 978-0-8050-9569-2 (hardback)—ISBN 978-0-8050-9570-8 (electronic book)
    1. Network (Motion picture)   2. Chayefsky, Paddy, 1923–1981—Criticism and interpretation.   I. Title.
    PN1997.N385I89 2014
    808.2'3—dc23   2013018292

Henry Holt books are available for special promotions and premiums.
For details contact: Director, Special Markets.

First Edition 2014
Designed by Meryl Sussman Levavi

Printed in the United States of America
1   3   5   7   9   10   8   6   4   2

For Amy, who makes me happy as hell

Slowly, the world we're living in is getting smaller, and all we say is, "Please, at least leave us alone in our living rooms. Let me have my toaster and my teevee and my steel-belted radials and I won't say anything. Just leave us alone."

Well, I'm not going to leave you alone.

I want you to get *mad*.

—HOWARD BEALE, *Network*

Contents

MAD AS
HELL

PROLOGUE

He was at his best when he was angry. It wasn't simply that so many things bothered him, or that when they did, they irritated him to the fullest possible degree. But where others avoided conflict, he cultivated it and embraced it. His fury nourished him, making him intense and unpredictable, but also keeping him focused and productive. He was not generally the sort of person who felt the need to clench his fists in violence or submerge his sorrows in drink. But he knew what it was like to have desires and see them denied; he knew how it felt to cry out and not be heard. His outrage simmered in his spleen and surged through his veins, collecting in his fingertips until it pushed his pen across paper and punched the keys of his typewriter. He wrestled his rancor into words and sentences and speeches. When Paddy Chayefsky's characters spoke, they spoke with his aggravated, articulate voice, and yet they seemed to speak for everyone.

While his career was in ascendance, he was hailed as the dramatist of the common man, whose ear for the language of the underclass was so uncanny that it was said he must have transcribed it from a tape recorder. His best-known characters were thwarted people who feared nothing so much as unfulfillment, whose most emphatic and memorable dialogue poured out of them in aggressive bursts, arriving in explosive climaxes after scene upon scene of unvoiced frustration and unresolved conflict. Whether he was imagining the inner life of a lowly, lovelorn butcher or the impotent chief of medicine at a major metropolitan hospital, Chayefsky could relate to these men. Their struggle for even a minimal amount of autonomy mirrored their creator's refusal to cede any amount of control in his life and especially in his work.

He had all the accumulated resentments of a man of his time and place, who had lived through the Great Depression and fought in World War II, and who strived to fulfill the dreams of his immigrant parents and outpace anyone he regarded as a rival or a colleague. He was a short, stocky Bronx-born Jew, a son of the Grand Concourse with narrow eyes framed by large, owlish glasses, and a head of unkempt brown and white hair, with an impish goatee to match. He had no regard for fashion or convention and possessed a mischievous, cantankerous personality. A sincere compliment directed his way could trigger his venomous invective as easily as a well-deployed insult or dirty joke could earn his respect.

Chayefsky was the rare writer whose reputation earned him absolute authority on his projects—supremacy above even the directors and producers he worked with—and he sought only projects where he was allowed this authority. But what defined his writing now, in 1974, was that none of it was working. Back in the 1950s it had taken only a few years of toiling in that newly created format of television for him to cast it aside in favor of a more respectable and lucrative career in motion pictures; and only a few more years of disappointment there to leave film for the theater, where he was certain he would retain total control over the material he created; and only a few more years of total discouragement in that field to abandon the stage and return to the movies.

At the age of fifty-one, he could get his film scripts commissioned but not produced; he could get his television pilots shot but couldn't get them on the air; and it would require the collective disappearance of every other form of dramatic art before he ever wrote another play for Broadway. The Academy Award he had won for his screenwriting two years earlier seemed less like an affirmation of his talents than a solemn, faceless bookend to the Oscar he had received back in 1956: one statue to signify where the journey of a once-promising screenwriter started and the other to mark its termination.

It was not only the repeatedly obstructed ambition to have his work seen by audiences again that was bothering Chayefsky, although that was a concern. The mission that consumed him with unusual urgency was to say something universal and definitive, to make the lasting statement that the compass of his career had always pointed to and that would make him worthy of the attention he had commanded at his peak. Every rung he climbed on his way up had given Chayefsky a higher perch to see the world more clearly, and all he saw were problems he could not solve. At his Central Park West apartment awaited a wife who almost never ventured outside, as she suffered from a mysterious malady neither he nor any doctor could help with, and a self-destructive teenage son he could not understand. He feared constantly for his livelihood and was struggling with tax problems, while he watched with resigned astonishment as the city he called home and the country he loved appeared to be unraveling. Revolutions were springing up everywhere—politically, socially, artistically, cinematically—and he wanted no part of them.

Then there was television, a blossoming medium he had helped to define and popularize, with the potential for connecting every person on the planet in an instant. But in two quick decades it had become hopelessly, irrevocably corrupt, devaluing truth and alienating viewers from one another.

With so many threats stirring, it seemed irresponsible to Chayefsky for him to ignore them in his writing. Was he the only one who felt a growing risk of terrorist attacks by suicidal militants? Who saw a rising tide of anti-Semitism and hostility against Israel? Who felt the creeping influence of foreign powers—Arab powers—in the American economy? Yet the more frantically he sought to clarify the message he believed was being transmitted to him from a hundred different sources, the more certain he felt it was eluding him.

Take, for example, the screenplay that he had started researching a few months earlier. Having cast his gaze on the television business that had provided the springboard for his career, he had drawn up a roster of characters to populate the world of a fictional broadcasting company: producers, executives, underlings, corporate tycoons, political radicals, and a mentally unstable news anchor named Howard Beale. But Chayefsky could not determine how they fit together. Were they allegorical figures in a larger narrative about power and decadence, or were they just a bunch of grotesque caricatures? What did any of them have to do with the love story he was trying to thread through his script, and was that too conventional even to belong there?

Across the top of a piece of paper he had torn from a notebook, Chayefsky wrote in jagged capital letters nearly impaled by an aggressive underline: THE SHOW LACKS A POINT OF VIEW. Then, in a gentler, pleading cursive handwriting, he filled both sides of that page with his unflinching self-analysis of the project, which he believed was drifting into chaos.

"I guess what bothers me is that the picture seems to have no ultimate statement beyond the idea that a network would kill for ratings," he wrote.

Most crucially, he wondered, what was he even trying to say in this screenplay? Were there identifiable sides to this argument, and whose side was he on? Because if he couldn't answer that, what was he creating, if not more fuel for his pyre of curtailed efforts and unsatisfied aspirations?

"We are making some kind of statement about American society," he wrote, "and its lack of clarity is what's bothering me—Even more,

I'm not taking a stand—I'm not for anything or anyone—If we give Howard a speech at the end of the show, what would he say?"

Sometime later, on a piece of the blank yellow paper he more commonly used for his writing, Chayefsky started to answer this question by sketching out a few handwritten phrases: "I want you people to get mad—You don't have to organize or vote for reformers—You just have to get mad."

Within months, Chayefsky would harness his boundless capacity for anger and channel it into his script for a motion picture called *Network*, investing it with all the angst, anxiety, and paranoia he had ever felt. The resulting film, released in 1976, would become a potent document, instantly incendiary and wildly popular.

Network was a bundle of contradictions, the last gasp of an era of populist Hollywood filmmaking as expressed by a man who never subscribed to the movement; it used the resources of one mass medium to indict another and, beyond it, the degradation and emptiness of contemporary American life. *Network* scandalized the television news business, inflaming the influential denizens who took more offense at the cartoonish portrayal of their world than its author intended or expected. But by arriving at a moment of maximal national frustration, the movie made itself the center of an argument about society and personal identity and inserted itself into the cultural lexicon, earning money, winning awards, and lifting its creator to new heights of acclaim.

The eerie and uncanny prescience of *Network*—dismissed in its day even by some of its admirers as an impossibly absurd satire—was not limited to the moment in which it made its portentous debut. Not only did it seem to foretell the tragic death of one of its lead performers; it provided a road map for the unraveling of the monolithic broadcasting companies, the diminishment of their once-mighty news operations, and the path to a fragmented and unrecognizable media environment that the industry would follow, almost to the letter, over the next forty years.

The film also carried a personal warning to Chayefsky, who spent most of his professional life fearing that the messages in his writing were not being received by their audiences. *Network* was indeed his magnum opus, and the last movie that he would willingly put his name on. It would cost him nearly everything to make it exactly as he wanted it to be, and when it was done it would leave him with a stark lesson about the ultimate price of self-expression.

1

THE IMPOSTER

The problems, plural, with television, as enumerated by Paddy Chayefsky, included but were not limited to: its crassness, its stupidity, its chasing of fads and its embracing of gimmicks; its reduction of all that was distinctive and worthy of celebration in American culture to the basic food groups of game shows, songs, and dances; its compulsion to force everyone watching it to think the same thing at the same time; and its overall lack of artistic integrity. Also, it paid him too little.

He would recite his list of charges whenever he was given a platform, whether in a newspaper or magazine interview, on the radio, or, especially, on television itself. But on this day in 1969 he happened to be delivering his latest version of the familiar tirade amid the clanging of silverware and the clattering of plates in the dining room of the Carnegie Deli. The bustling, boisterous Midtown Manhattan restaurant, next door to the gray-brown brick building where Chayefsky kept his office in room 1106 at 850 Seventh Avenue, and a short walk from its esteemed namesake, Carnegie Hall, was a frequent site for the week-day court he convened at lunchtime. There, the deli's adoring maître d', Herbie Schlein, gave him linen napkins to wipe the coleslaw and Russian dressing from his face while other patrons had to make do with paper, and his table was reliably populated by pals such as Bob Fosse and Herb Gardner—office neighbors who rented their work spaces down the hall from his—and other select peers who could keep pace with his accomplishments, his mind, and his mouth.

At this particular session, he was joined by Howard Gottfried, a producer with whom he had been working to figure out a new project ever since Alan Jay Lerner fired Chayefsky as the scriptwriter of his musical Western *Paint Your Wagon*. (The songs, Chayefsky had told the celebrated lyricist of *Camelot* and *My Fair Lady*, were no good, and anyway his stars Lee Marvin and Clint Eastwood couldn't "sing for shit," and that was the end of that assignment.) Their companion was Mel Brooks, who had lately withstood some tough reviews for his directorial debut, a polarizing film satire about two shysters peddling a Broadway musical about Adolf Hitler, only to have the last laugh by winning an Oscar for his screenplay of *The Producers*. They were three Jewish show business veterans kibitzing around a table, and naturally there was some commiserating about which industry they had worked in was the worst of the bunch. It didn't take long for television to rise to the top of the heap.

Television, Chayefsky argued, offered the least creative control for writers and the lowest return on their investment. Where was its dignity? Where did it draw the line, and what wouldn't it do for a rating?

Surely it wasn't all bad, said Gottfried, the conciliatory industry professional. What about that first-rate production of *Death of a Salesman* with Lee J. Cobb that CBS ran a few years ago?

Irrelevant, Chayefsky countered. Television was a parvenu industry, constantly conscious of its image as a cultural wasteland. A passion for prestige trembles through the business, and suddenly all the networks race out to do meaningful programming. *Death of a Salesman* had been just a seasonal attack of respectability, like hay fever.

"What's next?" wondered Brooks, reaching for the darkest and least appetizing idea he could think of, one rife with murder, rape, and depravity. "A television show based on *The Threepenny Opera*?"

Were the rights still available? Gottfried wondered.

What difference would it make to a programming executive? Chayefsky said. He wouldn't know if *The Threepenny Opera* was written by Bertolt Brecht or Hy the plumber. He probably wouldn't know that Bertolt Brecht had been dead for seventeen years.

"Leave it to me," said Brooks, his eyes agleam as he stood up from his seat. "I'll call one of the networks."

"Now, don't pile it on," Chayefsky warned his friend while offering him a dime. "Remember, you're not Doctor Krankheit," he said, citing an old vaudeville sketch.

"Are you trying to tell me how to play this?" Brooks protested. He made his way to a phone booth and a few minutes later came back with the following report.

Having dialed up NBC, where both he and Chayefsky had long-standing relationships, he was connected to the programming department and asked for a certain executive there.

"Hello dere," Brooks had said, slipping into an old stage accent. "Dis here is Berrrrrtolt Brrrrecht. I vanted to talk about der TV rights to my musical mit Kurrrrt Weill, der *Thrrrreepenny Operrrra*."

"One moment, please," said the secretary who had taken the call. "Let me see if he's available." The receiver was placed down, but a conversation was still audible from within the office.

First, the secretary: "There's a Bertolt Brecht calling for you. Something about *The Threepenny Opera*?"

Then the executive: "What are you talking about? Bertolt Brecht is dead!"

And then the secretary again: "How can Bertolt Brecht be dead? He's on the phone for you right now!"

"Oh, well, that's different—put him on!"

And that was what Paddy Chayefsky thought of television.

There had been a time when Chayefsky could convince himself that television would sustain him for his entire career. In his foreword to a hardcover collection of his television dramas that was published in 1955, he affectionately observed that "television has been a kind medium" to him. Though it was his intention at some point to resume creating works for the stage, Chayefsky said then, "I have never written a script in television of which I was not at least partially proud. I hope to continue writing for the medium as long as I can."

Yet Chayefsky was unambiguously displeased by the restrictions he said TV imposed on his creative freedom, and in that same foreword he bluntly registered his annoyance. "In television," he said, "the writer is treated with a peculiar mixture of mock deference and outright contempt. He is rarely consulted about casting, his scripts are frequently mangled without his knowing about it, and he is certainly the most poorly paid person in the production."

With years of creative output still ahead of him, Chayefsky observed with foreboding awareness that his fellow writers were the sort of people who live "in a restrained terror of being unable to think up their next idea." "Television," he wrote, "is an endless, almost monstrous drain. How many ideas does a writer have? How many insights can he make? How deep can he probe into himself, how much energy can he activate?"

To readers of that slim volume, which contains six of Chayefsky's hour-long scripts for *The Philco-Goodyear Television Playhouse*, it must have seemed like an astonishing introductory statement from a man who, at just thirty-two years old, had come to epitomize this unfamiliar but exciting new occupation of professional television writer. His words are surprising in their candor and precocious bitterness, reflecting not only the self-assurance Chayefsky felt at that age, but also the authority he possessed in his field and the rapidness with which he had accrued it.

All told, Chayefsky wrote ten plays for *The Philco-Goodyear Televi-*

sion Playhouse, an NBC anthology drama that alternated between those two title sponsors. The era, in which some twenty-six million households possessed TV sets, was dominated by comedies: first Milton Berle's *Texaco Star Theater* on NBC, and then *I Love Lucy* on CBS. Dramas, modeled on the legitimate theater, provided a more traditional if less flashy foothold for emerging talents, with *The Philco-Goodyear Television Playhouse* offering a proving ground for actors such as Grace Kelly, Steve McQueen, Joanne Woodward, and Walter Matthau and writers such as Gore Vidal and Horton Foote.

Chayefsky's installments in the series, shown between 1952 and 1955, were visually unsophisticated by contemporary standards: broadcast live from NBC's Rockefeller Center headquarters, they were transmitted in black and white, as shaky cameras captured sweaty performances under hot studio lights, in limited locations and minimalist settings. With words such as *videotape* and *rerun* not yet standard parlance, these programs were crudely preserved for future airings, if they were expected to be shown again at all. You watched them in real time on Sunday night—and about seven million to nine million viewers did each week—or you listened forlornly as your friends talked about them on Monday morning.

The format was too young to have established rules, and the harder Chayefsky pushed on its boundaries and with a writing talent that had not yet found its upper limits, the more his recognition grew. His teleplays were socially conscious if politically prudent narratives whose heroes were underappreciated and unseen strivers who sometimes won and sometimes lost, while their day-to-day struggles were elevated to the level of the cosmic. Whether they prevailed or were vanquished, these protagonists were always allowed their moments in the spotlight to rail passionately and persuasively against the hopeless, demoralizing complexities of modern life.

As Mr. Healy, the old, obsolete employee of a drab Manhattan printer's shop, laments to a young apprentice in a Chayefsky teleplay called "Printer's Measure," "Are people any wiser than they were a hundred years ago? Are they happier? This is the great American disease, boy! This passion for machines. . . . We've gone mad, boy, with this mad chase for comfort, and it's sure we're losing the very juice of living." The play culminates with his smashing a linotype machine with a sledgehammer.

Three installments on *The Philco-Goodyear Television Playhouse*, broadcast in 1952 and 1953, had made Chayefsky a writer whom audiences could identify by name. His fourth drama, called "Marty," was shown on May 24, 1953, and it made him a star.

During preparations at the Abbey Hotel earlier that year for a teleplay called "The Reluctant Citizen," Chayefsky wandered away from rehearsals and encountered a leftover sign from a dance event held by a local lonely hearts club. Lettered by hand, it read, GIRLS, DANCE WITH THE MAN WHO ASKS YOU. REMEMBER, MEN HAVE FEELINGS, TOO. He contemplated the poster and returned to pitch his director, Delbert Mann, and producer, Fred Coe, on an idea for a play about a young woman—no, wait, a young man—who attends one such event.

With their encouragement, Chayefsky crafted the story of a thirty-six-year-old butcher from the Bronx named Marty Pilletti, whose social life is summed up by the sad refrain he ritualistically exchanges with his only friend, Angie: "What do you feel like doing tonight?" Embarrassed to be the last unmarried member of his family, Marty is persuaded by his mother to attend a dance at the Waverly Ballroom, where he meets a girl who is as isolated and vulnerable as he is. Marty brings her back to the home he shares with his mother, and he and the girl engage in an awkward romantic dalliance. Over the objections of his overprotective mother and the envious Angie, Marty resolves to call the girl again some night.

That is the entire action of "Marty," but then "Marty" is not really a work of action. Behind the deceptively inert and half-mumbled performance of Rod Steiger, who portrayed the title character in the *Goodyear Television Playhouse* production, lurks the classic formulation of the Chayefsky hero, who has been held back for too long and who explodes with emotion when pushed to his breaking point. Urged by his mother to prepare for what he can only anticipate will be "a big night of heartache," Marty responds with a barrage of self-loathing. "Sooner or later," he declares, "there comes a point in a man's life when he gotta face some facts, and one fact I gotta face is that whatever it is that women like, I ain't got it. I chased enough girls in my life. I went to enough dances. I got hurt enough. I don't wanna get hurt no more."

In the scenes that follow his first meeting with the mistreated, unnamed girl (played by Nancy Marchand in her television debut), Marty hears her mocked once too often by people who are supposed to care about him. These provocations set loose his verbalized anger, which he aims at anyone who dismisses his feelings for her. As he tells off Angie in a concluding speech, whose stage directions call for it to be delivered in "a low, intense voice":

> You don't like her. My mother don't like her. She's a dog and I'm a fat, ugly little man. All I know is I had a good time last night. I'm gonna have a good time tonight. If we have enough good times together, I'm going down on my knees and beg that girl to marry me. If we make a party again this New Year's, I gotta date for the party. You don't like her, that's too bad.

Marty wins his freedom by casting Angie aside with the line that every disapproving housewife and busybody had previously used to humiliate him: "You oughtta be ashamed of yourself."

Of all the plays he wrote for *Philco-Goodyear*, "Marty" was not Chayefsky's personal favorite, and the praise and admiration it received took him by surprise, although he suspected it somehow resulted from the play's expression of feelings that viewers were not used to seeing on television. As he told *TV Guide* in 1955,

> I think it was because it tried to show love to be a very real emotion which very real people enjoy and experience in their

normal lives, instead of the gauche, contrived and intensely immature thing that the movies and current fiction have made of it. Love is a very common business, really; it does not require special settings or extreme circumstances or any particular face or body or income tax bracket. I think most people liked "Marty" because it tried to tell them that they have as deep and tender and gentle and passionate a soul as Tony Curtis.

Steiger may have come closer to identifying the reason for its emotional resonance when he surmised that his character and the play itself were somehow surrogates for its author. "We thought that 'Marty' was based upon, a lot, on Paddy Chayefsky," he later said. "Of course we didn't go up and ask him because since it was about such a lonely man, and such a man hungry for love, it would have been a rather embarrassing situation for all of us." Even audiences with no access to Chayefsky and only a vague sense of him as an individual felt certain they were seeing the honest unfurling of a real life, and all the undignified truths that came with it.

Sidney Aaron Chayefsky was born on January 29, 1923, in the Bronx home of his parents, Harry and Gussie Chayefsky, one block away from the Grand Concourse. His father, a dairyman, and his mother, a housewife, were Russian-born Jews who met on the beaches of Coney Island, where, family legend had it, Harry rescued Gussie from nearly drowning. Sidney, the youngest and smallest of three brothers, was raised primarily in Bronx tenements—the family had to sell a comparatively spacious house in Mount Vernon when the Great Depression hit—but he did not consider himself underprivileged. As an adult he would say he grew up in "the rich Bronx—in the Riverdale section—not the Odets Bronx. But I guess there's not too much difference."

His bar mitzvah was held at a storefront synagogue on West 234th Street, and his youth was filled with visits to the Yiddish theaters around New York City. Known at DeWitt Clinton High School by the nickname Chy, he preferred to add an affected middle initial when giving his full name, Sidney Q. Chayefsky, as on the masthead of the student literary publication, *The Magpie*, which he edited his senior year. Though he stood only five foot six, his barrel-chested build suggested the raw material of a potential athlete. But aside from a short stint at age seventeen as an offensive lineman on a semiprofessional football team, his ambitions, he knew, were on a more cerebral playing field, even if he could not quite say why. Asked years later where his writing talents came from, Chayefsky could only shrug. "You got me," he said. "In an ordinary Jewish middle-class home there's a great prestige to being a writer. My parents weren't writers but they were great readers. I read everything I could put my hands on."

After his graduation from City College in 1943, the twenty-year-old Sidney was drafted into the army and never came back. Roused one Sunday morning during basic training at Camp Carson, Colorado, the young private told his superior officer he could not perform his KP duty because he had to attend Catholic Mass. "Sure you do, Paddy," the officer sarcastically replied. This rechristening stuck, and Chayefsky enjoyed the distinctiveness of his new name: as unlikely an appellation as Sidney Chayefsky was, he could feel certain the world would never see another Paddy Chayefsky.

His other fateful encounter, as a machine-gun-wielding infantryman in the army's 104th Division, was with a land mine he sat on in Aachen. (As the dramatist Garson Kanin, then a captain at a U.S. military hospital in Cirencester, England, later recounted, Chayefsky told him, "We were out on patrol and I had to take a dump.") Chayefsky was awarded the Purple Heart, and during his convalescence he worked with another soldier, a composer named Jimmy Livingston, to write a bawdy musical send-up of their armed service experiences called *No T.O. for Love*. (A T.O., or table of organization, is a military chart illustrating a chain of command.)

Joshua Logan, already an established Broadway director at the time of the war and the future cowriter of *South Pacific*, was among those who took notice of this formative work, and he became fast friends with Chayefsky, whom he regarded as "a square"—not socially but physically. "Paddy is built like an office safe, one that fits under the counter and is impossible to move," Logan would later observe. "He is the only man I know who was that way when he was in his late teens and is still that way in full-fledged manhood."

The musical caught the attention also of Curt Conway, then a Special Services staff sergeant who was producing shows for GIs in London. So, too, did Chayefsky. "I thought I was the sloppiest soldier in the Army," Conway said. But Chayefsky, he found, outdid him. "Bedraggled is the best description—his shirttail always riding out of his pants and one trouser leg always out of the boot. He was generally unimpressive until you found out he had a charming sense of humor." Chayefsky struck Conway as shy and socially awkward. "He seemed to know very little about girls," he said.

Garson Kanin, a noted motion picture director at the time of his enlistment, put Chayefsky to work on Carol Reed's film *The True Glory*, an account of the Allied victories on the Western front that won the Academy Award for documentary feature in 1945. Returned to civilian life one year later, the two men crossed paths on the streets of Manhattan: Kanin was thriving as the celebrated playwright of the Broadway comedy *Born Yesterday*, while Chayefsky was working in his uncle Abe's printing shop on West Twenty-Eighth Street, yearning to resume his literary pursuits. Kanin and his wife, the actress Ruth Gordon, gave Chayefsky a $500 advance to write a play of his own—a gift, essentially, to get him out of his print shop job. Not knowing how proper dramas were composed, Chayefsky bought a book of plays by Lillian Hellman, sat down at his typewriter, and retyped *The Children's Hour*. "I copied it out word for word and I studied every line of it," he said. "I kept asking myself: 'Why did she write this particular line?'"

His first original play, *Put Them All Together*, about a Jewish family in the Bronx, was not produced, and this was a great disappointment to him. But the narrative treatment he wrote next, called *The Great American Hoax*, was, and this was an even greater disappointment. The treatment, about an older man being forced out of a printing job, earned Chayefsky a $25,000 option from 20th Century–Fox and a $250-a-week job at the Hollywood studio to write the screenplay, which eventually became the Monty Woolley comedy *As Young as You Feel*. But long before that, the young writer (who dubbed the end product "a real stinker") grew exasperated with the changes sought by Fox, which seemed to respond only to his irritation. "I stormed and ranted," Chayefsky said, "and the more I raved, the more they 'respected' me." With all the esteem of the studio, he took his substantial paycheck and stormed back to New York.

The year 1949 was doubly momentous for him: February saw the opening of the play *Death of a Salesman*, Arthur Miller's elegy for the misplaced values of the overlooked American middle class, an event that profoundly reshaped the perspectives of dramatists both established and aspiring. That same month, Chayefsky was married to Susan Sackler, a slight, slender ballet student who, like her new husband, came from a Jewish family in the Bronx. He found steadier employment adapting plays for radio broadcasts, and as television blossomed in the early 1950s, he was one of many writers enlisted by the networks to feed the public's growing hunger for new programming. But his first produced script, for the CBS suspense anthology *Danger*, directed by a young prodigy named Sidney Lumet, did not mark an auspicious debut. "Nobody called me to tell me what night they were putting it on, so I missed it," Chayefsky recalled. "Never saw it."

The 1953 broadcast of "Marty" brought an outpouring of appreciation and recognition for its author. If, as the future *Twilight Zone* creator Rod Serling wrote, Chayefsky regarded television plays as "the most perishable item known to man," then "Marty" was the exception that gave the form value and longevity. As Serling's widow, Carol, later said when she spoke of her husband's esteem for Chayefsky, "He had the gift of melding significance and meaning and humor into one play, often into one single situation. He gave stature to television. And that was really Rod's feeling."

"Marty" also attracted renewed interest from the motion picture industry. The original teleplay, which Chayefsky had written in a matter of days and for which he was paid $1,200, was purchased for a film adaptation by Burt Lancaster and his producing partner Harold Hecht, with Chayefsky receiving a $13,000 option and a percentage of its earnings to write the movie script. Wary of another Hollywood fiasco, Chayefsky negotiated that he be allowed to do his work in New York, that advance rehearsals be held prior to filming, and that Delbert Mann, who had directed the television production, also direct the movie.

Though he worked with an agent, Bobby Sanford, at the start of his career, Chayefsky made his later business deals on his own, and his lawyer, Maurice Spanbock, reviewed his contracts. As he would later explain, "My position is nonnegotiable. That's how much I want and what kind of controls I want. It is up to the other side to figure out how to make it palatable to themselves, because there is plenty of room left for everybody to make all the money they want." Most crucially with *Marty*, the movie, Chayefsky insisted that he be allowed to participate creatively throughout the filmmaking process. All his demands were accepted, and he was given an additional credit as associate producer.

Marty, starring an ebullient and eminently likable Ernest Borgnine and featuring a jaunty pop theme song by Harry Warren, is more eager to please and less rough around the edges than its television predecessor. But it was no less a cultural sensation when it was released by United Artists in 1955. In an early review, *Variety* wrote, "If *Marty* is an example of the type of material that can be gleaned, then studio story editors better spend more time at home looking at television." *Time* praised the film for telling "the whole truth and nothing but the truth about the unattached male," adding that Chayefsky "can find the vernacular truth and beauty in ordinary lives and feelings. And he can say things about his people that he could never get away with if he were not a member of the family."

In a marketplace of extravagant, widescreen Technicolor and CinemaScope presentations, the simple, black-and-white *Marty* was a surprise winner of the Palme d'Or at the Cannes Film Festival, and in 1956 it won the Academy Award for best picture and Oscars for Borgnine, Mann, and Chayefsky, who, after receiving his statuette and a kiss from Claudette Colbert, declared, "If I hadn't won, I'd have been disappointed."

By this time, Chayefsky had seen the birth of his son, Dan, and the TV broadcasts of his last scripts for *The Philco-Goodyear Television Playhouse*, including "The Bachelor Party," "Middle of the Night," and "The Catered Affair." He was also growing more assured in his abilities and more strident in his criticism of television. In a *New York Herald Tribune* article matter-of-factly headlined CHAYEFSKY ASSAILS TV AS STUPID AND DOOMED, he said, "The industry has no pride and no culture. The movies, with all their crassness, can point to something they've done with pride during the year."

Where he had once boasted that he wrote the dialogue in *Marty* "as if it had been wire-tapped," he now snapped at reporters who dared to ask if the words uttered by his characters came from surreptitious tape recordings. In an essay in the *New York Times*, he wrote that he was "frankly demanding to be relieved of the epithet of 'stenographic writer' or 'slice-of-life' writer and that my writing be recognized as more than an ability to put down recognizable idiom."

"Truth is truth," Chayefsky proclaimed, "and it is not made into poetry by artificial pungency. Life is life. It breathes for itself, and it contains the exaltation of true lyricism just in its being."

The press, meanwhile, found him a reliable sparring partner, latching on to his ostentations and mocking his physical shortcomings. Profiles of Chayefsky customarily tagged him as "chubby," "stocky," and "smallish," sometimes in concert, as in "a short, stocky and heavy-shouldered chap who'll never be a serious threat to Gregory Peck." In *Vogue* he was presented as "a squarish, hefty young playwright," and in the *New York Post* he was rendered "a chunky, Bronx-born, reformed éclair addict." When he swore to the *Herald Tribune* that he would eat his hat if the film version of *Middle of the Night* were not a hit, the writer retorted, "On the way from the movie studio in a near-by Italian restaurant where he devoured a huge hero sandwich, Mr. Chayefsky did not wear a hat. Perhaps he had eaten it because he had lost some other bet." The same article trumpeted in its headline that Chayefsky had recently grown a beard, while mentioning only in passing his admission that he had been in psychoanalysis for the past three years.

Over time, Chayefsky's eccentric if entertaining fussiness gave way to a reputation for being impossible to satisfy. A television series he planned to produce about the American Psychiatric Association fell apart in 1958 when he refused to cede any control to the networks interested in it. "Once they got control, it would be so dehydrated that it wouldn't be worth doing," he said. "They would try to make the subject matter more palatable, and it can't be done that way; it can only be done as art."

On a monthlong visit to the Soviet Union in 1959 with Alfred Kazin, Arthur Schlesinger Jr., and *Atlantic Monthly* editor Edward Weeks, Chayefsky insisted that the group set aside its planned itinerary so he could visit his mother's birthplace in Velikiye Bubny, a small village five hours from Kiev. "They did everything possible to divert our attention from the request," Weeks recalled. "Then Paddy said to them, 'All right, you've lied to me consistently. I'm pulling out of the conference and going home.'" In the end, Chayefsky got his visit to Velikiye Bubny.

Before the 1950s were out, Chayefsky vowed he was quitting television for film, where he could have more control over his work and earn more money. When movies such as *The Goddess* and *Middle of the Night* did not nearly match the triumph of *Marty*, he turned to the stage, earning Tony Award nominations for his plays *The Tenth Man* and *Gideon*. By 1962 he had concluded that he was "sick of" Broadway due to "economic futility." But his suffering was not yet through.

Chayefsky's 1964 directorial debut, *The Passion of Josef D.*, his stage drama about the Russian Revolution starring Peter Falk as the young Stalin, elicited some of the most brutal reviews of his career ("an almost unbroken and seriously unlucky succession of wrong choices"—Walter Kerr) and closed after eleven days. Months later Chayefsky would sheepishly admit, "I should never have tried to direct it, too."

After writing the screenplay that same year for *The Americanization of Emily*, adapted from William Bradford Huie's novel about a scheming navy officer thrust into the middle of the D-day invasion, Chayefsky returned to the theater in 1968 for one last play. For this stage satire, called *The Latent Heterosexual*, starring Zero Mostel as a gay man who marries a woman to escape an exorbitant tax bill, Chayefsky brought the production to the Dallas Theater Center, hoping it would avoid the glare of the powerful national and New York–based critics. He was wrong, and while some reviews were merely mixed, Chayefsky was most infuriated by the notices that praised Mostel's performance above his own writing. The actor "was so rich, deep, comic and pitiable," Clive Barnes wrote in the *New York Times*. "Not particularly the play, which is more interesting than totally successful."

A planned national tour was called off, and Chayefsky, the fading former sage of the Grand Concourse, was left contemplating a return to TV, "the best platform to express meaningful drama." But having renounced every artistic avenue available to him, he had to wonder where he truly belonged and which, if any of them, might still take him back.

There were no perfect matches for Paddy Chayefsky, but Howard Gottfried was as close as they came. The New York–born and –bred Gottfried, a former lawyer, had made his reputation as a producer of Off-Broadway theater in the 1950s and '60s. For a few years he decamped to Los Angeles for a job at United Artists Television, the studio behind shows such as *Gilligan's Island* and *The Fugitive*, but he decided that West Coast living wasn't his style and returned to New York to develop television projects for Ed Sullivan Productions. Gottfried set up shop at 1650 Broadway, near the Winter Garden Theater, and was soon introduced to Chayefsky by Noel Behn, another writer who kept his office on the illustrious eleventh floor of 850 Seventh Avenue. The lean and dapper Gottfried enjoyed dressing up for his work, and his personal manner was genial and accommodating. He could fight the battles Chayefsky wasn't equipped for and put out the fires his partner started; he encouraged his ideas and abided his temper.

Chayefsky's writing process was solitary and largely opaque to Gottfried, but their brainstorming sessions were cooperative and relaxed. Together, the two men would walk the streets of Manhattan, up Seventh Avenue and along the perimeter of Central Park, talking about whatever came to mind—news, sports, women. Over conversation, ideas would take shape, often from source material culled from day-to-day experiences. They were still laughing over their recent lunch with Mel Brooks when they struck a deal with CBS in July 1969 for Chayefsky to create the pilot script for a weekly series of "socially satiric" dramas.

Also fresh in Chayefsky's mind was a three-part *TV Guide* series he had been reading that summer about Mike Dann, a forty-seven-year-old senior vice president at CBS who had developed shows such as *The Smothers Brothers Comedy Hour*. As Dann weighed the possibilities of new television projects, canceled others, and fought with Tommy Smothers over a comedy sketch about astrology, the profile presented Dann as principled and thoughtful, but also overextended and arguably overqualified—all in all, a man Chayefsky could get behind.

Thus inspired, Chayefsky wrote a pilot script for a proposed CBS television series called *The Imposters*, focused in part on a fictional television executive named Eddie Gresham, who held the title of vice president in charge of program development, East Coast, for an invented network called United Broadcasting System, or UBS. Like his real-life counterpart, Gresham is idealistic and well educated, with a degree from the Yale School of Drama, but he realizes deep down that television is no place for his erudite designs. As Chayefsky's narrative description for the show puts it, "He knew by now that Eugene O'Neill wins the Nobel Prize but *Bonanza* draws a thirty-eight share in the ratings."

The other protagonist of *The Imposters* is a comic actor named Charley Peck, "a real katzenjammer kid if there ever was one," who is introduced to viewers over a lunch with Mel Brooks at the Carnegie Deli, where he "smokes a cigar, which never seemed to burn out." Informed by Brooks that the ignorant UBS, in trying to keep pace with CBS's hit broadcast of *Death of a Salesman*, has been trying to get in touch with the late Bertolt Brecht, Peck calls the network, impersonates the deceased playwright, and leaves his own phone number. Months later, when Gresham decides to create a television series based on *The Three-penny Opera* (one set in Harlem that will star Harry Belafonte as a modern-day Mack the Knife), he calls that number and arranges a meeting with the ersatz Brecht, but upon encountering him in person, he immediately sees through Peck's deception.

Gresham, in spite of it all, is disappointed only in himself and confesses to Peck everything he believes to be wrong with the television industry.

> We're not in the business of good drama. We're in the boredom-killing business. That's what my job is, that's what I do all day, think up ways of killing the boredom of two hundred million Americans. I concoct game shows and soap operas and schedule professional sports programs. I think up musical entertainments and talk shows for people who have forgotten how to talk to each other. What the hell has happened to us Americans anyway? We seem to have lost whatever identity we ever had. We used to be pioneers, homesteaders, farmers, craftsmen, shopkeepers, robber barons, bohemians, Whigs, Tories, rail-splitters, immigrants. Now, we're two hundred million whiter-than-white, softer-than-soft, deodorized, standardized, simonized, plastic and programmed things, totally indistinguishable from each other, any one of us replaceable by just ordering another part from the factory. . . . Some curious integrity has gone out of

Americans that made them curiously American. They don't want drama, especially good drama. They just want their boredom killed.

Peck replies to him: "It's not their integrity that's at stake; it's yours."

Gresham's *Threepenny Opera* idea is dismantled by his colleagues and turned into a show about "a colored junkie rock musician and a young business exec who leaves his wife and kids to go wandering around the country looking for reality." Then, at a dinner of broadcasting industry executives at the Americana Hotel, Gresham is mistaken for the evening's keynote speaker, Senator John O. Pastore of Rhode Island, then the powerful chairman of the Senate's subcommittee on communications. Taking the dais, he makes one last pitch for his Belafonte show, now about a Harlem congressman who's also a preacher; this stunt saves the series but costs Gresham any future in the television business.

Later, as he and Peck take stock of these improbable events, Gresham wonders if the two of them could make a career of pretending to be people they are not. Posing a classic Chayefskyian question, Gresham asks Peck, "Well, Charley, what do you feel like doing?"

"I don't know, Eddie," he replies. "What do you feel like doing?"

"I feel like going to Paris," says the invigorated Gresham, "and straightening out the peace talks."

The Imposters was bold; it was subversive; it was trying to use the mechanisms of television to criticize television itself—and it never had a prayer of getting made. A few weeks after Chayefsky finished writing the pilot, he and Gottfried went to CBS to meet with Mike Dann, the executive who had inspired the script and who would now decide its fate. As Gottfried recalled, "We're sitting there, and he looks us in the eye and he starts laughing. And he says, 'You don't really think I'm going to do this, do you?' He meant on the air. Mike said, 'I'm sorry—we can't do this.'"

Television had no place for Chayefsky's next pitch, either, a drama with the simple title *The Hospital*, which he described in a proposal as "a microcosm of society series"—"That is to say, the hospital represents American society, and all the stories in the series, which will be told through the hospital and its personnel, will nevertheless be satirical comments on the society as a whole."

CBS rejected this idea, too. But he and Gottfried were committed to it, and to setting a tone that Chayefsky said was grounded in "the hardness of comedy which is based on total authenticity, and the fact that the institution itself is the star." They decided they would instead produce it as a film, even though they had never made a movie together— Gottfried had never made a movie at all—and they brought the project to United Artists, where Chayefsky had made *Marty* and *The Bachelor Party*, and which was lately finding success with provocative contemporary dramas such as *In the Heat of the Night* and *Midnight Cowboy*. In 1970 the studio gave Chayefsky and Gottfried a two-picture deal whose first entry, the collaborators decided, would be this film, which they variously called *The Latent Humanitarian* and *Right Smack into the Wind*, though in time they came back to the original title, *The Hospital*. Their working arrangement with the studio offered them considerable freedom from its supervision and almost total control over their output.

"They didn't bother you," Gottfried said. "Once you got going, you were on your own."

There was the usual behind-the-scenes butting of heads. United Artists wanted Walter Matthau to play the lead character, Dr. Herbert Bock, whose asphyxiation-by-bureaucracy at the Manhattan hospital where he is chief of medicine parallels the isolation, depression, and sexual impotence he endures in his personal life; but Chayefsky and Gottfried got their choice: George C. Scott. The filmmakers wanted Arthur Hiller, who had directed *The Americanization of Emily* and was a hot commodity coming off *Love Story*, to direct; the studio wanted the less costly and less accomplished Michael Ritchie. United Artists briefly prevailed, until Chayefsky declared that he "just couldn't work" with Ritchie, and Hiller was in.

The setting of *The Hospital* is the interior of the Metropolitan Hospital Center at 1901 First Avenue, a dilapidated labyrinth of green tiles, cream-colored walls, and rusty steel beds that was nearly one hundred years old at the time of the film's 1971 release. Scott, who offscreen was fighting the collapse of his marriage to Colleen Dewhurst (for the second time, after they had divorced in 1965 and remarried in 1967) and a lifelong battle with alcohol, gives a commanding performance as the supremely disillusioned yet steadfastly resolute Bock; he earned an Academy Award nomination for the performance and might well have won, had he not refused the honor the previous year, when he was named Best Actor for *Patton*. There is even an uncredited cameo from Chayefsky himself, who, with amused detachment and his avuncular Bronx dialect, narrates the opening story of a freshly arrived hospital patient who in a matter of hours is misdiagnosed to death.

Still, the star of the film is Chayefsky's screenplay, a self-sustaining ecosystem of perfect frustration in which each of the three dozen speaking characters—doctors, nurses, administrators, patients, police officers, political radicals, subordinates, and flunkies—possesses a set of desires, vexations, and excuses that thwarts the wishes of someone elsewhere in the chain. This engine boils over in a few eruptive monologues, none more furious than one delivered by Bock on the night of an ominous and fateful rainstorm, just before he beds a free-spirited visitor played by Diana Rigg and explains to her why he has "lost even my desire for work, which is a hell of a lot more primal a passion than sex."

> I've lost my raison d'etre, my purpose, the only thing I ever
> truly loved. It's all rubbish anyway. Transplants, antibodies,
> we manufacture genes, we can produce ectogenically, we can
> practically clone people like carrots, and half the kids in this
> ghetto haven't even been inoculated for polio! We have assem-

bled the most enormous medical establishment ever con-
ceived, and people are sicker than ever! We cure nothing! We
heal nothing! The whole goddam wretched world is strangu-
lating in front of our eyes!

When his original screenplay for *The Hospital* won an Academy
Award in April 1972, Chayefsky gave a brief acceptance speech, offering a mere forty-seven words about privilege, gratified feelings, and a
spirit of solidarity with Ernest Tidyman, who had just won his own
Oscar for the adapted screenplay of *The French Connection*. (Tidyman,
whose mother had told him she wanted to see him victorious that
night, said he replied, "Those other four guys, they got mothers, too.")
It would be years before the public again heard Chayefsky express
himself in any meaningful way.

With the second Oscar of his career in hand, Chayefsky once
again found himself the recipient of Hollywood's awkward and unwanted
advances. Warren Beatty, who had befriended Chayefsky along with
his office neighbors Bob Fosse and Herb Gardner, recalled the screenwriter as shying away from schmoozy West Coast gatherings, too
retreating or befuddled to accept an invitation to visit the Playboy Man-
sion and its pajama-clad proprietor, Hugh Hefner. "I remember he told
me that someone had asked him to go up to Hefner's," Beatty said. "It
was not I who asked him to go, he was just telling me someone had
asked him to. There was a time at Hefner's when every political columnist, et cetera, was up there—you know, studying. And he said, 'Why
would I want to go up there, and sit in a Jacuzzi and be pushed away
from the wall?'"

Prior to the months he spent researching the screenplay for *The
Hospital*—surveying scientific journals, interviewing professionals,
and reviewing documents to learn the structure and language of such
institutions—Chayefsky had gained some personal familiarity with
modern medicine. He had been diagnosed with depression and had

moved on from traditional psychoanalysis and cognitive therapy to newer and more unconventional treatments, including the drug Elavil, a pill prescribed to treat depression, anxiety, and bipolar disorder, as well as the occasional attempt at transcendental meditation.

Like her husband, Susan Chayefsky had tried psychoanalysis in the 1950s, a period when she also enrolled in and withdrew from Columbia University and attempted working as a children's photographer before giving up the pursuit. This peripatetic pattern became the norm in the years and decades that followed, during which she was unable to settle into a steady vocation, beyond her role providing constant support to Paddy in his own career. "She was very, very talented," said Dan Chayefsky, the couple's son, "and remarkably unfulfilled in expressing that talent. And it made her very unhappy. I think it must have been hard for her to be part of that era, of women that didn't have a voice of their own."

As Dan Chayefsky would later recall, his mother had always been an introverted and reclusive person. "She was a perfectionist, and that made life impossible for her," he said. "If she wanted to go out with my dad, she had to look perfect. And that makes it too exhausting, after doing that a lot." But then she started having outright panic attacks, losing control of her body when she became overwhelmed from being out of doors or simply from the fear that she might have to leave her home. In one instance she went into a frenzy inside a public telephone booth; in another, a doctor had to be summoned to the living room of the Chayefskys' apartment, where he found Susan on the floor writhing in pain from the muscle spasms shooting through her legs. Eventually, she was diagnosed with an adult-onset form of muscular dystrophy—untreatable at that time and most assuredly incurable—and this disease, Dan said, "reflected her fear of people. It almost gave her withdrawal a cause."

Dan himself had been growing into a strong-willed teenager, and though he was hardly the "shaggy-haired Maoist" whom Bock decries in *The Hospital*, his father was finding it increasingly difficult to relate to him. The values of this new generation were a mystery to Paddy

Chayefsky, and he was equally enigmatic to the young and vocal son who saw him as a sullen, withdrawn father. "He was a fortress, my dad," Dan later said of Paddy. "He would occasionally come out and talk to people from the window. And sometimes he'd invite them into the fortress, and then at the end of the day, you'd leave the fortress again."

Dan could sense "a tremendous amount of combustion" at home, created by the tense dynamics of the stubborn Chayefsky family, and felt that even though his father loved him, Paddy was never completely satisfied with him, either. "He had a very, very strong agenda of what he wanted to see his child grow up to be," Dan said, "and I never fulfilled that for him. It was very, very hard for him and it was very, very hard for me, failing, and him being disappointed."

In his late teens and early twenties, Dan began to exhibit self-destructive tendencies that were at times so fierce that his parents could not be around him. At one point, the family even attempted a trial separation of sorts: for about three months, Dan remained by himself in the family apartment, while Paddy and Susan moved into a room at the Hotel Navarro on Central Park South. On other occasions, Dan was sent to a rehabilitation facility to be monitored and to undergo treatment, which required him to drop out of college while his father told friends that his son had gone to live on a commune. "I was just very self-destructive and very lost," Dan explained. "It was considered advisable that I would get residential treatment at the time. So I was there for a couple of years."

Paddy Chayefsky was attracted to many forms of chaos, but not the kind he encountered on his own doorstep; he found it sufficiently difficult to work from home when it was calm, and as his family life became more volatile, he turned increasingly to his office and to his writing for sanctuary. "It's almost like he took what was not working in the world around him and he brought this bonfire to his office, and he made something out of it creatively," Dan said. "And the only time he was really happy was when he wrote. Even my mom said she had to get used to the fact that he loved writing more than his marriage."

In his personal politics, Paddy Chayefsky rarely aligned himself with particular causes or parties for very long, and resisted efforts to apply simplistic labels to him. He was simultaneously a veteran of World War II and the screenwriter of *The Americanization of Emily*, which did not present the U.S. military in an entirely star-spangled light. And when he had strong feelings about affairs of state, he took his complaints to the top of the chain of command. In drafts of a letter to President Richard M. Nixon in 1971, Chayefsky wrote that he was not some "new-Mobe militant or placard carrier," but rather "a careful man who keeps his own counsel and has almost a horror of making a public issue of my principles or my conscience." He went on to say, "I have had and do not have now any simplistic feelings about the war in Vietnam. I have been against it for years because I thought it was a stupid and utterly unnecessary war whose principal victim would be the United States." Even so, Chayefsky said he had to speak out about horrors such as the My Lai massacre because, as he wrote, "We are becoming a nation of good Germans, and if we don't watch out we're going to become a nation of bad Germans."

At the same time, a growing fixation on the affairs of Israel was becoming increasingly apparent in his public remarks. Themes of Jewish culture and history had recurred throughout his work, but Chayefsky, who had traveled to Israel in 1960 and again in 1968, for Dan's bar mitzvah, possessed a more aggressive and admittedly paranoid streak. He revealed this side of himself in a long, discursive interview with *Women's Wear Daily* in 1971. In it, he said he believed all Jews around the world were in danger of imminent genocide. "Six million went up with a snap of the finger last time, and there is little reason to assume anybody's going to protect the other 12 million still extant," he said, adding that the risk was especially great in the United States: "There's a lot of anti-Semitism in America, real gutter Munich stuff. You hear it in the New Left: 'Kill the kosher pigs.'"

"Somebody wrote it—a Jew is a man with one bag packed in the hall closet at all times," Chayefsky went on. And, he said, "Israel is that place you go when you have to grab the bag."

During this period, Chayefsky changed the title of his personal company from Sidney Productions, reflecting his given name, to Simcha Productions, in honor of its Hebrew equivalent. On a visit to Washington to see a performance by the stand-up comedian David Steinberg, Chayefsky heard someone in the audience call Steinberg a "mocky," an obscure Jewish slur. At the end of the night, Chayefsky and Steinberg found themselves in an elevator with the man who Chayefsky presumed was the heckler.

"I don't know that it's that guy," Steinberg would later recall, "and Paddy recognizes the guy immediately. And he says to him, 'Are you the guy that was heckling him?' This is a big guy, and he starts stammering. Paddy goes, 'You call him a mocky, you call all of us a mocky.' And he didn't put him up against the wall like you do in the movies, but he had his finger right in this guy's chest.

"This guy was bigger than Paddy," Steinberg added, "and [Paddy] just was at him."

Privately, Chayefsky channeled his fervor into uncredited advertisements for the Anti-Defamation League, such as an announcement published at the height of the 1973 oil crisis that warned, "These Arabs would like you to believe that if we give in to their blackmail and change our Mid-East policy everything will be just like it used to be." After an earlier trip to Israel in 1971, he had started writing a screenplay set in the West Bank about a pair of police officers, one Israeli and one Arab, whose amicable partnership collapses as they investigate a murder case. Then he dropped this idea and started over with a different scenario.

For the screenplay he called *The Habakkuk Conspiracy*, Chayefsky opened his story in the autumn of 1947, during the final, anarchic days of the British Mandate in Palestine. A prologue introduces a young scholar named Yakov Amiel, a Palestinian Jew who is traveling to Jerusalem in possession of three ancient leather scrolls. He is harangued on a bus ("There is a Jew dog here! Jew dog! Jew dog! I shall slice his Jew head off!" screams one excitable merchant), is beaten by Arab men, and finally has his throat slit "from ear to ear" by an assassin who makes off with his priceless artifacts: these turn out to be no less than the Dead Sea Scrolls.

The action then shifts to two other characters. One is Yakov's younger brother, Micha, a nineteen-year-old militant who is hungry to avenge the murder and reclaim the stolen treasures. The other is Yakov's widow, Elizabeth, a twenty-five-year-old British woman torn between her loyalty to her dead husband and her desire to escape the Middle East entirely. She is gradually won over to the Jewish cause by violent circumstances and the passions of Micha, who argues like a man more than twice his age. In a speech he delivers as "his ascetic passion explodes," he tells Elizabeth:

> I'll tell you about your civilized world! For two thousand years, we Jews have depended on the civilized world for our survival. And for two thousand years, Jews have been cruci-fied, burnt at the stake, thrown to the lions, to the ovens, to the gas chambers, crushed into ghettoes, forcibly converted, exiled, deported, slaughtered by Cossacks and peasants, Turks, Greeks, Romans, Spaniards, Frenchmen, Englishmen, anybody and everybody, popes and Protestants and every mad minister from Haman to Hitler—and I'm tired of it! There's just a couple million of us left, goddamit! We're an endangered species! So we don't trust the civilized world any more! We'll take care of our own survival! Don't come to me with your bloody Christian hands and scold me about killing. We don't kill for conquest and empire, for profit and power! All we want is our home, the land of our forefathers, a patch of desert and swamp smaller than the state of Connecticut you're going to live in. Where a Jew can walk in his own streets and not tremble before every gutter politician and

street mob! We kill to survive! We kill so that we and our descendants shall live! When you're stripped to survival, maybe you'll understand that!

The film ends with Elizabeth striking "the figure of the fighting guerrilla, committed, triumphant," as she shoots dead the last of a squad of British police officers pursuing her; and then a scene showing the Dead Sea Scrolls, the Jewish birthright, safely on display in the present day at the Israel Museum in Jerusalem.

Chayefsky and Gottfried made one more trip to Israel in 1973, to scout locations for *The Habakkuk Conspiracy*, which they planned to make as the fulfillment of their two-movie agreement with United Artists. But the project was halted before work could go any further. For one thing, the studio had an arrangement with Otto Preminger to make his suspense film *Rosebud*, which similarly featured undercover Israelis and Middle Eastern terrorists and dealt with issues of Zionism in its story of a hostage crisis on a luxury yacht. Additionally, Chayefsky and Gottfried had become uncomfortable with the United Artists deal, whose terms required them to apply their profits from *The Hospital* to the production of their follow-up film. "Now, one might say it was in the contract," Gottfried said. "But at that time, we wanted to make *The Hospital*. And I was unknown, so to speak."

Maurice Spanbock, Chayefsky's lawyer, said that rapid modernization in the Middle East had made it all but impossible for Israel to stand in for its pre-independence self. "They could have made it elsewhere," Spanbock recalled, "but they said they couldn't make it in Jerusalem because there were television antennae all over the place." And the volatile nature of the script was also a strike against it. "One could read into it the fact that it wasn't done," said Spanbock. "You knew it obviously was coming up in a political world. But I never heard that articulated. You could make whatever surmise you elected to."

The outbreak of the Yom Kippur War in October of that year ensured that *The Habakkuk Conspiracy* would not be filmed soon, though United

Artists retained ownership of the screenplay and regarded its deal with Chayefsky as completed. With nothing going forward at the studio, he and Gottfried began to question why United Artists was selling the television broadcast rights for *The Hospital* in a package with other less successful (or unsuccessful) features, a common industry practice that they said cheapened the value of their film. "Each of the movies in that package would get a sum of money," Gottfried explained. "But the result of the bundling was that they broke up the fee for the whole bundle, and the bundle usually consisted of maybe one or two hit films, and some of their bum films that were not worth a nickel. They certainly weren't worth what *The Hospital* was worth." He and Chayefsky threatened legal action, putting a chill on their relationship with United Artists.

Meanwhile, the Internal Revenue Service had begun tightening its rules about commercially failed independent films and set its sights on Chayefsky's 1958 movie *The Goddess*. The film, which stars Kim Stanley as a distraught screen idol not unlike Marilyn Monroe, had lost more than $700,000 when it was released by Columbia Pictures. Chayefsky produced it through an independent company using money from Columbia, and then spent the next decade and a half writing off the loss on his taxes as if it were a conventional loan from the studio. But now the IRS said *The Goddess* was Columbia's property and thus Chayefsky, who had stood to receive half the film's profits if it made any, had nothing to depreciate. When a court ruled against him in February 1973, Chayefsky was stuck with a tax bill of $86,770, plus a $5,248 penalty for late filing.

With his back to the wall, Chayefsky resumed pitching television projects, but a set of ideas he presented to NBC in 1974 were dispiritingly conventional and rang with the desperate echo of a man who was writing for his life. They included *The Rabbi Mystery Show*, which he described as "an hour mystery show in which the main character is a revered and retired old rabbi, a scholar and a mystic, one of whose sons happens to be an officer in Homicide Manhattan South or North. (Or

Queens or the Bronx or whatever)," and *The Stage Mother*, "a half-hour sitcom about a woman with two daughters, one of whom is a model and the other (a teenager) is being hustled by her mother for commercials and movie bits."

The concept that came closest to the airwaves was a situation comedy that would have starred James Coco as a newly divorced man adjusting to the unfamiliar singles scene in New York City. The project, which was essentially Chayefsky's attempt at re-creating *Marty* twenty years after the fact, was originally titled *Starting Over*, and then, in a familiar mouthful, *So What Do You Feel Like Doing Tonight?*, and finally, *Your Place or Mine*. It was produced as a pilot for NBC in March 1974 and directed by Delbert Mann, who had handled both the television and film versions of *Marty*. But somehow, Chayefsky's heart was not in the material. "He said he could not master it," Dan Chayefsky recalled. "He was very involved in it, and then, after a certain amount of time, he didn't see it—he couldn't bring it to fruition." Nor could NBC, which chose not to commission a series from it.

Paddy Chayefsky wasn't welcome at home, he wasn't wanted for the only work he knew how to do, and he wasn't certain there would be a future for the world in which he lived. He was running out of options, and something, somewhere, had to give.

2

STRANGELOVE-Y AS HELL

As the president of the news department of the NBC network, Richard Wald was a man entitled to some respect. He ran one of only three operations in the country with the privilege, the duty, and the means of gathering the events of the day and transmitting them to the television sets of some fifty million viewers in homes across the country. As such, he held a share of the power of deciding what was worth communicating to America and what was not. The division he oversaw commanded an annual operating budget of $100 million and employed a thousand people in roughly thirty domestic and foreign bureaus. It was his custom, as it was for many of his peers, to arrive for work each day at 9:00 A.M. sharp, attired in a neatly pressed suit, shirt, and tie, and polished shoes. He would enter his corner office on the fifth floor of NBC's art deco headquarters at 30 Rockefeller Plaza, take off his jacket, roll up his sleeves, loosen his tie, and begin to read the morning's newspapers in preparation for the day.

On one such morning in the spring of 1974, Wald's routine was interrupted by a visitor: a small, disheveled-looking man shabbily dressed in a sweatshirt with an undershirt poking out through its collar, baggy corduroy pants, and a beat-up pair of boots. Through large glasses, this bearded man looked at Wald expectantly, as if waiting for him to say something. Wald looked back at him with similar uncertainty. Awkward seconds passed silently until the visitor spoke.

"I'm going to spend the day with you," Paddy Chayefsky told him.

"Okay," Wald replied. "What the hell."

A few days earlier Wald had received a call from an executive in NBC's entertainment division, vouching for Chayefsky as a friend and asking if the writer could spend some time observing the operations of the news department while he researched a new project. Without inquiring much further, Wald agreed, and now he directed Chayefsky to a chair in the corner of his spacious office and proceeded to conduct his work. Throughout the day, colleagues buzzed in and out to discuss arcane matters—labor relations at NBC, personnel problems, the possibility that another network was pirating NBC's broadcasts. Chayefsky took notes, sketching out the department's floor plan, counting the number of desks, and jotting down bits of lingo that tickled his ear: *HUT ratings. Audience flow. The dark weeks.* He asked no questions, and at no time did Wald explain to anyone who he was or what he was doing there.

The next morning, Chayefsky returned to Wald's office wearing the same clothes he had worn the day before and repeated his practice of silently watching the news department transact its business. At lunchtime Wald invited Chayefsky to a dining club on the sixty-fifth floor for a meal and a conversation he did not expect to be particularly scintillating. Based on what he'd seen of Chayefsky so far, Wald said, "I expected grunts."

Instead, when Wald asked Chayefsky what he was up to, the writer replied, "Well, I'm doing a movie." Chayefsky said he had been visiting the various television networks to see if there was a cinematic story to be told about them, and he had narrowed down his screenplay plans to one of two approaches: one, a documentary-style, day-in-the-life look at a single network over a twenty-four-hour period; the other, in the style of *The Hospital*, would be a more "far-out" satire.

How, asked Wald, would he decide which route to take? "From the way it appears," Chayefsky explained. "The way you look at it and you talk to the people and everything else. And it develops, one way or the other." Chayefsky indicated that he did not have a strong feeling either way but, Wald recalled, "He was very charming, and he was very funny about some of the people he'd seen. Which led me to believe that he was not going to treat them kindly."

As early as December 1973, Chayefsky had started to revisit the core idea of a story set within the television industry, as he had laid out in his pilot script for *The Imposters*. But he recognized that its Bertolt Brecht setup was out of date and, if anything, did not treat its intended target seriously enough. The medium had evolved substantially since the era of "Marty," as the infatuations of TV programmers and audiences vacillated from game shows to Westerns to the cornpone comedies of *The Beverly Hillbillies* and *The Andy Griffith Show* to the social satire of *All in the Family*. More crucially, television had grown into an invisible nexus capable of linking all Americans instantaneously—more than 90 percent of the country had tuned in to witness historical moments such as the raucous 1968 Democratic National Convention or the Apollo 11 moon landing—and Chayefsky had deep misgivings about this power.

"The thing about television right now is that it is an indestructible and terrifying giant that is stronger than the government, certainly Nixon's and Agnew's government," he wrote in a preliminary treatment. "It is possible through television to take a small matter and blow it up to monumental proportions."

Starting fresh, he sketched out the premise of a fictional news anchor he variously called Holbein, Munro, Kronkhite, or Kronkheit (whether intentionally or accidentally, he did not use the more customary spelling), who has a "crack up on the air" in prime time, unexpectedly boosting the ratings of his show and creating expectations for more extreme behavior in future broadcasts. This could provoke his TV rivals to have to keep pace with his outrageousness or provide the framework for a story about his network being swallowed up by a sinister multinational corporation. "So far," Chayefsky wrote, "Kronkheit hasn't done anything but express outrage." But: "What would happen if he started inventing news—The basic joke is that the networks are so powerful they can make true what isn't true and never even existed—The networks are so powerful they make the ravings of the maniac Kronkheit true."

Still, Chayefsky felt that a basic "satirical clarity" was so far missing. "The only joke we have going for us," he wrote,

> is the idea of ANGER—the American people are angry and want angry shows—they don't want jolly, happy family type shows like Eye Witness News; they want angry shows—so they base their programming on ANGER . . . the American people seem to be hungering for happier days like the Depression, note The Waltons—Programming sets up depression shows with happy, starving families.

Months later Chayefsky made his visits to NBC News and took private meetings with John Chancellor, the stentorian anchorman of *NBC Nightly News*, and CBS to meet his industry rival Walter Cronkite, the trusted anchor of *CBS Evening News*, either of whom might find himself, on any given weeknight, the victor in an ongoing race for ratings supremacy. In his notes from those meetings, Chayefsky recorded the clockwork precision of their schedules—hours set aside for reading, writing, reviewing, lunches, afternoon walks—the physical layout of their workplaces, and their vocabularies filled with industry argot.

What it all added up to wasn't clear. Yet as Chayefsky delved deeper into the basic operations of television news, exploring reports in trade publications and research papers from scholarly journals provided by his roster of industry contacts, a certain central tension began to emerge. Atop the TV news pyramid sat the networks' national evening broadcasts, thirty minutes of serious, straightforward content presided over by serious, straightforward men. The early 1970s had provided a torrent of significant events that perfectly matched these programs' maturing ability to deliver immediate, up-to-the-minute coverage: the Senate Watergate hearings, the downfall of the Nixon administration, the withdrawal from Vietnam, crisis upon crisis in the Middle East. Given the vital role that these news programs played in informing the American populace (and protecting, via their public service, the near-monopolistic status of the networks), they were not expected to be profitable and were managed by a hierarchy of executives wholly separate from those responsible for entertainment content.

But national network news was not the only game in town. Each regional channel in the constellation of marketplaces where these networks operated had its own local newscast, leading into the national broadcasts and then returning for another half hour or hour at night. They had chirpy, cheerful, bantering coanchors and dynamic titles such as *Action News* and *Eyewitness News*; and in their vigorous competition with their local rivals, they were far from the "jolly, happy family type shows" that Chayefsky dismissed. Many of these news programs did not necessarily see it as their sacred obligation to dispassionately provide facts and knowledge to an uninformed audience. They were more like the Wild West, and some of them even reveled in this comparison.

Among the materials that Chayefsky reviewed was the transcript of a *60 Minutes* segment from March 10, 1974, titled "The Rating War." For this report, a skeptical and unamused Mike Wallace visited with *Channel 7 News Scene*, the increasingly popular 11:00 P.M. news show of KGO-TV in San Francisco, hosted by a quartet of male anchors who dubbed themselves "The Four Horsemen" and who could be seen in a popular series of on-air advertisements that cast them as bronco-riding cowboys arriving in a lawless frontier town. Wallace reported that 55 percent of the stories on *News Scene* "fell into the tabloid category—items on fire, crime, sex, tear-jerkers, accidents and exorcism." Other recent segments on the program had included a report on a Florida heiress who was hacked to death by a machete-wielding assailant on the porch of her St. Augustine home; an interview with the mother of a nudist; and the story of a severed penis that had been found in the rail yards of the East Bay. ("Male genital found on railroad track," viewers were advised. "Stay tuned!")

The success of *News Scene* had decimated morale at KPIX, a more straitlaced competitor, but the general manager of KGO, a silver-haired industry veteran named Russ Coughlin, was unrepentant. "Isn't fire, crime and sex news?" he said to Wallace. "When did that get out of the news business? . . . We could sit around and do pontifical kind of news day in and day out. We'd be back where we were in the old days, when we were trying to be very clever and profound about news, and died, and nobody watched it."

This sensibility wasn't exclusive to evening and late-night newscasts. For his research, Chayefsky clipped an April 1974 *New York Times* profile of Chuck Scarborough, a young anchorman recently delivered to WNBC in New York from WNAC in the cutthroat Boston marketplace. As compelling as the article itself was an advertisement on its second page for an NBC daytime show called *Not for Women Only*, promoting an upcoming episode called "Cats, Dogs and Underdogs." "What kinds of animals go with what kinds of people?" the ad read. "Should your pet have a pet? How can you test a dog's IQ? Barbara Walters and a panel of animal psychologists and other specialists discuss everything from guppies to puppies."

In May 1974 Chayefsky and Gottfried flew to Georgia to meet Pat Polillo, a creator of the *Action News* format and a widely traveled news director who had previously worked in Baltimore, Pittsburgh, Philadelphia, and at KGO in San Francisco before arriving at WAGA, a local Atlanta station. "You win because you have a competitive edge," Polillo had told a convention of television executives earlier in the year. "Finding and developing that competitive edge in a market where the other stations are doing a good job in news is one hell of a fight."

As far as Gottfried could tell, all that this inquiry yielded were more sketches of newsroom floor plans and head counts of cameramen and assistant directors. "The Atlanta trip made it clear that there was nothing that exciting, as far as a movie was concerned, that we could find to do about a local station," Gottfried said. "Not the kind of thing that would make a formidable movie, in any event. You'd probably end up with some kind of soap opera or something."

But in his personal notebooks Chayefsky was mapping the architecture of a structural behemoth he identified as THE NETWORK, whose internal configurations he had never closely contemplated, despite having earned his living from several of them. Each such entity had a corporate division (which, for narrative purposes, could provide a "theme relating to power + profits uber alles"), a programming division ("theme related to ratings"), a news division ("theme relating to ratings vs truth"), divisions for sales, sports, and so on.

What he needed, Chayefsky realized, was a "basic incident that ties all these units together—around which the various definitive characters revolve and interplay on one another's story." His preference, he wrote, was that this incident "evolve out of NEWS": "Thematically, we have to reconcile the concept of RATINGS UBER ALLES and whatever statement about power we can find."

Starting again with the incident of the television anchor who snaps on air, Chayefsky piled all the knowledge he had accumulated in his travels and research into a story that was ambitious to the point of oversaturation. There would be a young hotshot news producer who is brought in to boost a show's sagging ratings ("What he did in Detroit was to tabloid the news, featuring sex, scandal and sports + slighting hard news"); resistance and consternation from the network that runs this show, which is on the verge of being bought out by an international corporation or maybe by "Arab oil sheiks"; conflict with the Federal

Communications Commission, which turns out to be owned by the corporation or the sheikhs anyway. And then: "We are shooting for a third act," Chayefsky wrote, "in which the NETWORK becomes so powerful it is an international power of itself and even declares war on some country."

Lest he lose sight of his characters, Chayefsky reminded himself: "The Basic story is the destruction of a buccaneering independent TV HOTSHOT by surrendering his identity, patriotism and self to the dehumanized multi-national conglomerate." At the close of act 2, he wrote, would be "where HOTSHOT submits, is sold the inevitable necessity of multinational and sells his soul in exchange." What he envisioned, in short, was nothing less than "FAUST + MEPHISTOPHELES today."

Even the author seemed to realize the preposterously high stakes he had set for himself. As he wrote in a separate set of notes, "Now, all this is Strangelove-y as hell, can we make it work?"

Chayefsky approached his writing like any other trade; the most crucial requirement to completing a task was not ingenuity or talent, but the application of persistence over time. "If you can get in four good hours a day," he said of his work, "you're in terrific shape." Each day, after stopping off for his morning Sanka, he would arrive by 9:30 or 9:45 at his eleventh-floor office, a converted efficiency apartment indifferently decorated with worn gray carpet and haphazardly furnished with a piano, a complete collection of *National Geographic* magazines from January 1965 onward, an L-shaped desk to support his Olympia manual typewriter, and a swivel chair with stuffing spilling out of a torn armrest. The view his workspace offered, through tattered, yellowing paper window shades, was of a tenement across the street where a man could be seen at all times of day standing in his underwear and washing his hands in a basin. While his neighbor attended to his tasks, Chayefsky turned to his own solitary labors.

He wrote on whatever paper he could find, with whatever implement was available to him. Sometimes he expressed his ideas in complete and properly punctuated sentences. Other times they emerged in fragmentary bursts that ended on uncertain dashes. But whenever he had a thought or self-criticism, he reflexively committed it to paper, preferring unlined pages that were colored a canary yellow.

Before Chayefsky commenced on a proper screenplay it was his practice to prepare detailed organizational outlines and write novelistic, narrative prose treatments. Then he would rewrite them, and rewrite them, practically from scratch, as if testing himself to see how much of the previous draft he could still remember. Frequently he would stop in mid-summary and, in his writing, speak aloud to himself as he took stock of the situation: "What have we got?" "Okay let's follow that through." "Let's just push through the story and see just what our basic premise demands." In these necessary pauses he would decide whether he was satisfied with what he had or whether it was time to clear the table.

At the outset of his latest, nameless project, Chayefsky did not have characters so much as concepts. There was HOTSHOT, his "young (35) news producer" who is hired to bring his hit tabloid format to an ailing network newscast; KRONKITE, the fading anchorman whose on-set episode is broadcast across the nation due to a "fuggup"; and the NETWORK, on the verge of being or already bought out by an international conglomerate. Or maybe, Chayefsky speculated in capital letters, "BY THE END OF THE PICTURE, ALL THE NETWORKS WILL HAVE BEEN BOUGHT BY OTHER MULTINATIONALS."

Within a few weeks, Chayefsky had changed some of these parameters. His young HOTSHOT hero had metamorphosed into a fifty-year-old president of the network's news division, "a tough, but righteous fellow" who, alongside iconic broadcasters such as Edward R. Murrow and Fred W. Friendly, had been "involved up to his neck with the breaking of Senator McCarthy's reign of terror," and who, despite a disintegrating home life—"His wife divorced him years ago, and his children have grown further and further away from him"—still regards himself "as a man with the highest traditions of journalism." Soon this character would also have a name, Max Schumacher, a nod to the baseball pitcher Harold "Prince Hal" Schumacher, who in Chayefsky's youth had won the World Series with the 1933 New York Giants.

The "Krazy Kronkite" character also gained a name, Howard Beale— Howard as a tribute to Howard Gottfried and Beale for the mother-daughter duo of "Big Edie" and "Little Edie" Beale, the eccentric cousins of Jacqueline Kennedy Onassis who had lately clashed with Long Island health inspectors over their garbage-ridden Grey Gardens estate. The fictional Beale now had a back story, too, as a man in his late fifties, "benign, magisterial, the archetypical network anchorman, but declining in stature and audience," though still "an old friend and a man of genuine stature" in Max Schumacher's eyes.

A few supporting characters began to take shape as well: a hungry young corporate executive named Hackett, and a regional news director, maybe named Gianini or De Filipo, who would clash with Schumacher after previous successes at stations in Detroit, San Francisco, and Atlanta. ("His method of doing this is to adopt a tabloid attitude towards the news, sacrificing hard news, especially international and national news, for filmed stories on sex, scandal, nudity, sports, crippled children and dying animals and lots of religion.")

The film would begin on a typical day as Howard Beale comes in to prepare for the evening network news. But, Chayefsky wrote, "ten minutes into the news cast he flips out. He begins cussing his co-anchorman in Washington as being full of shit, throws a chair at one of the other newscasters, and generally carries on in a way startling, to say the least, for the benign, objective, pontifical dean of television anchormen."

Six months later, Beale returns refreshed from his stay at a sanitarium, and when he is put back on the air, he loses it again.

> But this time, his flip is not an unruly, profanity-ridden flip out, but an angry outburst against some piece of news. Beale erupts out of his benign, objective, pontifical image and turns into a roaring editorializing Jeremiah. Let's say, the

news is about inflation, and Beale warns in prophetic rage of
what will happen if we allow inflation to proceed uninhib-
ited. In the course of his eruption, he will call Nixon full of
shit for pretending the economics of the country are being
taken care of because it's a congressional election year and
Nixon is lying to the country to keep his party electable.
Something like that.

The crucial twist here, wrote Chayefsky, "is instead of objective
reporting, we put a raging prophet on the air, a prophet in the biblical
sense, who will prophesy doom and disaster every day, who will roar
out against the inequities, hypocrisies and absurdities of our times."
The problem, he realized, "is a man doing the raging prophet every day
can get to be repetitive and dull and a pain in the ass, so the trick is to
keep Beale straight but letting the audience know that you never know
when and where he will erupt."

"Okay, let's push on," he wrote. "Maybe the incidents will clear
themselves up."

While he cycled through possible endgame scenarios for the
screenplay—the networks versus Nixon? the multinational corporations declare war on Chile?—Chayefsky decided to add a love interest
for Schumacher, "a no bullshit girl who sees through all of Max's high
principled bullshit," whom he would dislike at first but who would, in
the long run, come to represent the virtuous path he needed to follow.
He also devised an early scene in which Schumacher and Beale "get
smashed" together as they contemplate their dispiriting professional
futures, in which Schumacher jokingly suggests to Beale that he commit suicide on the air—after giving the network a week to promote the
event—so that the anchor can depart with the best ratings he's ever
had. Beale, who is more depressed than Schumacher realizes, announces
on the air the next day that, in one week's time, he is going to commit
suicide on his show.

This scenario eerily paralleled a tragic real-life incident that occurred while Chayefsky worked on the screenplay. On the morning of July 15, 1974, viewers of WXLT-TV 40 in Sarasota, Florida, watched as Christine Chubbuck, the auburn-haired twenty-nine-year-old host of the morning show *Suncoast Digest*, appeared to be wrapping up a brief news report. Instead, Chubbuck looked into the camera and said, "In keeping with Channel 40's policy of bringing you the latest in blood and guts and in living color, you are going to see another first—an attempted suicide." She then drew a .38-caliber Smith and Wesson pistol from a shopping bag hidden behind her desk and shot herself behind the right ear. Chubbuck, who had a history of depression and had been discussing suicide with friends and coworkers in the preceding days, died later that night.

Whether Chayefsky was aware of Chubbuck's death at the time he was writing his screenplay is unclear. Months later, he wrote a line for Beale in which the anchor declares he will "blow my brains out right on the air, right in the middle of the seven o'clock news, like that girl in Florida," then deleted it from the script. But a set of screenplay notes dated July 16, 1974—the day after the horrific broadcast, when news of Chubbuck's suicide would have been widely known—makes no reference to her or the incident.

In that same set of pages, however, Chayefsky determined that the rising hotshot and the romantic interest for Schumacher were to be the same person, a female programming executive he called Louise Dickerson, then Diana Dickerson, and finally Diana Christensen. (He did not discard the name Louise entirely, giving it instead to the faithful wife Schumacher abandons to pursue his affair.) In an early description of the character that would carry through in future drafts, Chayefsky said Diana was "tall, willowy and with the best ass ever seen on a Vice President in charge of Programming." As she pursued her seduction of Schumacher, she would also try to capitalize on Beale's unexpected success, bringing his show and the increasingly unstable newsman under the umbrella of her department. She "encourages Howard to get mad-der and madder and more and more prophetic," Chayefsky wrote. "Howard doesn't need the encouragement. He gets madder and madder and finally achieves a state of grace and beatitude." In pencil, he added to this: "He is no longer a prophet; he has become a messiah."

Then followed the increasingly familiar muddle of intramural backstabbing and deal making among the network, its corporate par-ent, and the U.S. government, until Beale, Schumacher, and Diana are left "wandering the streets of the country preaching goodness, forgotten, ignored, even despised." Within these notes Chayefsky also sketched out a formative encounter between Schumacher and Diana in which, he wrote, "She looks him up and down, says: 'You're married, aren't you?' He says, yeah. She says: 'Then we better go to my place.'" On this page, Chayefsky wrote in red ink and underlined the words "*LOVE STORY.*"

All along, Chayefsky had wanted to tell a story that was global in its scope, from the continent-spanning clashes of governments and corporations to the atomic-level collisions of mere people, but the over-whelming sprawl of his narrative was becoming apparent. The harder he pressed himself to figure out how his characters fit together, the larger his roster of dramatis personae grew, and the longer he toiled without success to bring his story to an end—what logical conclusion was suggested by the inherently illogical universe he had built?—the more frustrated he became.

His cast had been expanded to include a female radical who leads a left-wing revolutionary group and her second-in-command, a sort of "Leader of the People guy, a hot-headed impulsive terrorist who wants to shoot it out with the cops all the time." At the other end of the spec-trum is the chairman of the corporation that owns the network, an executive named Arthur Jensen, who is to have a meeting with How-ard Beale and tell him "the revealed truth as it really is": "The world will soon be totally technological and the individual human will be just a piston rod in the whole vast machinery, a world dominated by the ultimate laws of production and consumption." Beale not only will be persuaded by this line of thought, but will embrace Jensen "as his new god to replace his voices."

In his notebooks, Chayefsky wrote year-by-year biographies for his characters. Schumacher doggedly worked his way up through the army's *Stars and Stripes* newspaper, local papers, radio, NBC morning news, *See It Now*, *CBS Reports*, and network documentary and news departments to become the president of his division. Diana, by contrast, had just five previous television credits—at a children's show, in audience research, and in daytime programming—before she reached her own vice president post. He drafted for himself a twenty-three-person roster of nonexistent executives at the fictional network he called UBS (a detail recycled from *The Imposters*), from its chairman of the board down to its vice presidents of programming, legal affairs, public relations for the news, and public relations for the network. He drew up a seven-night programming grid for UBS, inventing every show that aired from Monday through Sunday, 6:00 P.M. to 1:00 A.M., with such evocative and snidely reductive titles as *Surgeon's Hospital*, *Pedro and the Putz*, *Celebrity Canasta* (paired on Wednesday evenings with *Celebrity Mah-jongg*), *Lady Cop*, and *Death Squad*. None of this information would make its way into the screenplay.

For more practical purposes, Chayefsky wrote out a page-long list of synonyms for the verb *corrupt*—*adulterate*, *debase*, *dilute*, *suborn*, *defile*, *befoul*, *taint*, *tarnish*, *contaminate*, *degrade*, *debauch*, *putresce*— which he would surely need to draw from as his writing proceeded. For unclear reasons, he also created a separate, three-page list of the increasingly ominous political calamities he could imagine befalling the United States ("racist hysteria + jingoism"; "police violence in the ghettos + barrios"; "a consolidation of a United Front joining together all sections of the revolutionary, radical + democratic movements"; "the sheer numbers of the prisoner class and their terms of existence make them a mighty reservoir of revolutionary substructures and infrastructures").

Over lunches at the Russian Tea Room with his friends Bob Fosse and Herb Gardner, Chayefsky conjured up new screenplay concepts to distract him from the matter at hand. Starting from the semi-facetious suggestion that the three of them collaborate on a movie for Dino De Laurentiis, the deep-pocketed producer of a coming remake of *King Kong*, Chayefsky hit upon the idea of reinventing another classic horror tale, turning *Dr. Jekyll and Mr. Hyde* into the story of a latter-day character who experiments with an array of drugs, devices, and therapies as he studies "the states of human consciousness." For now this idea was little more than a literal sketch, a doodle of his imagined hero: pinched, peanut-shaped head, comb-over hairdo, pointy nose, and prominent chin.

Turning back to the screenplay he was supposed to be writing, Chayefsky tossed aside potential endings as fast as he could imagine reasons why they wouldn't work. What if the revolutionary group kidnapped Beale as a way of attracting attention for their group? But, wrote Chayefsky, "If their show is a hit, they already have attention— Ransom? They're already rich from TV—in fact, we are trying to say their revolutionary ideals have already been corrupted by TV—in what way?" None of this sounded like the American counterculture he thought he saw sprouting up all around him, which, he wrote, "wants chaos, depression + disaster to produce the popular discontent necessary to the creation of a revolutionary class."

An especially grim possibility considered by Chayefsky centered on a radical he named Achmed Abdullah, who is being groomed by Diana for a television show of his own and whom she convinces that "if he assassinates Beale and takes film of it—doing it right on camera during a Beale show," it "would give his show a tremendous kickoff for his first season." Chayefsky was at one point so certain he was on the right track that he wrote the following words, drew a black box around them, added a red box around the black box, and placed six red check marks next to the red box: "So the terrorist story is really the story of Achmed Abdullah, the mad terrorist who is slowly corrupted into a

TV star and finally winds up slaughtering everybody + HB just to give his TV show a terrific looking audience for his first show."

Had this version of the story come to pass, it would have ended with Achmed Abdullah using himself as a suicide bomb to blow up Beale and his studio audience, leaving only Diana "alone in the shambles wondering if there can be another way for the world to go."

The conclusion that Chayefsky instead settled on was milder, if only slightly. "We've got to replace Beale," he wrote to himself. "They replaced Allen with Paar—they replaced Paar with Carson and that show's still killing everybody—It's not Beale—it's his bullshit that sells." The solution was to have Diana get her up-and-coming terrorist group to assassinate Beale—"It not only gets Howard off the air, but it gives terrific promotion for the counter-culture hour"—and in the final joke of the movie, "they kick this idea around just like any other network decision."

If Chayefsky felt any sense of confidence or closure after reaching this conclusion, it was short-lived. It was here that he pulled a sheet of lined paper out of a notebook and dejectedly wrote to himself across the top of the page: "THE SHOW LACKS A POINT OF VIEW." Whatever this thing was that he had been laboring on all these months, it had "no ultimate statement beyond the idea that a network would kill for ratings, and even that doesn't mesh with the love story and whatever the love story says thematically." Maybe there was something darkly funny about these futile characters and the dehumanizing institutions they occupied, but he had not created them "just for laughs." "They are allegorical figures in a social satire—extreme social forces trying to get power through the medium of television—But, at the same time they are corrupted and eventually dominated by the medium they are trying to exploit." Chayefsky berated himself for not taking a clear stand in the narrative—"I'm not for anything or anyone"—and seemed to believe that the correct path to a meaningful message would necessarily lead him back to Howard Beale. But this created further problems: "If we gave Howard a speech at the end of the show," he asked himself, "what would he say?"

Acknowledging his self-doubt did nothing to overcome it; the anxiety had not been staved off so much as set down on a page. In the same routine and workmanlike way, Chayefsky typed out a blunt piece of text that, with a bit of revision, would become the opening lines of his screenplay.

> This story is about Howard Beale who was the network news anchorman on UBS-TV. In his time, Howard had been a mandarin of television, the doyen of anchormen, silver-haired, magisterial, dignified to the point of divinity, and with a HUT rating of sixteen and a twenty-eight per cent audience share. In 1969, however, his preeminence was yielded first to Walter Cronkite and then to John Chancellor, and, finally, in 1972, Howard K. Smith and Harry Reasoner took pretty much of what was left of Howard's audience. In 1973, his wife died, and he was left a childless widower whose ratings were sinking. He began to drink heavily, he became morose and isolated, and, on September 23, 1974, he was fired, effective in two weeks.

Dialogue was Chayefsky's single greatest talent. He was a conduit for spoken words—words as they were authentically spoken and as he wished to hear them spoken—and they emanated from him at variable speeds. Some lines came quickly, and some speeches seemed to pour out of him fully formed, ready for camera on the first draft. Others developed at a more deliberate pace, requiring extensive revisions and evolving over time as his thoughts about his characters changed.

As during the organizational stage of his scriptwriting, Chayefsky sometimes preferred to write in a straight prose style. These exercises could generate dialogue or stage directions that would carry over into a formal screenplay, or simply reveal the mood of a scene, as in a late

exchange between Schumacher and Diana showing that they are drifting apart emotionally.

> She sank into an overstuffed chair, submitted to its comfort,
> closed her eyes. "I'm dead" she said, "worn out. I'm trying to
> get some kind of season together for January, and I think I'm
> going nuts in the process." She opened her eyes and regarded
> Max now sitting across from her. "I can't tell you how good it
> is to see you, Max. I've missed you terribly, thought about
> you. Do you still hate me for taking over your network news
> show?" "Me," said Max, "In fact I've become quite a fan. I
> watch Howard every night. In a curious way, he's become a
> solace to me. I suppose I'm going through a menopausal panic.
> All of a sudden, I've begun contemplating death and disease.
> I've become conscious of every twitch, stitch, twinge and
> creak."

Or a decisive confrontation between Schumacher and Hackett, the
ruthless executive enforcer.

> "I mean, what the hell! What was this, some kind of demented
> gag!" "Oh, stop screaming, you monkey," growled Max.
> "You've been after my ass ever since you joined this network,
> and now you've got it. You'll have my resignation tomorrow
> and I'll be out of here by Friday." "The enormity of it!"
> screamed Hackett. "I mean, do you have any understanding
> of the enormity of what you Katzenjammer kids just did!" "I
> don't have to take your shit!" roared Max. "Your reorganiza-
> tion plan isn't effective till January, and I'm not accountable
> to you! I'm accountable to Mr. Ruddy and Mr. Ruddy only!"

These words did not all survive to the finished script, but it was in
the course of working through this exchange that Chayefsky penciled

in, almost as an afterthought, a bit of vulgar marginalia that became one of Hackett's more lasting utterances: "He was hoping I'd fall on my face with this Beale show, but I didn't. It's a big, fat, big-titted hit, and I don't have to play footsie with Ruddy any more."

Some ideas and characters fell out of the screenplay completely at this stage: a scene following the opening narration in which Howard Beale is found by his housekeeper "still wearing the clothes he wore last night, curled in a position of fetal helplessness on the floor in the far corner of the room"; Beale's nineteen-year-old daughter, Celia, who bemoans her fate as having "a nut for a mother and a drunk for a father"; a psychiatrist, Dr. Sindell, who examines Beale and suggests to Schumacher that he be institutionalized for his catatonic trances and manic delusions that "are traditional to schizophrenia, not that any of us know what the hell schizophrenia is."

Chayefsky's internal editor excised dialogue when it tended to be too overtly didactic—for example, a line spoken by Hackett in private to his fellow television and corporation executives: "Television is the most powerful communications medium that has ever existed. Its propagandistic potential hasn't even been touched. I sent several confidential memos to you about just that, Clarence."

But when his sense of humor was allowed to expand to its fullest dimensions of cynicism and morbidity, he did not always recognize when he had gone too far. In the scene where Beale and Schumacher drown their sorrows after the anchorman has been told of his firing and they drunkenly brainstorm the terrible TV programs that could follow his on-air suicide, Schumacher's imaginary pitch for *The Death Hour* is to be accompanied by additional suggestions for *The Madame Defarge Show* and something called *Rape of the Week*.

The rise and fall of Schumacher and Diana's love affair, from devious flirtations to smoldering passion to burned-out ashes, is a trajectory Chayefsky worked out over numerous revisions. When the female lead of his screenplay was still called Louise, she was a more romantic soul who, with dewy eyes, confesses to Schumacher that she'd previously met him when he gave a guest lecture during her senior year of college: "You and Ed Murrow and Fred Friendly had knocked off McCarthy, a craggy man, about thirty-eight, tie askew, collar unbuttoned—I think you were affecting the manners of the hard-bitten, hard-drinking, tell-them-like-it-is reporter. You made a terrific hit with the kids. I fell instantly in love with you. I had never had a crush on anyone before."

When she became Diana, her temperament changed, too. Like her namesake, she had the unattainability of a goddess and her animal wiles, but she was also volatile, joyless, and depressed, telling Schumacher that she lived "on the brink of despair" twenty-four hours a day.

> If I could stand the taste of liquor I'd be a lush. I had three wretched years of marriage and four futile years of psycho-analysis. I've tried hallucinogen drugs, commune living, activist politics. . . . In order of appearance, I've tried to believe in God, the dignity of man, love and marriage, drugs and feminism and even the absolutism of sex, and I was lousy at all of them, especially sex. I can't tell you how many men have told me what a lousy lay I am. I seem to have a masculine temperament. I arouse quickly, consummate prematurely, and promptly lose interest.

As the relationship turned physical, Chayefsky's prose was at times prurient, and he was unabashedly direct that Diana's presence in Schumacher's office, her lithe form "lit only by his desk lamp," was enough to give the old newsman an erection: "it was nipple clear that she was bra-less; when she leaned to his desk to flick an ash from her cigarette into the tray, he could see the assertive swells of her body, and, damn, if he wasn't reacting to all this like a schoolboy."

Over the course of an evening's seduction, the action moves from the UBS office building to a deserted Hamptons beach to a romantic Italian bistro to the dimly lit bedroom of a highway motor lodge—but the conversation, even in flagrante delicto, never changes from the subject of the TV business. Schumacher and Diana were, in a prelude to their lovemaking, meant to exchange more of Chayefsky's acidic and willfully awful ideas for new programming. She suggests a show adapted from *The Exorcist* ("I think that occult shit just might go very big as a series"), and he replies, "Sounds like good family entertainment. A ten year old girl who masturbates with crucifixes every week." She says, "I also want to do a soap on homosexuals," and he answers, "We'll call it *The Faggots*—the heartrending saga of a man's helpless love for his wife's boyfriend." All of these lines would be rewritten before Diana and Max moved on to their "accumbent embrace and intensified foreplay."

When their affair began to buckle under the intruding weight of reality, Chayefsky toyed with the possibility that Christensen and Schumacher's coupling might somehow remain intact, as in a set of handwritten lines that begins with her offer to marry him.

DIANA

I'll try to make a home with you. If I have to, I'll bear
children for you. And if that isn't love, it'll have to do.

MAX

It'll do.

DIANA

Until the real thing comes along.

MAX

It is the real thing—

But the hopefulness of this denouement must have surely rung false to Chayefsky, who instead prescribed for his two lovers to break apart with maximum brutality. Before the author extracted some of the venom in the scene, Schumacher's last words to Diana were to be

"We're born in terror and we live in terror. Life can be endured only as an act of faith, and the only act of faith most of us are capable of is love. And you're a vast wasteland, Diana. You haven't got a single cell of living emotion in you! Goddam right I'm going back to my wife!"

This, too, was discarded in favor of a kiss-off that more fluently spoke the language of television, in which Schumacher declares "a happy ending" for himself: "Wayward husband comes to his senses, returns to his wife with whom he has built a long and sustaining love. Heartless young woman left alone in her arctic desolation. Music up with a swell. Final commercial. And here are a few scenes from next week's show."

In his stage direction, Chayefsky adds, "We can hear the CLICK of the door being opened and the CLACK of the door closing" as Diana is left "alone in arctic desolation."

Chayefsky's monologues did not necessarily go through as much revision as his dialogue. The only substantial edits made to a speech given by Arthur Jensen, the chairman of UBS's parent company, the Communications Corporation of America (CCA), that wins Beale over to his "corporate cosmology," were for length. At its top, Chayefsky amputated a long windup in which Jensen argues that human suffering is not only unavoidable but a natural and necessary element in the reaction that produces progress: "Our generation fought two world wars in which we killed thirty more million men to uphold their dignity," he was to tell Beale. "We have barely endured two world-wide depressions, and, this year alone, twenty-five million people will starve. There's something less than efficient about all that."

At its end, Chayefsky lopped off a section in which Jensen lays out his vision for "a world of total orderliness, Mr. Beale, a planned and programmed world without war and famine, oppression and brutality, crime and disease, one massive, global tutelary corporation where all men can serve their specific functions, their necessities provided, their anxieties tranquilized."

From its midsection, Chayefsky cut a portion where Jensen observes that mankind may still get "hit with a tidal wave now and then, an earthquake, a tornado, and we still depend somewhat on natural snow for our ski weekends. But on the whole we control nature. We control everything." But he left behind the very next line, in which Jensen gives his grand summation: "You have meddled with the inexorable"—no, make that *primal*—"forces of nature, Mr. Beale, and I won't have it, is that clear?!"

Another speech, this one designed for Beale—the moment that would transform him from a madman ranting at sixty million viewers to a true prophet of the modern day—contained some of the rawest, most unrelenting language Chayefsky would write, even as it was composed in a methodical and incident-free manner. A hint of it appeared on a handwritten note made for himself, on a mostly blank page bearing only these words: "I want you people to get mad—You don't have to organize or vote for reformers—You just have to get mad—"

A more fleshed-out version of the speech appeared in one of Chayefsky's narrative treatments, with its most crucial expression still not fully formulated and pivoting on Beale's metaphor that, though nobody could seem to explain what television ratings were, his viewers themselves were the ratings. To that, he added: "Open all your windows. Everybody. The whole family. Fathers, mothers, lovers, kids. Everybody. Stick your heads out. Now, I want you to yell. I want you to yell: 'We're not going to take it any more. We're mad as hell, and we're not going to take this any more.' Yell that out into the streets."

A further refinement of the monologue dropped the too precise television jargon. Instead, Beale warns his viewers that he won't let them retreat into anesthetized isolation and orders them to unleash their anger, not in the form of physical violence but through the expression of language.

> I don't have to tell you things are bad. Everybody knows things
> are bad. It's a depression. Everybody's out of work or scared
> of losing their job, the dollar buys a nickel's worth, banks are

going bust, shopkeepers keep a gun under the counter, punks are running wild in the streets, and there's nobody anywhere who seems to know what to do, and there's no end to it. We know the air's unfit to breathe and our food is unfit to eat, and we sit and watch our teevees while some local newscaster tells us today we had fifteen homicides and sixty-three violent crimes, as if that's the way it's supposed to be. We all know things are bad. Worse than bad. They're crazy. It's like everything's going crazy. So we don't go out anymore. We sit in the house, and slowly the world we live in gets smaller, and all we ask is, please, at least leave us alone in our own living rooms. Let me have my toaster and my teevee and my hair dryer and my steel-belted radials, and I won't say anything, just leave us alone. Well, I'm not going to leave you alone. I want you to get mad.

I don't want you to protest. I don't want you to riot. I don't want you to write letters to your congressmen. Because I wouldn't know what to tell you to write. I don't know what to do about the depression and the inflation and the defense budget and the Russians and crime in the streets. All I know is first you've got to get mad. You've got to say, "I'm a human being, goddammit. My life has value." So I want you to get up now. I want you to get out of your chairs and go to the window. Right now. I want you to go to the window, open it, and stick your head out and yell. I want you to yell, "I'm mad as hell, and I'm not going to take this any more!"

The truncated stage direction that now followed Beale's speech only hinted at the power of the national reaction that his sermon was supposed to have generated. But in a narrative treatment, Chayefsky spelled out more emphatically his vision of what happened next.

Thin voices penetrated the dank rumble of the city, shouting: "I'm mad as hell, and I'm not going to take it any more!" Then, suddenly it began to gather, the edges of sounds and voices, until it all surged out in an indistinguishable roar of rage like the thunder of a Nuremberg rally.

To the outside world, which believed that the once-prolific and fiercely outspoken Paddy Chayefsky had exhausted his energy and had nothing left to say, the screenwriter did not mind helping to perpetuate the illusion. A brief report published in the *New York Times* in January 1975 pointed out that he had not presented anything on the stage since *The Latent Heterosexual* and that his last new work of any kind was *The Hospital*, a film released in the bygone era of 1971. "Since that production," the article said, "nothing." Speaking from his office at 850 Seventh Avenue, Chayefsky mentioned that he was "in the middle" of a new screenplay, and when the *Times* reporter inquired if the project was, perhaps, a comedy, the screenwriter was poker-faced. "I always think of them as comedies," he replied.

The article mentioned that Chayefsky's fifty-second birthday was just a few days away and that his son, Dan, was now nineteen, but there was no mention of his wife, Susan. Even his close friends and collaborators knew not to ask about her, and that such inquiries would produce half-mumbled responses, shrugs, or no answers at all. She was forty-eight now, and though she had been an often reliable presence by the author's side at public events in the 1960s and a reluctant entertainer and sandwich maker at his late-night poker games, members of the Chayefskys' social circle noticed that they had been seeing less and less of her over the years and that their interactions with her were mostly over the telephone.

Gwen Verdon, the actress and wife of Bob Fosse, estimated that she saw Susan a total of five times in her life, and Ann Reinking, Fosse's mistress, was surprised by Susan's beauty on the rare opportunities she was allowed access to her. "She had the kind of skin that doesn't need powder or makeup," Reinking said. "She changed her hair color when I knew her. One time she was blond and the next time she was brunette." She added, "My impression was that she had her own life, which from all appearances remained largely separate from Paddy's."

Mary Lynn Gottfried, Howard's wife, was newly married to her husband in 1973 when he and Chayefsky took what would be their final trip to Israel before work was halted on *The Habakkuk Conspiracy*. (As Mary Lynn would continue to joke thereafter, "I got the wedding; Paddy got the honeymoon.") Before the intrepid filmmakers embarked on their journey, the Chayefskys and the Gottfrieds all excitedly piled into a car that delivered them to the airport, where everyone kissed and hugged good-bye and the wives watched from the ground to wave at the plane that carried their husbands off beyond the horizon. Susan, as Mary Lynn recalled, was bright, vivacious, engaged in events and conversations, and not looking forward to the long absence of her spouse and the late-night, long-distance phone calls from seven time zones away. This was to be one of the last times Mary Lynn would see Susan Chayefsky in public.

Paddy Chayefsky could do nothing to cure Susan's ailments and hardly much more to ease her suffering. But he tried to integrate her into his professional life as best he could, and cared for her opinion enough that he sought her input on the screenplay he had nearly completed. In broad cursive strokes that were looser and less regimented than her husband's handwriting, Susan offered Paddy her comments, recorded on a memo pad that one might keep on a nightstand to jot down telephone messages. Whether she was directed by her husband's instructions or her own personal preferences, Susan gravitated in her notes to the scenes that involved female characters, and commented frequently on the distress these sequences stirred up within her.

After reading the argument between Max Schumacher and his wife, Louise, in which Max confesses that he has been conducting an affair with Diana Christensen while suspecting deep down that she is not "capable of any real feelings," Susan wrote to Paddy that it was "not comforting in reading it." Similarly, Susan wrote that she was "uncomfortable" with the series of caustic, businesslike remarks made by Diana throughout her overnight getaway with Schumacher, but "It pays off tho" when the two characters tumble into bed with each other. The scene, which Paddy later toned down, was "funny," Susan wrote, but you "almost don't want it that brutal."

A conversation between Diana and Laureen Hobbs, the leader of the revolutionary radicals, laden with swear words, TV-industry jargon, and references to left-wing political figures, was flagged by Susan for its "Very 'in' talk—think audience will not comprehend." She added that this scene "should be cut substantially—viewers won't understand it." When Beale resurfaces in a following scene to decry the CCA's clandestine takeover by a Saudi Arabian investment group, Susan observed, "you feel Howard is no longer in the picture. It is Diana + Max's picture." "By this pg," she wrote, "we feel we know what Howard is going to say," when what was needed was "a scene in which he 'relates' to other people." Responding to the climactic moment in which Schumacher harshly dismisses Diana and leaves her for good, Susan wrote, "love speech but wished I could see her through his eyes, so that when he makes the speech I believe it more."

There is no precise way to determine which of Susan's suggestions were directly incorporated into the script, which ones may have influenced its author in more oblique ways, and which may simply have caused him to chuckle or stroke his beard. But when Paddy Chayefsky arrived at what he felt was a complete version of the screenplay, which he had by now named *Network*, he took a marker and wrote its title across the cover page in block capital letters. Beneath this, he added in pen a parenthetical dedication: "(The original version for my Suzy)."

Chayefsky's first attempt at selling *Network* to Hollywood, in the summer of 1974, while the screenplay was still a work in progress, yielded a deal so quickly that he must have been suspicious. Following a discussion with David Begelman, the president of Columbia Pictures,

Chayefsky received an offer on June 24, guaranteeing him $100,000 for the *Network* script—$50,000 on signing and $50,000 on delivery—and as much as $300,000 in total screenwriting fees if the film were produced. By July the deal was dead when Columbia balked at a profit-sharing proposal that would have given Chayefsky and Gottfried 50 percent of the film's net proceeds. Suddenly a reconciliation with United Artists did not seem like such a bad option.

When Chayefsky and Gottfried were not feuding with United Artists and when it was not crushing their hopes and squandering their efforts, their relationship with the studio could be fruitful. In the 1950s, United Artists had released both *Marty*, one of the few filmmaking experiences Chayefsky did not regard as a psyche-scarring trauma, and his less successful movie adaptation of *The Bachelor Party*. More recently it had released *The Hospital*, but it frustrated Chayefsky and Gottfried with its handling of the television rights for that film and by putting the brakes on *The Habakkuk Conspiracy*. Once the dispute over *The Hospital* was settled, however, United Artists emerged as a good fit for the sort of scathing social indictment that *Network* offered.

By the end of 1974, the American motion picture industry was in the midst of a systemic transformation. Hollywood had not abandoned the bloated big-budget spectacles it had been turning out for the past twenty-five years, if films such as *Airport* and *The Towering Inferno* were anything to judge by. But a new species of cinema was arising, one that tapped into the tumultuous changes taking place in the country. These films were stylish and spoke with a cool, contemporary vocabulary; also, several of them made money. The financial success of features such as *Easy Rider*, a 1969 release that took in more than $40 million on a budget of $360,000, had shown that movies could be anti-establishment and pro box office.

Profitability and prestige were not mutually exclusive, either. It was not uncommon to see movies such as *Midnight Cowboy*, *MASH*, *The French Connection*, and *The Last Picture Show* atop lists of the year's high-grossing releases while also being nominated for—and winning—Academy Awards. Mike Medavoy, a veteran producer who was then the vice president of production at United Artists, would later summarize the prevailing philosophy of the day: "People thought about making good movies to make money."

United Artists had taken only partial advantage of this shift in values, during which time it was led by Arthur B. Krim, a former adviser to Presidents John F. Kennedy and Lyndon B. Johnson, and by David V. Picker, a third-generation movie industry executive whose uncle Arnold M. Picker had revitalized the company alongside Krim in the 1950s. The studio's eclectic offerings included Woody Allen comedies such as *Bananas* and *Sleeper* and the James Bond movie franchise; its highest-grossing release in 1971 had been *Diamonds Are Forever*, and its second-highest was *The Hospital*. The studio saw sweeping potential in the independent film adaptation of Ken Kesey's *One Flew Over the Cuckoo's Nest*, which it had recently acquired, and its executives were not afraid to get their hands dirty in support of more esoteric offerings: Picker and Krim had fought with the studio's parent company, the Transamerica Corporation, to allow United Artists to release X-rated features such as *Midnight Cowboy* and *Last Tango in Paris*.

A deal offered by United Artists for the *Network* screenplay in the fall of 1974 gave Chayefsky highly favorable terms, similar to those he would have received at Columbia: he would be paid $300,000 in total, receiving $100,000 for the finished script, $150,000 on commencement of principal photography, and a final deferred payment of $50,000. While United Artists retained final approval on the film's budget, director, and principal cast, the studio gave a substantial 42.5 percent of any net profits from the picture to Chayefsky's Simcha Productions.

The studios nonetheless retained private reservations about what kind of movie *Network* would turn out to be. An internal MGM memo cited "an off-the-record speculation" from the manager of the Hollywood Code Office at the National Association of Broadcasters, expressing concern that *Network*'s depiction of the television industry raised "serious doubts about the property's acceptability to U.S. networks for exhibition on television." Also problematic in this regard was its use of words such as *Chrissakes*, *fucking*, *shit*, *son of a bitch*, and *cocksmanship*. And when Chayefsky delivered a finished draft of the screenplay in May 1975, Marcia Nasatir, the head of script development at United Artists, wrote in a memo that it was "very funny" and "very pertinent," but she worried that it offered "no hero" and "no hope." If *The Hospital* presented the portrait of "a committed man," Nasatir wrote, *Network* "is all madness and bullshit philosophy. Accurate picture of TV and U.S.A. life but Chayefsky is too much of a do-gooding humanist to write a totally successful black comedy."

A few subsequent discussions about the project would soon discredit such a generous assessment of its creator. That spring, Mike Medavoy met with Chayefsky and Gottfried over lunch to talk about possible directors for *Network* and was surprised that they had enthusiastic designs on Sidney Lumet, the onetime wunderkind of television who was now the revered director of feature films such as *Serpico* and *Murder on the Orient Express*.

As Medavoy recalled the conversation, "I turned to both of them and I said, 'Are you serious? Sidney Lumet? To do a funny movie? When was the last funny movie you saw from Sidney Lumet?'" Reminding Chayefsky and Gottfried of the agonizing scene from Lumet's movie *The Pawnbroker* in which Rod Steiger penetrates his own hand with a nail, Medavoy told them, "That ain't funny." At which point, Medavoy said, Chayefsky "took his matzo ball soup and it went, a little bit, flying. And I looked at Paddy and I said, 'You know what? If you feel that strongly, he's probably a really good director for this.' And that ended the conversation and it was time to leave. It's one of those moments that is indelible in my mind, because I can't remember ever having anybody turn a plate of soup on me."

Chayefsky's resentment of the studio personnel, whose interference with *Network*, he felt, could only diminish the final product, grew, with one frustrating interaction after another. Summarizing a May 15 meeting with the United Artists executive Dan Rissner, Chayefsky recounted in a letter to his lawyer, Maurice Spanbock, some of the studio's suggestions for revising the script, including:

1. That Diana seduce Howard Beale for some not too clear reasons.
2. That Howard Beale and Max turn up at the affiliate convention and kick up some kind of comic ruckus.
3. That the characters of Althea and the Great Aga Khan [the domestic terrorists who would become Laureen Hobbs and the Great Ahmed Kahn] be merged into one character.

"All these suggestions are so amateurish and counter-productive they are hardly worth commenting on," Chayefsky wrote, "but I maintained my temper."

A few days later, Chayefsky and Gottfried were summoned to the studio's offices in New York to see William Bernstein, the head of its business affairs department. The meeting began in a friendly manner, with Bernstein complimenting Chayefsky on the *Network* screenplay. There was, of course, a qualification coming.

"He says, 'Listen, guys, it's a great script, but there's something about it that bothers me,'" Gottfried recalled Bernstein saying. "This is what he opens our meeting about. So I said, 'What about it bothers you?' So he looks at us, particularly Paddy, and he says, 'There's something about Howard Beale that I don't think works.' So, Paddy looks him in the eye. He says, 'Let me get this straight: There's something about Howard Beale that bothers you?' He said, 'That's it.'" Without speaking a single word more, Chayefsky stood up and exited the meeting, leaving Gottfried behind with Bernstein.

"I'm still there and I look at him," Gottfried said. "I knew the guy well. I said, 'You dumb son of a bitch.' Paddy really was an easy guy, but it was coming from the wrong place."

When Gottfried completed his own solitary journey from the aborted meeting back to Chayefsky's office, he found the author on the phone with Spanbock, asking that the United Artists deal for *Network* be dissolved.

It was a bold but not totally self-destructive move on Chayefsky's part. By this time, news of his volatile and exciting screenplay had reached other studios. Among them was Metro-Goldwyn-Mayer, which had once dominated the industry with a leonine might with epic films such as *Gone with the Wind*, *The Wizard of Oz*, and *Ben-Hur*, but which had not had much to roar about since 1960s-era hits such as *The Dirty Dozen* and *2001: A Space Odyssey*. Under its head of production, Daniel Melnick, MGM in the 1970s released about five to ten films a year, finding modest success with *Westworld*, a science-fiction thriller, and *That's Entertainment*, a feature-length compilation of vintage music and dance numbers celebrating the studio's fiftieth anniversary. But awards and credibility had recently proved elusive.

Melnick wanted to make *Network*, even if his corporate superiors did not. "They didn't want to have anything to do with it," he later recalled. "They were very scared, which was understandable. At that time MGM was working on a very reduced budget. To get their money back on a movie they had to sell the ancillary rights to television. And their network division said, 'Forget this, it will never be shown on national TV.'" Warner Bros. was interested in Chayefsky's screenplay as well, giving MGM the necessary encouragement to overcome its apprehension and pick up the project, if for no other reason than to keep it out of the hands of a competitor.

For Chayefsky and Gottfried there was an additional incentive to choose MGM. At that time, the studio's own distribution muscle was so atrophied that for significant releases it often sought support from United Artists. If United Artists joined in as a production partner now, it would be doing so in supplication, on Chayefsky and Gottfried's terms. And Gottfried was certain that Arthur B. Krim, the studio's chairman, would make the case to his colleagues that they did not want to lose out on the same movie twice. "I don't know Arthur's exact words,"

Gottfried said later, "but he made it plain that UA would look like ass-holes."

On July 2, 1975, *Variety* reported that MGM and United Artists had made a deal to release *Network* as a coproduction. The announcement declared that the "television industry is the target" of the film, adding that "Few specifics are offered about *Network* but one is that it will be 'a dramatic yet comedic view of the television medium.'" It would take more than a year for the movie to be made and released in theaters, at which time audiences could decide for themselves if that synopsis offered an adequate summary of what Chayefsky had wrought.

3

A GREAT DEAL OF BULLSHIT

"This story is about Howard Beale." The matter-of-fact observation was not only the first spoken phrase in Chayefsky's screenplay for *Network*; it became a mission statement for the author and his producer, Howard Gottfried, as they began the brick-and-mortar work of making the movie. They had the support of two studios and a budget of about $4 million, and now they needed to find a director, hire actors, scout locations, and fill every post from cinematographer to editor to costume designer to key grip.

But what they wanted most of all was an anchor. The actor playing Howard Beale would have to not only master large volumes of material and perform several intense monologues, but also substantially dictate the tone of the motion picture and establish a center of gravity around which its entire fictional world revolved. If they could have their way, they would cast this part first, and then move on to the remaining roles.

But while cinema may be the art of bringing dreams to life, this partic- ular fantasy would go unfulfilled.

As Chayefsky and Gottfried negotiated their deal with MGM and United Artists, they held wide-ranging discussions with the studios about a suitable director for *Network*. One list of candidates compiled by Chayefsky noted nearly every working filmmaker of the day—not only his preferred candidate, Sidney Lumet, but also accomplished screen veterans such as Elia Kazan, John Huston, and George Roy Hill; mem- bers of the next generation's New Establishment, including Francis Ford Coppola and Robert Altman; and foreign directors who had crossed over to the American marketplace, such as Roman Polanski and Marcel Ophüls. Another list seemed to emphasize Lumet, Bob Fosse, and Mike Nichols, whose personal telephone numbers were written next to their names, while adding Sydney Pollack and a relative new- comer named Martin Scorsese—whose name was sufficiently unfamil- iar to Chayefsky that he misspelled it as "Scorcese."

One viable contender strongly opposed by Chayefsky was Hal Ashby, whose hit social satire *Shampoo* had opened in March 1975. In a draft of a letter that did not mention Ashby by name but whose subject was clear, Chayefsky wrote that the directing of *Shampoo* was "blunt and obvious," made by a filmmaker who was weak "on scene and setting and shoots everything—even his crowd scenes—up tight on the actors throughout." "He never pulls back and lets you see where the hell you are," Chayefsky added. "With the exception of the beauty salon, which was blatant, none of the sets and locations had any comment or char- acter in them." Dispensing with any lingering uncertainty about whether he would let this person touch *Network*, Chayefsky wrote, "If you're asking me if this director is the right one for a high-style film, filled with lengthy set-pieces and theatrical monologues, a film that is totally satiric and especially politically satiric . . . I'd have to say no I don't think so."

The studios also made their preferences known. Before his rela- tionship with Chayefsky could go completely sour, William Bernstein, the United Artists executive whose indelicate remarks about Howard Beale had sent the author storming out of his office, wrote to Chayefsky's lawyer, Maurice Spanbock, suggesting "that any submissions be limited only to those directors whom we specifically discussed last week, i.e., Stanley Kubrick, Mike Nichols, Arthur Penn and Bob Fosse."

But in a letter to the actor Paul Newman dated May 21, Chayefsky wrote, "All other factors remaining constant, Sidney Lumet will probably direct this picture." He continued: "As far as Sidney is concerned, you can have any part in this picture you want. From the selfish interest of the production, however, I'd like you to consider the part of Howard Beale. It's the most difficult part to cast; you and a very small handful of other actors are the only ones I can think of with the range for this part. Anyway, please read this script and see if you have any interest in starring in it. Needless to say, I would consider it a privilege to have you star in anything I write." He added his home and office numbers, but his entreaty to Newman was unsuccessful.

Around this same time, Chayefsky and Gottfried had an audience with George C. Scott, the truculent star of *The Hospital*, who was preparing to play Willy Loman in a Broadway revival of *Death of a Salesman* that he was also directing. They delivered a copy of the *Network* screenplay to Scott in his dressing room at the Circle in the Square Theatre, hoping that he would be interested in playing Howard Beale.

"We said, 'Here it is. You name the part,'" Gottfried recalled. "Because at that point, we were just anxious to get him, and we'd figure out how to get him to play the role." A few days later, Scott summoned the partners back to the theater.

"He said in that voice of his, 'Who's playing Diana?'" Gottfried recounted. "And we said we haven't cast it yet. And he says, 'How about Trish?'"—the actress Trish Van Devere, Scott's fourth wife, whom he had married in 1972, after his second divorce from Colleen Dewhurst.

Van Devere had appeared in films such as *Where's Poppa?* and *One Is a Lonely Number*, but neither Gottfried nor Chayefsky could envision her carrying the central female role in *Network*. "I spoke up,"

Gottfried said, "because I didn't want to put Paddy in any position. I said, 'George, that's impossible. I'm sure that the studio's going to insist on a star.' We had to give him some reason." Nonetheless, said Gottfried, "He was devoted to her and wanted to get her a part. I said, 'George, you know the business, it's impossible, we can't do this.' And he said, 'Then I'm not interested.'"

In a letter dated June 8, Van Devere wrote directly to Chayefsky, praising him for having come a long way "from not one woman doctor in *Hospital* to the executive broad of all times heading your cast in *Network*!" She added, "George felt that role and I would be very good for one another—I seldom agree with George but in this case I tend to."

It took nearly two months for Chayefsky to respond to Van Devere; on July 31 he finally wrote to her, saying that his response had been slow because "I had nothing to tell you." He went on to say that "the preliminary processes of casting have started; that is, a great deal of bullshit is going on between us and M.G.M. and United Artists. I will keep you informed on what's happening."

In further handwritten lists, Chayefsky cycled through the many esteemed actors he could imagine playing his carefully crafted *Network* characters. For Beale, his mad prophet of the airwaves, he envisioned Jimmy Stewart, Henry Fonda, Gene Hackman, Sterling Hayden, or Robert Montgomery; Max Schumacher, too, could be played by Fonda or Hackman, or by William Holden; and Diana Christensen seemed ideal for Candice Bergen, Faye Dunaway, Ellen Burstyn, or Natalie Wood. On another sheet of his telltale yellow paper he ranked his top choices for the three principal roles. For Beale, they were: 1. Hackman, 2. Fonda, 3. Hayden, 4. Stewart; for Diana: 1. Dunaway, 2. Bergen, 3. Burstyn; and for Schumacher: 1. Lee Marvin, 2. Fonda, 3. Holden, with Burt Lancaster and Walter Matthau listed, unnumbered, in reserve.

These standings were arrived at after much crossing out and many revisions, and with the use of several crisscrossing arrows that suggested last-minute changes of heart. For Chayefsky they represented personal tastes rather than the actual attainability of the actors, and he could not invest himself too deeply in these preferences. He had worked in show business long enough to know that for every available role and responsibility, a dozen or more options must be floated, and that no one ever gets his first choice. But some crucial pieces soon began to fall into place.

The life of Sidney Lumet had advanced on a track that was often parallel to Chayefsky's, intersecting only occasionally. Born in Philadelphia in 1924 to Russian-Jewish parents, Lumet was raised in the tenements of Manhattan's Lower East Side and in Astoria, Queens. As a teenager he attended New York's Professional Children's School while acting in Broadway plays written by Maxwell Anderson and William Saroyan, and filled his personal notebooks with precocious guidance such as: "I advise all the children who want to go on the stage to try first to find a profession where the hours are more regular and the pay is better. The theatre is no place for sissies or people who can't take it." With his inner fire came feistiness; as Lumet would later observe, "As a Jew, I'm very judgmental. As a street Jew, doubly so."

After serving in World War II, Lumet resumed acting and then focused on directing as the rapid expansion of television created new opportunities and mobility. Before he was thirty years old he was working seven-day weeks, splitting his time between two CBS programs: *Danger*, on which he shared directorial duties with Yul Brynner and which had been the venue for Chayefsky's first produced teleplay; and *You Are There*, a weekly series of historical reenactments hosted by Walter Cronkite. A 1953 feature in *Life* magazine showed the spry, five-foot-five-and-a-half-inch bespectacled director clad in a dress shirt and a skinny tie as he threw himself, quite literally, into morning rehearsals for a *You Are There* episode about the Battle of the Alamo, demonstrating for a Texan defender how to fall over a wall and die; and inspecting a hug between Nina Foch and Stephen Elliott during afternoon scene work for *Danger*. "In this rat race I ought to be having a nervous breakdown every week," Lumet said in an accompanying interview. "But I feel just great."

In 1957, two years after Chayefsky's successful leap from television to motion pictures, Lumet made his film directing debut on a feature adaptation of *12 Angry Men*, Reginald Rose's sweltering jury room drama, which had first been presented on the CBS anthology series *Westinghouse Studio One* in a live production directed by Franklin J. Schaffner. For the movie, which was budgeted at $350,000 and boasted a star-studded, cinema-ready cast led by its producer Henry Fonda, Lumet made the unusual if pragmatic decision to film its many speeches out of sequence and instead shoot juror by juror, chair by chair, as he worked his way around the deliberation table. In advance, he sketched out all the necessary camera angles and lines of sight and decided the amount of sweat that should appear on each actor as conditions grew increasingly heated.

"I spent nights puzzling the problem and my script became a maze of diagrams," Lumet explained at the time. "We had arguments on the set as people tried to explain to me that I was crazy. But the diagrams came out right 396 times in 397 scenes. One we had to reshoot because I had the stockbroker looking the wrong way as he spoke to another actor." Released by United Artists, as *Marty* was, *12 Angry Men* was a commercial disappointment but a critical success, earning Lumet an Academy Award nomination for best director and propelling him toward a full-time filmmaking career.

As he graduated from romantic trifles such as *Stage Struck* and *That Kind of Woman* to more assured and ambitious features such as *Long Day's Journey into Night* and *The Pawnbroker*, Lumet lived as passionately as he worked. The director made front-page news in the summer of 1963 when, the day after his second wife, Gloria Vanderbilt, got a quickie divorce from him in Juárez, Mexico, firefighters were dispatched to his Manhattan apartment to revive him from an apparent overdose of sleeping pills. (Lumet later joked that what he'd indulged in that day "was only seven vodkas, a Miltown and idiocy.") That

November he married Gail Jones, a journalist and author who was the daughter of Lena Horne, though the couple would spend another month publicly denying that they'd wed before finally admitting to their nuptials in December.

In a lengthy *Life* magazine feature on the making of *The Group*, Lumet's 1966 adaptation of the Mary McCarthy novel, Pauline Kael described the director as being "cheap, fast and reliable," but also lacking in intellectual curiosity. Kael, who had been given extensive access to the production of the film, wrote that Lumet was "everybody's second choice, the driving little guy who talked himself into jobs and then finished them before the producers even got to know him."

But by the mid-1970s, Lumet had solidified a cinematic reputation for his quintessential depictions of claustrophobic urban angst and New York City in all its grimy, garbage-strewn glory. As he would later explain, he had shunned Hollywood to avoid the intrusion of studio bureaucrats, and discovered that living and working in New York offered further benefits. "I found that I was getting something back," Lumet said. "For example: I think I'm a better director because I saw Jerry Robbins's ballet last night. Why leave that? The city is always changing and always remains the same, and that's what I hope about myself." In movies such as *Serpico* and *Dog Day Afternoon* he was also developing a less mannered and more naturalistic, vérité approach to filmmaking, which appealed to Chayefsky and Gottfried as they narrowed the field for a director for *Network*. So, too, did his experience in television—as well as a certain resentment he carried with him after leaving the medium. Lumet was fond of saying, "I never left television; it left me."

Yet despite Chayefsky's interest and the many times Lumet was mentioned as the presumptive director of *Network*, a delay preceded his officially signing on. "It had a somewhat tortured beginning," said Philip Rosenberg of the project. Lumet's longtime production designer, Rosenberg would serve in that same capacity on *Network*. Though Lumet had mentioned the project to him several months before work began on it, Rosenberg said, "There were some very tense waiting periods for it to actually start up, and Sidney seemed to be quite nervous about something. I wasn't privy to what the difficulties were, but it was several weeks where Sidney was doing nothing but worrying and staying in his house and stripping the windows to pass the time while he was waiting for something to get settled."

Lumet may simply have been waiting for the resolution of financial matters or other points relating to his *Network* deal. (His production company, Amjen Entertainment, would ultimately receive 12.5 percent of the film's net profits.) Or he may have been contemplating just how much autonomy he was willing to concede on the film, knowing that he would not have final approval over the finished cut of the movie and that his wishes would have to be subordinate to Chayefsky's. "Paddy is a tough writer and creator," Rosenberg said. "He feels justifiably possessive of the entire work. So for a director to work for him is—I don't know if anybody else could have directed this picture without it becoming a debacle."

Other longtime colleagues said that Lumet was not overly concerned with final-cut approval. "Most of the directors who worked in New York basically did what they wanted," said Alan Heim, who edited *Network* and numerous other Lumet features. "A good director—you make a good movie, nobody's really going to meddle too much."

For all the qualities he shared with Chayefsky, Lumet began to pick up on differences in their attitudes and approaches to their work once he formally came on board *Network* that summer. Lumet was known for his on-set charm and spirit of camaraderie, but he said of Chayefsky, "His cynicism was partly a pose, but a healthy dose of paranoia was also in his character." More precisely, Lumet described the writer as "litigious": "His answer to conflicts very often was, 'Can I sue?'"

The arrival of Lumet meant that Chayefsky's initial ideas for casting *Network* would have to be tempered with his director's proposals, and the two men did not always see eye to eye. Recalling one brainstorming session with Chayefsky, Lumet said, "I suggested Vanessa Redgrave. He said he didn't want her. I said, 'She's the best actress in the English-speaking world!' He said, 'She's a PLO supporter.' I said, 'Paddy, that's blacklisting!' He said, 'Not when a Jew does it to a Gentile.'" But they found common ground elsewhere, and with it the first major star of their film.

"I think of Faye Dunaway as an enchanted panther in a poem," a person identified only as "an actor who admires her" told *People* magazine at the end of 1974. "She's tawny and elegant, and her eyes are like big mysterious emeralds. I want to stroke her but I want bars between us when I do. She looks hungry and dangerous. Whatever there is to want, she wants it all." Protected by a cloak of mystery, this unnamed enthusiast identified the essentially feline nature of the actress: Dunaway was alluring and graceful, with sharp features that, before she even expressed herself, could make her seem exotic or aloof. Underneath that simultaneously tantalizing and intimidating exterior lurked a curious intellect, boundless passion, and a mercurial mood. No one could question Dunaway's talent or her devotion to her art. But as the anonymous author of this appraisal surely knew—why ask for anonymity otherwise?—when she felt she was cornered, she could pounce.

In a decade's worth of motion pictures, Dunaway had won international fame, lost it, and then recaptured it. *Bonnie and Clyde*, the New Wave–inspired Arthur Penn drama that paired her and Warren Beatty as the doomed Depression-era bank robbers, had been a showcase for Dunaway, from her nearly naked but discreetly framed frolic at the start of the film to its bullet-riddled finale. Released in 1967, it was only her third movie role; it made her a sensation (along with her slightly anachronistic beret and midi-skirt look, created by the costume designer Theadora Van Runkle) and earned her the first Academy Award nomination of her career.

The next year, in *The Thomas Crown Affair*, Dunaway faced off against Steve McQueen in the sexiest chess scene ever committed to celluloid. But by 1970, gossipy newspaper columns and their readers were already asking, "Where Did Faye Fade To?"—the answer being that she had been working on challenging if not always widely seen films such as *Little Big Man* and *Puzzle of a Downfall Child*.

Then, just as abruptly, Dunaway was generating talk of a comeback for her performance as the enigmatic Evelyn Mulwray in the 1974 crime noir *Chinatown*, where her vintage looks made her a perfect fit for Roman Polanski's vision of Southern California in the 1930s. Dunaway was once again called upon to shed her clothes, for a postcoital scene with costar Jack Nicholson, and she received her second Oscar nomination. (A *People* magazine profile from that year offered a poetically apt summation of the actress, calling her "a gossamer grenade.") But in the process, she was also saddled with the most withering criticism of her career. In an interview with *Rolling Stone*, Polanski described an incident on the *Chinatown* set where Dunaway called filming to a halt so she could air her grievances to the director. Of the actress, he said, "You have, I guarantee, never seen such certifiable proof of craziness. Working with Faye, I might eventually have actually questioned my own methods had I not known that she has had the same confrontations with *all* her directors, and gained the reputation as a gigantic pain-in-the-ass."

Years later, Dunaway responded to Polanski's charges by suggesting that the world did not permit women to pursue perfection in their work in the same way that men were allowed to. "The fact is a man can be difficult and people applaud him for trying to do a superior job," Dunaway said in a memoir called *Looking for Gatsby*. "People say, 'Well, gosh, he's got a lot of guts. He's a real man.' And a woman can try to get it right and she's 'a pain in the ass.' It's in my nature to do really good jobs, and I would never have been successful if I hadn't."

Dorothy Faye Dunaway was born in 1941 in a one-room frame house on the Florida farm where her father worked as a hand, located between the Panhandle community of Two Egg and the town of Bascom. She was raised primarily by her mother and extended family while her father worked odd jobs and was drafted into the army. He reenlisted after World War II and brought his wife and children with him to Germany, where in 1952 he disappeared from his base on a bender.

Dunaway's father was listed as AWOL, then found the next day and court-martialed. He would be convicted on charges of drunken driving and resisting arrest and sentenced to six months in a stockade, but before his trial his eleven-year-old daughter made herself a fateful promise to become a self-sufficient adult, requiring no one else's help. "I determined that no matter what I did," Dunaway vowed, "I would never allow myself to be in the position of needing financial support from a man."

Dunaway graduated from a Tallahassee high school, and a teaching scholarship led her to Florida State University and some of her earliest stage roles, including Olivia in *Twelfth Night* and the title character in *Medea*; she then transferred to Boston University's School of Fine and Applied Arts, portraying Hypatia in Shaw's *Misalliance* for the Harvard Summer Players and Elizabeth Proctor in Miller's *The Crucible*. In 1962 she passed up a Fulbright Scholarship to join the Lincoln Center Repertory Company, newly formed by Elia Kazan and Robert Whitehead, and two days after graduating college she signed a one-year contract to replace Olga Bellin in the role of Margaret More in Whitehead's Broadway production of *A Man for All Seasons*.

To each of her screen characters Dunaway sought to bring careful reflection and confident choices, sometimes to the befuddlement of filmmakers who expected their instructions to be followed without question. In her eyes, Bonnie Parker was "a creature who wanted freedom, and a bra just didn't fit"; Vicki Anderson, in *The Thomas Crown Affair*, was the archetype of "a woman pushing the envelope." "These were women who found out who they were," Dunaway said, "who expressed who they were, and who were able to function as complete human beings, the way men do in the world." She also paid a financial price to get the recognition she felt she deserved: to share the over-the-title billing that Warren Beatty enjoyed in *Bonnie and Clyde*, she had to give back $25,000 of her $60,000 salary.

When J. J. Gittes gazes upon Evelyn Mulwray in *Chinatown*, he notices a tiny flaw in her eye. But when Dunaway looked at herself as closely, she saw a mass of imperfections. After watching herself in daily film footage from *Bonnie and Clyde*, she wrote, "I couldn't stand how I was—my manners, my gestures. . . . This was the first time I had seen myself on this big screen, with its millions of silver dots, and I just thought I was sadly lacking."

In her off-camera life, Dunaway had romantic affairs with Lenny Bruce; Jerry Schatzberg, the photographer turned director who oversaw her on *Puzzle of a Downfall Child*; and the Italian actor Marcello Mastroianni. "I used men as buffers against the world," she would later explain. "I never walked away bleeding from a relationship, because I allowed them to continue long after they were over so I could prepare myself for the moving on. My bleeding took place while they were ending . . . But I couldn't let go. I was so afraid of being alone."

Mastroianni, the libidinous star of *La Dolce Vita* and *8½*, shared Dunaway's aptitude for cutting analysis. In an essay published in *McCall's* magazine after the two had parted ways, Mastroianni said of her, in remarks he apparently considered to be affectionate:

> She wasn't beautiful. Or she was beautiful because she wasn't perfect. She was full of imperfections, edges, mistakes. She had the hands of an old woman. The first time I saw those hands, I thought: "What a pity, those bony hands! I like soft hands with tapering fingers." . . . She had the knees of a Christ, sharp and lean and strong. And her nose was squashed, broken on the septum—even her face had something wrong. Yet it was so shining, pale and shining, lunar.

These imperfections notwithstanding, Dunaway married Peter Wolf, the lead singer of the Boston-based rock group the J. Geils Band, in the summer of 1974. She wrapped film roles in *The Towering Inferno* and *Three Days of the Condor*, performed in stage revivals of *After the Fall* and *A Streetcar Named Desire*, and then began a hiatus from acting that would last nearly a year.

Dunaway, who knew and respected Chayefsky's writing, was

excited by his screenplay for *Network* and eager to play the character of Diana, recognizing her as a woman who "was driven, more driven in her career than I was in mine, but I knew what fueled that sort of ambition." She pursued the role over the objections of her new husband and of confidants such as the playwright William Alfred, who regarded Diana as too heartless, and were concerned, Dunaway said, "that people would think badly of me, would confuse the character and the actor, and come to believe I was like that."

Among those who encouraged Dunaway to sign on for *Network* was her agent, Sue Mengers, a powerful Hollywood player who also represented Barbra Streisand, Ali MacGraw, and Cybill Shepherd, and who said she persuaded the actress despite Dunaway's insistence that she didn't feel like working at the time. "I sat her down and told her I could no longer represent her if she didn't do this film," Mengers would later say. Dunaway herself said that she believed Diana was "one of the most important female roles to come along in years." "If you wanted to succeed as a woman in a man's world, you had to beat them at their own game," she later wrote. "Diana, I knew, would end up right in the middle of that debate."

Before Dunaway had fully committed to the film, Lumet visited her at her Manhattan apartment on Central Park West. There, Lumet said, he gave Dunaway an ultimatum on the character of Diana.

> Crossing the floor of her apartment, before I'd even reached her, I said, "I know the first thing you're going to ask me: Where's her vulnerability? Don't ask it. She has none." Faye looked shocked. "Furthermore, if you try to sneak it in, I'll get rid of it in the cutting room, so it'll be wasted effort." She paused just a second, then burst out laughing. Ten minutes later I was begging her to do the part. She said yes.

Dunaway, by her own account, was already teeming with ideas for the film and made the case to Lumet that the part of Max Schumacher should be played by Robert Mitchum. But Lumet declined her pro-posal—he and Chayefsky had their own plans about how they were going to fill the role.

On September 24, 1975, MGM and United Artists issued a press release announcing that Dunaway would star in the film the studios referred to as "Paddy Chayefsky's *Network*," noting in the second paragraph that it would be directed by Lumet, who planned to shoot on location in New York and at the MGM Studios in Culver City, California. Recycling a turn of phrase from Chayefsky's screenplay, the announcement proudly said of Dunaway that "in her starring role, which Chayefsky believes to be one of the most important parts written for a woman in recent years, the actress will play a character described by the writer as tall, willowy, and with the best bottom ever seen on a Vice President in charge of programming." Not mentioned in the press release was Dunaway's salary of $200,000, though it noted that she "will be joined by two male stars in *Network*," a reference to the not-yet-solidified roles of Howard Beale and Max Schumacher. An item published in *Variety* that same day added the detail that William Holden was "close to signing" for the project.

Holden and Dunaway had previously appeared together one year earlier, in *The Towering Inferno*, the star-studded Irwin Allen disaster picture in which she had played the enticing girlfriend of Paul New-man's altruistic architect, Doug Roberts, and Holden had played the owner and builder of the 138-story skyscraper turned deathtrap of its title. They shared only a few on-screen exchanges, including one where, as she enters a party clad in a beige barely-there dress, Holden gives her the once-over and remarks, "Find me the architect who designed you, and who needs Doug Roberts?" A mild weariness pervaded this line reading, as it did much of Holden's delivery in the film, as if he were exacting quiet retribution on the producers who had given him lower billing than leading men such as Newman and Steve McQueen, and who placed his name last of the three on the movie's poster, at the end of a diagonal and decidedly downward trajectory.

Once, he had been called "Golden Boy," and not simply because he made his motion picture breakthrough in the 1939 film adaptation of that Clifford Odets play. In his prime, the ruggedly handsome Holden played the doomed screenwriter of Billy Wilder's 1950 film noir *Sunset Boulevard* (the movie for which everyone thought he should have won an Academy Award) and the suspected American turncoat in Wilder's 1953 prisoner-of-war movie *Stalag 17* (the movie for which he in fact received his Oscar). He was the best man of his close friend Ronald Reagan at his 1952 wedding to the actress Nancy Davis and, by his own account, nearly killed himself filming his own stunts on David Lean's *The Bridge on the River Kwai*, in a scene that required him to swim through rock-strewn rapids in the Indian Ocean and place dynamite charges at the base of the bridge. "I was halfway through when I hit a hidden rock headfirst," Holden said of the feat gone awry, which he still completed in a single take. "The blow dazed me and I was pulled under by the churning current. Somehow I managed to fight my way to the surface."

But as Holden was often reminded, and frequently to his face, he was not in his heyday anymore. A journalist taking stock of the actor in the 1970s commended him for possessing a jawline every bit as strong as it had been four decades prior, but added that "the hairline is receding, the skin has leathered, and basset-hound bags droop under mellow eyes." Another appraisal from this period described Holden as speaking "in commanding tones and well-enunciated repose, a whisky baritone buried by a coffee-table carton of Carleton cigarettes," while still another called him "world-weary" and said, as casually as if it were reporting the weather, that his "face started to deteriorate" some years ago and was now "old" and "shopworn."

All that Holden could do was accept these assessments with dignity and self-deprecation. "What am I?" he said. "A crazy-faced middle aged man. I can't grow younger." Fortunately for the people who put forth such blunt observations, he said, "they don't have reruns of their past on TV. They don't realize that when they see me playing the violin and trying to learn how to box on the Late Show it was 38 years ago and I was 20 years old. But at least I no longer have to sit on the edge of Gloria Swanson's bed with one foot on the floor and my overcoat on. The movies have grown up, and so have I."

By 1960, Holden had appeared in nearly fifty feature films. In 1975 he was regarded as an endearing relic, an old zoo animal to throw peanuts at, a charmingly obsolete vaudevillian who, gracefully or not, just needed to exit the stage. He was fifty-seven years old.

He was born William Franklin Beedle Jr. in the town of O'Fallon, Illinois, in 1918, to a family that claimed George Washington and Warren G. Harding among its relations. His father, a chemist, soon moved the family to Pasadena, California, where young William studied chemistry at the local junior college and, disliking the subject, joined the Pasadena Workshop Theater's production of a play about the life of Madame Curie. Playing the role of Curie's eighty-year-old father-in-law, he was discovered on opening night by a Paramount talent scout who signed him to a fifty-dollar-a-week contract with the studio. When its executives expressed concern that the actor's surname was too evocative of an insect, William took inspiration from an assistant managing editor at the *Los Angeles Times* and changed it to Holden.

Throughout his seemingly perpetual ascent, following from the moment that director Rouben Mamoulian chose him from among some three thousand contenders to star opposite Barbara Stanwyck in *Golden Boy*, Holden harbored a cynical attitude toward show business and rarely allowed himself to take much pride in his work or his iconic status. "For twenty-two years, I've put up with a lot of asinine suggestions made by various studio experts about how to change myself—to fix the shape of my eyebrows, and stuff like that—but I've always refused to do it," he wrote in the *New Yorker* in 1961. "I may not like the way I look, but I take myself the way I am and do the best I can with it. Being a movie star and seeing myself on the screen don't make me feel good. In fact, they make me feel kind of sad. But I do the best I can with all that, too."

In truth, Holden had done exceedingly well for himself. For his work on *The Bridge on the River Kwai* alone, he was guaranteed a salary of $250,000 against 10 percent of the film's gross revenue—a contract that paid him $3 million when the movie's ticket sales came to $30 million worldwide. By 1960 he had investments in nearly every part of the globe and a home in Switzerland that kept him close to productions such as *The World of Suzie Wong* and *The Counterfeit Traitor*, but that also fostered occasional accusations that he was a tax cheat. "I'm living in Switzerland for the same reason a Madison Avenue advertising man gives up his suburban home in Connecticut and moves to Central Park West," Holden explained at the time. "I just want to be closer to my work." By the 1970s he could be most often found at his estate in Palm Springs, or at the Mount Kenya Safari Club, the hunting lodge and rare-animal preserve he helped establish on 1,200 acres of ranch land near Nairobi (at a cost of $750,000), where he vacationed and played host to the likes of Bing Crosby and Lyndon B. Johnson.

For many years, Holden had been portrayed in flattering stories published by compliant Hollywood publicity magazines as sharing a wholesome family life with his wife, the former actress Brenda Marshall, their two sons, and Marshall's daughter from her previous marriage. But in 1963 the couple announced their separation after twenty-two years of marriage; they briefly reconciled a few years later and finally divorced in 1971.

In 1966, Holden was involved in a fatal car accident near Pisa, Italy, overturning the other car and killing its driver. Holden, who was not alone in his vehicle—his passengers were two American women in their twenties whom he said he was driving to visit some friends—was ultimately cleared of any wrongdoing in the crash. *TV Guide* wrote that "it was common knowledge" that Holden "had sought some solace in the bottle—too much solace, some said" while he and Marshall worked out their issues. The actor said in the mid-1970s that, after a few years of winnowing himself down to just beer, he had quit drinking altogether and didn't go out. But at least part of this claim was untrue: though he had yet to acknowledge it publicly, Holden had recently been seeing the actress Stefanie Powers, whom he'd met at a celebrity tennis match in 1973 and who was twenty-four years his junior.

For all his cultivated grouchiness about the film business, Holden truly despised only one thing about acting: love scenes. As many times as he had done them, Holden said they were "the most difficult feature of an actor's profession, the one real embarrassment, the chief invasion of privacy." "I've played my share of them with some of the most beguiling partners in the business," he said, "but I hope it will be taken as no reflection against these ladies that I'd rather be anywhere else than in their arms . . . Aside from the fact that there are upwards of 50 members of the crew looking on, there is also the little matter of turning up 18 times life size on the world's movie screens. This is too much. It's too personal."

Of the actors recruited for the principal cast of *Network*, Holden presented the least difficulty, in part, perhaps, because he was granted favorable terms very similar to Dunaway's: a generous bonus plan alternately paid each of the actors an additional $50,000 for every $2.5 million the film earned at the box office. The fact that Chayefsky's screenplay specifically called for a love scene between their characters did not dissuade Holden from accepting the role, nor did his announced aversion to such exercises discourage its creative team from offering it to him; the part was his if he wanted it. As Gottfried put it, "Bill Holden is Bill Holden." Besides, there were bigger problems to contend with.

Since the spring, Chayefsky and Gottfried had made it their highest priority to find an actor for the role of Howard Beale. Now it was autumn, and they were no closer to completing their search. They had exhausted their pie-in-the-sky candidates, their long shots, and their dark horses to find that, no matter how much polite praise the

Network screenplay received, it was not easy to convince any of Hollywood's leading men to play a part so iconoclastic, so morbid, and so vulgar. But while they had been knocking on every door in the business, someone else had been knocking on theirs just as persistently.

As the screenplay for *Network* circulated among agents and talent handlers, it eventually reached the desk of a Hollywood manager named Barry Krost. A bushy-haired man with a cherubic build and a gregarious manner, the London-born Krost represented an eclectic roster of British artists, including Angela Lansbury, Cat Stevens, and the playwright John Osborne, and he believed the role of Howard Beale was perfect for one of his lesser-known clients. For some time, Krost had been trying to persuade Gottfried to consider an actor named Peter Finch, but Gottfried wasn't interested in seeing anyone who spoke with an accent, and Krost was fearful of pushing the producer too hard. "I think I was so in awe of Lumet and Chayefsky, I kept a distance," Krost later recalled. But "being relentless," he added, "the office would call every couple of weeks to Howard, and he got, I think, frankly, a little bored of the calls. But that's my job, to irritate and bore people at times."

Finally, Krost was notified that the *Network* filmmakers were willing to meet with him and Finch in New York. He left word for his client, who had already been sent a copy of the script, and sometime later, Krost got a phone call from Finch in return.

"I'm all excited he returns my call," Krost said, "and to tell him there's a meeting. And he says, 'You mean they want me to *audition*? Tell them to go fuck themselves.' Really pissed, and he put the phone down. So I was a bit stunned and I didn't know what to do." Krost waited a few minutes that, to him, seemed like hours. When his phone rang again, he answered it and was offered an apology: "The voice at the other end said, 'Krosty'—that's what he called me—'Finchy here.' He said, 'Sorry, darling, I forgot I was an actor.'" He would take the meeting after all, as soon as he could get himself to Manhattan from his home in Jamaica.

By now the fifty-nine-year-old Finch was used to a nomadic and picaresque existence. Born Frederick George Peter Ingle-Finch in London in 1916, he was raised as the son of George Ingle-Finch, an Australian chemist who accompanied George Mallory on a 1922 expedition to Mount Everest, and Alicia Gladys Fisher, a young woman who met George Finch at an officers' dance during World War I. The Finches' marriage dissolved quickly, and at the age of six young Peter was sent to Paris to live with his paternal grandmother, a spiritual bohemian who three years later moved to the International Headquarters of the Theosophical Society in Madras, India, and put him in the care of Buddhist monks. As their initiate, Peter had his head shaved and was dressed in yellow silk robes, an experience he would later describe as an adventure, "sometimes in thinking and learning, but mostly in being spoiled by the monks, who were too good to me." But he was quickly pulled out of the apprenticeship—he recalled officers telling his grandmother, "You can't do this; it would destroy the British Empire"—and was sent off again to live with more responsible relatives in Australia.

By the late 1930s, Finch had worked as a cub reporter at the *Sydney Sun*, as a "jackeroo" at a sheep farm, and as an itinerant "swagman" in the Australian bush, sleeping outdoors while traveling from job to job by hitching rides or stowing away on trains. During World War II, he served as an anti-aircraft gunner and organized concert parties and revues that he wrote, directed, and starred in, known as "Finch's Follies." After his discharge, he worked with a traveling theater company that performed at canteens, snack bars, and factories, and it was on one such tour, during a lunch-hour production of Molière's *The Imaginary Invalid* at a glass-blowing shop, that Finch was noticed by two illustrious visitors, Laurence Olivier and Vivien Leigh, who suggested he come to England and pursue an acting career there.

After moving to London in 1948, Finch quickly made his name as an actor on the stage of the Old Vic theater, where Olivier was on its board of directors, and in films such as *Elephant Walk* (with Elizabeth Taylor and Dana Andrews), *The Nun's Story* (with Audrey Hepburn),

Walt Disney's adaptation of *Kidnapped*, and *The Trials of Oscar Wilde*, playing the title character. At Taylor's request, he was also slated to play Julius Caesar in *Cleopatra*, but he withdrew amid the film's legendarily lengthy delays.

Finch earned a reputation as one of the city's hardest drinkers, as a member of an informal fraternity of cavorting cronies that included Peter O'Toole, Richard Harris, Oliver Reed, and Errol Flynn. Years later, Finch would recall their antics as a bit of harmless hell-raising "and laughing a bit louder than the other people in restaurants—Errol used to say we were the last ones in London who could draw a sword and cut up a dark alley." But to others these escapades had a dark and dreadful underbelly. After meeting Finch for the first time, the Irish novelist Edna O'Brien thought she saw something "tormented" in him. "He had a streak of mad anger that one was always fearing would rear up," she said. "He was made very nervous at any signs of aggression around him and I think this is because, having had a great deal of aggression inside himself, he was nervous of it in others."

An affair that Finch conducted during the 1950s with Vivien Leigh, the troubled wife of his mentor, Olivier, led to his divorce from his first wife, the ballet dancer Tamara Tchinarova, and in 1965 he divorced his second wife, the actress Yolande Turner. The singer Shirley Bassey was named a corespondent at Finch's latest divorce trial, and Finch was named a corespondent at Bassey's—a legalistic way of saying that the two had been romantically intertwined. It was around this time that Finch learned from his mother that he himself had been the product of her adulterous liaison with another man, and that that affair had destroyed his parents' marriage.

Seeking a new start in 1966, Finch declared that he'd had "a complete clear-out" of all his possessions, save for a couple of sport coats. "Nobody can take away my car or my home or my swimming pool because I haven't got them," he said. "And I've just enough money so that if I want to stay up in the hills for the rest of my life, doing nothing, I can." He stated that he was working on a book of poems and had temporarily given up his drinking due to a case of jaundice. Furthermore, he was moving to Jamaica. "You can walk about without shoes there, and I like that," he explained.

Relocated to an eleven-acre farm of citrus, banana, allspice, and timber trees near a Jamaican settlement called Bamboo, Finch met a young woman named Eletha Barrett—depending on the story, their first encounter was either at a party or at a fence that Finch was climbing to retrieve his morning newspaper—and the two became inseparable. Finch raised her son, Christopher, by a previous relationship, and with her had a daughter, Diana, before he married Eletha in 1973 at a civil ceremony in Rome. To him, it did not matter that they were twenty-four years apart in age, or that he was white and she was black, or that her domestic drive was stronger than his. "All women want to nest a little, it's a part of the natural process of the species," he said. "I get frightened when they start picking up refrigerators and carpets in their beak." She didn't mind that he slept in the nude, though she did try to buy him pajamas.

But the world that Finch and his young wife inhabited was not nearly as open-minded about their relationship. A letter writer to *Parade* magazine would ask about Finch in a dispatch its editors considered suitable for publication in 1971: "I hear he has a fondness for black girls, keeps several of them simultaneously. Yes?" The magazine's response in no way challenged the author's underlying assertion, and simply noted Finch's relationship with Barrett, "a black hairdresser and telephone operator from Jamaica," adding that he was previously "enamored of Shirley Bassey, a black singer from Wales." In a tell-all biography called *Finchy*, his second wife, Yolande Turner, would claim that her ex-husband often expressed to her "his need for the gutter," and would throw himself into "the wet, wild woods"—his alleged euphemism for the "dark, noisy black clubs" of London—"whenever he felt threatened sexually."

Finch found himself an unexpected Academy Award nominee for best actor in 1972, for his performance in John Schlesinger's film *Sun-*

day Bloody Sunday as a gay doctor in a love affair with a bisexual man. (Finch's fellow nominees for the Oscar that year included George C. Scott in *The Hospital*, though both men would lose to *French Connection* star Gene Hackman.) But this brush with greatness gained him little in the long run, except perhaps the leading role in a notoriously dreadful 1973 musical remake of *Lost Horizon*.

To Finch's manager, Howard Beale did not register on the page as the role of a lifetime, but merely a role that his client could perform. "The truth is, you try to get actors jobs," Barry Krost said. "Sometimes you realize the importance of the job," but in the case of *Network*, "I can't say I knew it would be a great movie. No, I'm not that clever. It was a great, fun read, and what a great, fun part."

By the time Finch arrived in New York for his meeting in the fall of 1975 with Gottfried, Chayefsky, and Lumet, their greatest concern was whether the actor, with his Australian and British heritage, could pull off a convincing American accent. Their plan was to accompany him from the Sherry-Netherland Hotel, where Finch was staying, to a casual script reading at the Oak Room of the Plaza Hotel, across the street. But what little chitchat they conducted in their walk across Fifth Avenue was sufficient to seal the deal. "Before they sat down," Krost recalled, "Howard said, 'Bingo'—he'd got the part."

For Gottfried and his partners, the sudden endorsement reflected their confidence in Finch as much as the urgency with which they needed to fill the role. "He was very persuasive," Gottfried said of the actor. "Obviously, the reading he did was excellent. And to be perfectly candid, at that time, we were pretty ready to shoot the movie and we didn't have a leading man that we were happy with, certainly. So we decided to put Peter on."

Some strange charm seemed to be following Finch on his American sojourn. That same day, he later told his manager, he went for a walk in Central Park, dressed in his blazer and cravat, and a man there bumped into him. Immediately realizing that he was missing his wallet, Finch chased after the stranger.

Describing the encounter as Finch relayed it to him, Krost said, "He runs up to the man and says, 'Give me the wallet, you—' f-word, f-word, 'Give me my bloody wallet or'—and gets the wallet. Goes back to the hotel. Locks the door. Puts the chain on the door. And puts the wallet down on his dresser next to his wallet. He hadn't taken his wallet at all."

The tale, Krost acknowledged, was almost certainly apocryphal but, he said, "it's one of my favorite stories."

With the most vital members of the *Network* ensemble in place, the hunt was on to fill its many other parts—more than thirty additional speaking roles—in time for the start of filming in January 1976. To oversee this process the production hired Juliet Taylor, who had only recently graduated from a junior casting associate's position on films such as *Bananas* to the full-time casting director of movies such as *The Exorcist* and *Taxi Driver*, after taking over the business of her former boss, Marion Dougherty, the Hollywood star maker who had handled these duties on *The Hospital*. Working for Dougherty, Taylor had also helped cast Lumet's film *The Anderson Tapes*, but for *Network* she was brought in by Gottfried, acting on Chayefsky's behalf.

"Paddy did run the show," Taylor said. "He was an adorable man and hilarious, but he was very strong." In particular, Taylor understood she was to look for actors who could handle the sheer density of material in his *Network* screenplay, and who would respect it enough to read it as written. "Nobody writes screenplays like that, with monologues that are a page long," she said. "Brilliant monologues, and that not only required wonderful actors, but the word was the thing."

Some key hirings were made without much deliberation or the need for formal auditions. Robert Duvall, whose portrayal of the Corleone family consigliere in *The Godfather* and *The Godfather Part II* had lifted him into ever-higher echelons of fame and esteem (and earned him an Academy Award nomination), was offered the role of Frank Hackett, the corporate executive with the creatively vulgar vocabulary. He accepted. "He didn't have any of the Western thing going on at all," Taylor said of Duvall, the future star of *Tender Mercies*, *Lonesome Dove*, and *Broken Trail*, who was then living in the well-to-do enclave of Tuxedo Park, New York. "He was a totally New York guy back then. He didn't have a New York accent, but he was a solid New York actor."

Most of the remaining parts were settled in marathon casting sessions held in Gottfried's Broadway offices in November and December. Among the roles that had remained obstinately vacant was that of Louise Schumacher, Max's mistreated wife, described in Chayefsky's script as "a handsome matron of fifty." Lumet had had his eye on Candice Bergen, the star of his film *The Group*, who had also been considered to play Diana. But in a single appointment on the morning of November 10, the director and his colleagues were won over by Beatrice Straight. Straight was a granddaughter of William Collins Whitney, the patriarch of that powerful and wealthy New York clan, and a daughter of the progressive philanthropist Dorothy Payne Whitney Straight Elmhirst, who helped found the magazine the *New Republic*. She was also a cousin of Gloria Vanderbilt, the heiress and ex-wife of Sidney Lumet. Straight, now in her fifties, had appeared in only a handful of films (including *The Nun's Story*, with Peter Finch) but had starred in nearly a dozen Broadway plays over the past forty years. "When she came in to read for the part," Gottfried said, "she had us weeping."

Those tears would have to be wiped away quickly; in that same day's session, the *Network* filmmakers also saw Wesley Addy (cast as the UBS president Nelson Chaney), Lane Smith (the UBS news division vice president Robert McDonough), Kenneth Kimmins (an unnamed associate producer in the UBS control room), and Darryl Hickman (Bill Herron, the slick producer who introduces Max Schumacher to Diana), each in intervals of five to fifteen minutes. On November 18 they met Conchata Ferrell (who would play Diana's programming underling Barbara Schlesinger) and Marlene Warfield (the philosophi-cally pliable revolutionary Laureen Hobbs), whom they knew from the Broadway and film versions of *The Great White Hope* and from a curi-ous incident in London in which she was arrested for biting a police officer as she exited a nightclub in Chelsea. ("A bobby grabbed my wrist," Warfield later recalled, "and my first instinct was to bite him on his thumb. The next thing I knew, I was in jail overnight.") On December 2 they saw John Carpenter, who was hired to play George Bosch, another programming executive; and Roberts Blossom, who had portrayed the ill-fated patient killed off in the opening scene of *The Hospital* and whom they cast this time as Arthur Jensen, the persuasive tycoon seated atop CCA.

At another fateful late-autumn meeting, the *Network* filmmakers were introduced to Arthur Burghardt, who had played Frederick Douglass in a one-man show and had appeared on Broadway in *Sher-lock Holmes*. But when they invited him to read for the role of the Great Ahmed Kahn, the terse, hulking leader of the radical Ecumenical Lib-eration Army, and this six-foot-five-inch actor crossed the threshold of Gottfried's office, all they saw was a physically imposing black man cursing loudly and brandishing a toy firearm. "At one point, this char-acter bursts in the front door with a gun," Gottfried recalled. "And this big brute of a guy starts shouting at us, with the gun—it's not a real gun of course—but he was threatening us that he wanted the part. And we looked at this guy and we thought, that's the kind of guy we wanted."

Burghardt later said this had all transpired as he had planned it. "I went looking very much like a deposed street punk/gangster in the garb of a revolutionary guerrilla," he said. "I think I put a toothpick in my mouth. I always believe in going to auditions looking like the part. And I thought, this may be something."

Kathy Cronkite, a young actress who had appeared in the *Billy Jack* action movies, may not have auditioned at all for the role of Mary Ann Gifford, a Patty Hearst–like heiress who falls in with the radical group.

The fact that she was the daughter of Walter Cronkite, the CBS news anchor and former host of Lumet's *You Are There* series, may have assisted in this regard. "You have to wonder how much of that was Sidney's and Dad's old friendship, and throwing his daughter a bone," she later said. She had no reason to believe, however, that she was being cast specifically because of who her father was, or for the ironic purpose of having a Cronkite family member in a movie that satirized the television news business. "Nobody's going to risk a multimillion-dollar movie just because someone has a name that they like," she said. "And maybe that's naïve, but it's what puts me to sleep at night."

While its cast was being decided, the crew hired for *Network* was an intermingling of recruits brought in by Gottfried and by Lumet. The director chose his trusted editor Alan Heim, with whom he'd worked since *The Pawnbroker*, and his production designer Philip Rosenberg, who had already put in some pro bono hours on *Network* while a budget was hammered out. "I worked on nearly all the preproduction period without a deal," Rosenberg said. "The expense of my fee is absolutely inconsequential to the making of a movie, and still the negotiation took until the week before we were ready to start principal photography. I worked on the picture anyway because I knew ultimately it would get together."

Owen Roizman, the director of photography who used his training from commercials to give New York City a tactile and claustrophobic presence in films such as *The French Connection* and *The Taking of Pelham One Two Three* (and who had similarly given Georgetown its haunting Gothic look in *The Exorcist*), was selected by Gottfried. Of his two cameramen, Roizman hired one, Tom Priestley Jr., who had worked with him on *The French Connection* and *The Exorcist*, while Lumet hired the other, Fred Schuler, whom he'd come to trust on *Dog Day Afternoon*.

Despite the ad hoc assembly of this team, its membership shared the desire and the know-how to film outside of soundstages in practical, authentic settings. As Priestley recalled, "When I started in the business in 1961, basically the cinematographers were, for the most part, World War II vets. And it was a more burly, adventurous group that was accustomed to hard drinking and living and all those things." But newer, lighter-weight technology was providing camera crews the ability to venture more easily into the outside world, and audiences were increasingly expecting to see authentic locations on their screens.

"Television was demanding and the people were becoming more educated," Priestley said. "The public didn't want to see the old Bob Hope and Bing Crosby *Road to Morocco* kind of movies. They were all shot on a back lot, against a painted scenic piece or a backdrop. They wanted to see the real locations."

At the end of 1975, with rehearsals and filming for *Network* set to start in January of the new year, everything appeared to be in order. Only one small complication had arisen: Daniel Melnick, the MGM executive, was unexpectedly sent an invoice totaling $970.64 for a wig that Faye Dunaway had purchased for herself, in preparation for *Network*, and which she billed to the studio. Melnick, in turn, forwarded this expense to Gottfried, and with it the delicate diplomatic responsibility of explaining to Dunaway's agents why he would not be paying the charge—first in a phone call and then in this carefully worded letter dated December 4:

> To reiterate the substance of our phone conversation, I urge you not to interpret the return of this bill as any lack of confidence on our part in Ms. Dunaway's instinct as to what is right for her, nor as any lack of desire whatsoever, to accommodate her. The fact is however, that nobody from our production has had an opportunity to discuss the use of a wig for "NETWORK" with Ms. Dunaway or for that matter, any manner of her wardrobe, hair or makeup. On this basis alone my acceptance at this time, and or payment of the bill would

be premature. Far more important however, is my belief that it would be destructive and an affront to the other creative people engaged for "NETWORK" for such a decision to be presented to them, without prior consultation, as a fait accompli.

Gottfried added: "We are anxious for Ms. Dunaway to be comfortable and look her best at all times." That, he thought, should put the matter to rest.

4

THE DAILY PARADE OF LUNACIES

If the inhabitants of New York wanted to see a city in decline and on the verge of collapse at the dawn of 1976, they didn't have to go to the movies or turn on their television sets; all they had to do was stick their heads out their windows. Monday, January 5, found the city in the throes of multiple competing manias. A Christmastime bombing at LaGuardia Airport in Queens had killed eleven people and injured seventy-five more, and remained unsolved, and fires raged in South Brooklyn, where a series of fuel-oil tanks had exploded. An austerity drive imposed upon the financially struggling metropolis, two months after it teetered on the brink of default, had stripped its streets of more than 4,200 police officers, and a newly proposed budget sought to cut nearly 1,000 more. Meanwhile, on the Upper West Side, Zabar's had sold out its supply of a new home appliance called the Cuisinart—two hundred such devices and their gleaming, whirring blades at the discounted price of $135 each—in two days.

It was against this backdrop that the cast members and key personnel of *Network* gathered at the Hotel Diplomat in Times Square to begin two weeks of rehearsals for the movie. Paddy Chayefsky, Sidney Lumet, and Faye Dunaway each arrived from their Manhattan apartments, and William Holden and Peter Finch from their rooms at the Pierre hotel, to assemble at the sixty-five-year-old Diplomat, a single-room-occupancy hotel on West Forty-Third Street that had previously served as an Elks lodge but was now better known as the home of the Le Jardin disco and as the site, in 1973, of the notorious cocaine bust that drove the radical agitator Abbie Hoffman into hiding. The ensemble had hoped to use the hotel's ballroom for their inaugural read-through of the script, but they found the hall unheated and had to flee to a nearby room to begin their work.

For some members of the *Network* crew, the most anticipated meeting of the day was the introduction of Holden and Finch, its one-time marquee idols, who had never previously worked together. Susan Landau, a production assistant, later observed, "Bill and Peter took to each other instantly. I have never seen such love and recognition like that between two people; such mutual respect. Both men had been there and back in their lives, you might say, and both had been away from films for a long time. They shared so much together. Anger, and respect for acting, and pride in acting."

The more crucial dynamic, however, was the one emerging between Lumet, who as the director would customarily have the final say on all decisions, and Chayefsky, who held this authority by contract. The very presence of the screenwriter at this stage of a film's creation was highly unorthodox; Chayefsky knew this, and therefore demanded the access. He expected total control over events, and he expected things to go wrong. "I'm a pain in the ass and I know it," he said after the film was completed. "I'm a worrier. I'm used to panic and hysteria in a production. It's always there."

Lumet rallied his team on day one with his enthusiasm and an early instructional speech to the actors to keep their performances simple: they should emanate from "pure behavior" but should not be quite as naturalistic as his previous motion picture, *Dog Day Afternoon*, because the language of Chayefsky's script was not naturalistic. After day two of rehearsals, the film's script supervisor, Kay Chapin, recorded in her diary what she thought was the formation of a natural give-and-take relationship between writer and director. "Sidney knows specifically what he wants and is very adept at communicating his intentions to actors," Chapin wrote. "Paddy almost always agrees but if he doesn't he's specific about his objections. . . . It looks like it's a perfect combination all around: a terrific script; a director that totally understands the material; a writer who knows that he understands it and actors that are perfectly cast and adore the script and director. . . . It's the first time I've experienced this kind of intermeshing—a rare experience."

The company spent the next few days in the ballroom (where the heat had been restored), blocking out the physical action of their scenes in taped-off sections meant to represent the various locations of the movie: the UBS television studio and control room; the newsroom and offices; and the apartments of Diana Christensen and Max Schumacher. Lumet came armed with a notebook full of his hand-drawn diagrams for where he expected to place his cameras and how he expected each sequence to unfold, and he played all the parts not already assigned to his principal cast. His choreographed system left little to chance, yet it seemed to open the door to flexibility: if he came to a scene and could not remember his intended blocking, he told his actors, then it must have been bad.

While Dunaway immersed herself in her heavily annotated copy of the script, and Chayefsky laid out for the actors the intricate hierarchies of UBS and CCA, and where they were situated within them, Lumet seemed to keep a certain distance from his performers. As he privately told his crew, he had given up his own acting career because he realized that an actor has to reveal himself, and he didn't want to do that; nor did he want to get into the personal problems of anyone else in the cast.

In fact, Lumet was observing his players carefully. In particular, he identified an "emotional reticence" in Holden—something he noticed during Holden and Dunaway's rehearsal of Schumacher's "male menopause" speech, where Diana is distracted by telephone calls and the declining fortunes of *The Howard Beale Show*, while he is pleading for her to love him, "primal doubts and all." Lumet saw the scene as Schumacher's confession that he and Diana "came from very different worlds, that he was achingly vulnerable to her and therefore needed her help and support." But when Holden performed the scene with Dunaway, "he looked everywhere but directly into her eyes. He looked at her eyebrows, her hair, her lips, but not her eyes." For the time being, Lumet said, "I didn't say anything."

On Saturday, January 10, it was time for a field trip. At dawn, Lumet and his crew embarked for suburban Nyack, New York, about thirty miles north of the city, to produce the very first footage for *Network*: the black-and-white amateur film of a bank robbery conducted by the kidnapped heiress turned leftist radical Mary Ann Gifford, which would become the kernel of Diana's pitch for a new reality-based TV series called *The Mao Tse Tung Hour*. Outside a Main Street bank, Lumet staged the scene in about twenty minutes, stationing his camera behind a large rubber tree that partially obscured the action. Shooting began at 9:35 A.M., as Kathy Cronkite and Arthur Burghardt burst into the building wielding prop weapons and shouting swear words and slogans that would go unheard on the silent reel.

Cronkite, a relative newcomer to film acting and not much bigger than the gun she was firing, remembered being startled by the power of her firearm. "I shot it," she said, "and it scared the hell out of me. I did not expect it to be as big and as loud and have as much of a recoil—even though it was a fake. I just went, 'Uhhhhhh.' And then I thought, 'Man, I really screwed that up.' And they went, 'Oh, that was great!' I kept some of those little fake plastic bullet things." Lumet filmed a few more takes and wrapped for the day at 10:00 A.M.

The second week of rehearsals resumed at the Hotel Diplomat the following Tuesday, and the final rehearsal day, Friday, January 16, focused partly on Beatrice Straight and her wrenching confrontation with Holden, in which Louise Schumacher sorrowfully interrogates her husband about his "great winter romance." "She gave a printable performance," Kay Chapin observed, "tears and all, a marvelous actress." But Chapin also noticed a brewing disagreement between Chayefsky and Lumet over the work of Roberts Blossom, the gaunt and goggle-eyed character actor playing the thunderous CCA executive Arthur Jensen. Where the screenplay seemed to call for a confident pitchman who could sway Howard Beale to his doctrine of an "interwoven, inter-acting, multivariate, multinational dominion of dollars," Chapin noted that the author and his director "don't seem to be in perfect agreement on that role":

> Paddy wants it less theatrical, more like a Rotarian, Mr. Congenial, whereas Sidney appears to like Blossom's perfor-mance that is very theatrical. Sidney toned him down a bit, otherwise it would be like two maniacs together which throws the intent of the speech out the window. Blossom came back later with a rework of the speech and everyone seemed to like it.

Before the company was dismissed, Finch regaled some listeners with a story from his early days in the London theater. While playing a scene with Dame Edith Evans, Finch said he found himself overcome by a cough and unable to speak; his clever costar created a distraction with a coffee cup, got the audience to laugh, and underneath the mur-mur said to him, sotto voce, "All right, love: have a good cough now." The tale was hopefully some consolation to Roberts Blossom, who, unknown to most of the staff, was about to be quietly let go from the cast.

"With Sidney, you never traveled very far away from New York City," said Lumet's production designer, Philip Rosenberg. But in the case of *Network*, the director found it necessary to cross international borders to produce the portions of the film that were set within a working television studio and that depicted the oracular on-camera speechifying of Howard Beale. Prior to shooting, Lumet had arranged for Rosenberg to receive a tour of CBS operations in New York from his friend Walter Cronkite and to get a crash course in television news production. But it was instead decided that the television sequences would be filmed at the CFTO-TV facility in Toronto, for several reasons. In New York, it was simply not practical or affordable to build a working replica of a television control room and studio, and the existing spaces offered to the production did not allow for the needed interplay between the control room and the stage. Union rules, which would have required the paid presence of members from both the television and motion picture guilds during studio filming, created further financial complications.

There was also a growing sense among the *Network* crew that the American television industry wanted nothing to do with the movie and would make no effort to assist in its creation. "Because of the volatile nature of the screenplay, we couldn't get cooperation from any of the networks," said Owen Roizman, the film's director of photography. "We couldn't get anything in New York; nobody would cooperate. They didn't want that coming out, even if it was true. Especially because it was true."

Rather than risk any further estrangement, MGM and United Artists executives stated in a January 9 memo that Chayefsky and Gottfried had "placed an embargo on the showing of NETWORK scripts to all media contacts—whether they be visiting the set for interview purposes or requesting it for background/information on the picture. In addition, under no circumstances are we to reveal the ending of the picture in any publicity material, or in discussions with the media." The benign explanation provided in the memo was that "we all strongly feel that to do so would dissipate the element of surprise which Chayefsky strived so hard to achieve."

The Toronto studio offered several benefits, including an ample soundstage that would provide the setting for the expanded UBS *Network News Hour*, its live audience, and cohosts such as Miss Mata Hari and Sybil the Soothsayer. Less conveniently, the upper portion of a spiral staircase visible in its TV control room required that its lower portion be replicated on the *Network* newsroom set—which was being built in New York—to avoid continuity errors. "It took a lot of work for the script girl and Sidney to remember when they were in Canada and when they were in New York," Rosenberg said.

All *Network* talent and personnel were put up at the Hotel Toronto on University Avenue, where a little intermingling between nobility and commoners was not out of the question. On the evening of January 18, the night before filming began, Roizman headed down to the hotel restaurant, expecting to eat by himself.

"It was pretty empty," he recalled. "I was one of the only ones there. And I sat down and put my order in. And just then, Paddy and Bill Holden came walking by. And they said, 'Who are you eating with?' I said, 'Nobody. I'm alone.' They said, 'No, you're not. Come on, you're going to sit with us.' And I said, 'That's okay. You don't have to do that.' And they said, 'No, we want to,' and they picked up my place settings and took it to their table and said, 'You're eating with us.'"

"Two big icons," Roizman said, "and they treated me like royalty."

Principal photography for *Network* began on Monday, January 19, with a call time of 7:30 A.M. and cameras rolling at 9:45 on the first take of its first scene: executive producer Harry Hunter on the phone in the UBS News control room, assuring an unseen Max Schumacher that he believes Howard Beale is fine. The day's aggressive schedule called for portions of six different scenes to be produced, but only two, depicting Harry Hunter and Diana Christensen in the control room, were shot on film. The remainder, recorded on videotape, were two sequences involving Beale's fill-in anchor, Jack Snowden, played by Stanley Grover, and two that focused on Beale himself: a monologue known as "Last night I was awakened," in which he describes a revelatory conversation with "a shrill, sibilant, faceless voice," and the speech he would be seen delivering on the television sets and studio monitors in Scene 99, which was simply called "Mad as hell."

Lumet, in preproduction conversations with Roizman, had determined that he wanted the visual look of *Network* to proceed in three distinct phases. "The first phase," said Roizman, "should be 'naturalistic,' the second 'realistic,' and the third 'commercial.'" (As Lumet himself put it, "The movie was about corruption. So we corrupted the camera.") And as in rehearsals, the director arrived for each day of filming with a notebook in which, for every scene, he had already determined where his cameras would be placed and how his actors would move in front of them. Within his industry, Lumet was legendary for his speed and had a fairly earned reputation for shooting as few takes as he felt were necessary before moving on to the next camera angle or the next scene.

"If he only needed one shot for the scene, that was it, and he walked away," said his camera operator Fred Schuler. "'Cut, print, move on.' That was his slogan. And when he said, 'Cut,' he was most of the time in my shot before I turned off the camera."

"We used to joke about it," said Roizman. "We'd say he would wear out a pair of sneakers in the course of a shoot."

Watching Lumet reconnect with his roots while he directed scenes that were, in essence, live television broadcasts—snapping his fingers and pointing at cameras as he cued the performances of actors on screens within screens and instructed a console operator to switch from one shot to the next—could be dazzling to behold. "He was, like, in a frenzy," said his camera operator Tom Priestley Jr. "'Give me Camera A, give me Camera B, go back to Camera A.' At the end of those two minutes, he was soaking wet." Kay Chapin, in her diary, described Lumet as prowling "like a caged tiger; pacing, moving into everything, never rests. . . . When he runs out of directorial things to do he'll tell the grips how to move the crane, wet down Finch, or schedule all the actors for the next day. He has incredible energy and knows everything."

His rapidity had other advantages: if you were a member of his crew, you worked a consistent day, with lunch at noon or 1:00 P.M. (during which the director usually took a nap), and finished at a civil hour, generally 5:00 or 6:00 P.M. Additionally, Roizman said, "He wasn't a fusspot when it came to technical things. They didn't have to be perfect. He preferred them, I think, when they weren't perfect, and he liked things to be just a little off, here and there."

However, Lumet's certainty of his choices could be a source of frustration to his collaborators. "He knew exactly what he wanted to do all the time," said Roizman. "To a fault, I think, because very often on that film, there was no room for spontaneity. There was no improvisation. It was all planned ahead of time, and that bothered me. I always like to figure things out at the time, based on what I'm seeing in front of me. You just didn't have that luxury with Sidney. He knew exactly what he wanted, and there was no wavering from that, and it's too bad."

Lumet was more graceful in wielding his power than Chayefsky, whose mandate to be present during filming often left him out of place, underfoot, or otherwise in the way. Chayefsky's primary concern, more than seeing to it that *Network* was filmed imaginatively, or competently, or quickly, or on budget, was ensuring that all its dialogue was performed exactly as he had written it in the script. When it was not, he could be counted on to point out to his actors exactly where and how they had gone astray, often using Chapin, the script supervisor, as his emissary to dispense the corrections.

And in order to best observe the actors' work, Chayefsky felt it was necessary to situate himself as close as he could to their performances. As Schuler recalled, "Paddy had this keen sense to always be in the front of the key light"—that is, the principal light used to illuminate the object of a camera—"because that's where the person was best lit." Eventually, he said, "it became a joke. 'Where's Paddy? Oh, look for the key light.'" Chayefsky's small but bearish presence did not show up in the frame or affect the composition of shots, but it could interfere with the flow of communication (and people) in front of and behind the camera. So, said Schuler, an alternate arrangement was worked out: "At one point, they put a light up, a little soft light, and they called it the Paddy light. That's where his place would be."

This configuration did not prevent Chayefsky from turning around and offering instantaneous feedback to the director, but Lumet said he welcomed the input. For example, in a scene preceding Howard Beale's "Mad as hell" speech, in which the rain-soaked anchor arrives at the UBS studio and announces to a security guard, "I have to make my witness," there was disagreement over how the guard was to deliver his one-line reply: "Sure thing, Mr. Beale."

"In my heavy-handed way," Lumet said, "I told the guard to take in Peter Finch's disheveled state, then humor him as he said the line. Paddy was at my ear in a second. 'This is TV,' he whispered. 'He shouldn't even notice him.' He was right, of course. The line got the laugh it deserved. It wouldn't have been funny delivered my way."

Finch was the focal point for nearly all two weeks of the Canadian shoot, and he was happy for the challenge and for the attention. Before Howard Beale came into his life, he had been thinking of his migration to Jamaica as decidedly one-way. "In his mind, he wanted to retire," his daughter Diana Finch-Braley would later recall. "He was like, 'I found what I wanted, I had a baby, I'm raising a family so I think I'm going to settle down.'"

As had become his tradition when he traveled for his movies, Finch brought his wife, Eletha, and their young children, Christopher and Diana, with him on the road, and Eletha (with six-year-old Diana, whom he had nicknamed DiDinckles, in tow) became a familiar sight on the *Network* set. To some, Eletha's presence called attention to the differences between her and her husband, while her absence brought out his weariness. "The physical transformation of Peter on the set was remarkable," said production assistant Susan Landau. "He *was* Howard Beale. But slumped on a chair in the hotel lobby waiting for Eletha who was always late, he looked . . . well . . . he looked a lot older."

Others saw the role reinvigorating Finch, and offering him cause to wonder if there might be one more act left in a career he had been ready to accept as finished. He immersed himself in Beale's words and found himself connecting with the character's prophetic sense of conviction. "He was what you'd call a Method actor, without ever studying the Method," Diana Finch-Braley said. "He was the kind of person who would get so into character that he didn't know if it was real or not real." He was spiritual but not religiously observant, with a worldview shaped by Christianity, Buddhism, Theosophy, and the kaleidoscope of belief systems he'd encountered on his journeys.

But Finch believed that Howard Beale was doing something to his soul. One morning in their hotel room, he excitedly described to Eletha how, like his character, he, too, had been visited by a nebulous sacred presence. "I feel like I've had some kind of experience, I can't explain it," he told his wife. "Like Daniel and the burning bush."

Eletha, who had grown up in the church and studied her Bible more carefully, laughed and corrected her husband's errors: it was *Moses* and the burning bush, *Daniel* in the lion's den.

The Toronto portion of the *Network* shoot would demand much of Finch's body as well as his psyche. On the first day of filming, he was responsible for performing two of the character's most challenging orations, including four videotaped takes of the "Mad as hell" speech, only three of which he was able to complete in their two-and-a-half-minute entirety. (According to the official shooting log, Take 3 was halted at the one-minute mark for an unspecified reason.) January 20, the second day of shooting, called for Finch to deliver Beale's "Bullshit" speech—his on-air proclamation, during what is supposed to be his valedictory news broadcast, that he "just ran out of bullshit." January 21 saw the filming of Beale's introductory outburst, in which he tells his audience that he has been fired and plans to kill himself on next week's show. On January 22, it was back to "Mad as hell"—not the videotaped feed that would show up fleetingly on TV screens in the living rooms and offices of other characters, but the filmed version that was his to carry alone.

The completed "Mad as hell" sequence—from the moment the drenched and bewildered Beale, seated at his anchor's desk and wearing a trench coat over his pajamas, begins to address the camera ("I don't have to tell you things are bad. Everybody knows things are bad. It's a depression") to the moment Max Schumacher's daughter, Caroline, looks out a window of her family's living room to hear all of New York City shouting its cacophonous chorus of anger and despair—contains thirty edits: nine different reaction shots of Diana growing in her elation, racing out of the control room and into an office to discover that they are also shouting in Atlanta and Baton Rouge; three of Harry Hunter feeding broadcast data to Diana and instructing his director to keep his cameras on Beale; one of the director repeating Hunter's orders; and various shots of the speech (as previously recorded on videotape) playing on the Schumachers' home television while Max watches with his family in dismay.

The rest of the scene, when it is not being covered or elongated by these cuts, is a seemingly continuous take from a crane-operated camera, pointed from above at Beale ("Everybody's out of work, or scared of losing their job. The dollar buys a nickel's worth, banks are going bust"), then slowly zooming and pushing in on the increasingly agitated broadcaster ("We sit watching our teevees while some local newscaster tells us that today we had fifteen homicides and sixty-three violent crimes, as if that's the way it's supposed to be"), lowering its aim until it is almost even with his livid face and condemning blue eyes ("All I know is that first you've got to get mad. You've got to say, 'I'm a human being, goddammit. My life has value'"). Then it follows Beale around the studio as he emerges from behind his desk, past a startled stagehand and his floor director, to implore his viewers that they must get as upset as he is: "I want all of you to get up out of your chairs. I want you to get up right now and go to the window, open it and stick your head out and yell: *I'm as mad as hell and I'm not going to take this anymore!*"

Chayefsky may have been a stickler for the written word, but he was not able to prevent Finch from inserting an extra *as* into Beale's repeated expression of maximum frustration (the screenplay simply read "I'm mad as hell"). No changes were possible to Shot F of Scene 99, as the master shot of the "Mad as hell" speech was delineated in the official filming record of *Network*, because Lumet attempted it only twice, and Finch completed it only once.

Lumet had anticipated that the scene would be difficult for Finch, and he prepared by having an additional camera on set, already loaded with film and ready to go so that a second attempt at the speech could be filmed as soon as the first one was finished. ("No reloading," the director explained. "No time lost between takes.") But on Take 2, Finch halted himself one minute and ten seconds into his delivery, just as Beale was proclaiming that he didn't want his audience members writing to their congressmen "because I wouldn't know what to tell you to write."

"Between the length of the speech and the amount of emotion it took, he just ran out of gas," Lumet said. "He stopped halfway through. He said, 'Sidney, I can't do any more.'" That was as much as the director was willing to ask of Finch, whose portion of the scene was assembled from the first half of Take 2 and the second half of Take 1.

Beginning on Friday, January 23, and for the week that fol-lowed, the production moved to the CFTO-TV soundstage that housed the new, Savonarola-style UBS *Network News Hour*. The set was built upon giant turntables that Lumet chose to have rotated by stagehands who would be seen on-screen—partly to let the audience in on the illusion of television, and partly because a winch to spin the stage mechanically was not available—and it was decorated with what appeared to be a stained-glass window but was in fact a painted piece of canvas that production designer Philip Rosenberg had sprayed with gelatin and carried underneath his arm on his plane ride to Canada.

One morning during the week of January 26, a reporter for the *Toronto Sun* found Chayefsky in the CFTO-TV cafeteria. The screenwriter was poorly rested, having been awoken at 5:00 A.M. by his anxieties after a night of fitful sleep, and not much calmer as he tore into a plate of scrambled eggs and toast. When Kay Chapin, the script supervisor, sat next to him, he noticed her toasted cheese and tomato sandwich.

"That looks better than what I've got," Chayefsky said with ostensible purpose.

"Want me to get you one?" Chapin offered.

"No," he replied.

"I'll get you one," she said. "It'll only take a minute."

"No," he said, "I've got to go now anyway."

"Take mine," she said. "I'll get another."

"No," he said, abandoning his breakfast altogether. "I'm not hungry. I didn't sleep last night. Not at all."

On the *Network* set, Finch was running through the last substantial speech he would perform as Howard Beale, after the character's philosophy is corrupted by his pro-corporate lecture from Arthur Jensen ("The time has come to say, is dehumanization such a bad word?"). A studio audience of hundreds of extras watched him pace the stage while Lumet observed, from on high, in a control room suspended two stories above the scene.

The director's voice rang out from a studio loudspeaker: "Peter, would it be convenient for you to start from 'The world is mass-producing people the way we mass-produce our food'?"

Finch silently waved to the booth and performed the scene again. "Is that what you wanted, Sidney?"

The disembodied voice answered, "Peter my dear, we're just waiting for the playback. Just relax."

A fidgety Chayefsky had also been watching the retake from down below and was stewing, not so quietly, over one of Lumet's directorial choices. "There's a gag line in this speech that Sidney loves," he said, "and I'm afraid he loves it too much. It should be murmured, mumbled almost—not spoken. It's a throwaway line, see, and it's only funny when

it's done that way." When the *Toronto Sun* reporter asked him what precisely *Network* was about, Chayefsky was evasive, except to say that
"it's all fabricated, all fiction. And it's all true."

Once the journalist left the studio, conditions were clear to film
the climactic sequence that Chayefsky and Gottfried were determined
that the media not learn about in advance: Beale's assassination by the
Ecumenical Liberation Army.

Arthur Burghardt, who played the militant group's leader, the Great
Ahmed Kahn, was one of two actors in the studio audience directed to
rise up on cue and pretend to shoot Beale dead with prop machine
guns loaded with blanks. One impediment to his successful completion
of the task, Burghardt later recalled, was the gun itself. "The blanks
were spewing out cotton," he said. "Some of that was on fire, and I was
afraid that I would hit somebody with that. We got people to move
aside a little bit, so that no one's hair would be caught on fire."

The other obstacle was Burghardt's realization that, as usual, Eletha and Diana Finch were on set, and he hurried to tell Peter about the
oversight. "He was about ready to get killed," Burghardt said. "And I
told him, 'Peter, you know Eletha's up there and the baby's up there.'"
Once informed, Finch was just as determined to make sure his wife
and daughter did not see him violently murdered: "She's what? Eletha!
Eletha! Take her out! No, no, no, no, you can't see this!"

Then the Great Ahmed Kahn pulled his trigger, and Howard Beale
became "the first known instance of a man being killed because he had
lousy ratings." "Everybody in the place—everybody in the studio, everybody in the cast, everybody in the crew—that evening was very sad,"
said Burghardt. "There was a sadness. As they dollied up to look at his
wounds and to fade to black, we were just all dumbfounded. I was. I
went and drank myself to sleep that night. I didn't think that the
American people would understand what we were really saying."

At the start of February, *Network* resumed production in New
York. Despite the many hours of effort expended and reels of film

recorded in Toronto, it was not certain that all the members of its cast would continue on this itinerary. Nearly every actor, at some point or another, had choked on a mouthful of Chayefsky's magniloquent, pleonastic dialogue, but Dunaway seemed to be struggling with it more than most.

"If you look at the movie closely, you'll see that Faye fumbles a few places," said its editor, Alan Heim. "Those were hard speeches. But she worked. I mean, she *worked*."

Her dedication was almost not quite enough to satisfy Lumet, who began to consider firing her from the movie.

"At one point," said Heim, "Sidney came to me, early on in the shooting in New York, by the time we got there, and said he was thinking of replacing Faye. And I said, 'Why would you do that? She's so good.' And he said, 'Well, she's having trouble with the words.' I said, 'Who would you replace her with at this point?'"

Lumet named a specific actress, though Heim declined to say whom the director had in mind.

Heim, who had started to review the raw footage from the Toronto shoot, defended Dunaway: "I said, 'No, no, you can't do that—the energy that this woman is bringing to the part.' Sidney agreed with me on that. And the next thing I knew, she was not replaced." Almost immediately, Dunaway would make her allies regret this show of support.

Though the rehearsals for *Network* appeared to have gone smoothly for her, she was growing uneasy about a sequence with William Holden in which Diana enumerates to Schumacher the details of a federal investigation facing *The Mao Tse Tung Hour* ("Hackett told the FBI to fuck off. We're standing on the First Amendment, freedom of the press, and the right to protect our sources") and how she plans to use media coverage to the show's benefit ("I said, 'Walter, let the government sue us! We'll take them to the Supreme Court! We'll be front page for months!'").

Also, while Diana is providing this continuous one-way commentary, she and Max are enjoying a candlelit dinner at an Italian restaurant; undressing each other in a Long Island motel room; engaging in sexual foreplay; and, as Chayefsky's stage directions describe the scene, "groping, grasping, gasping and fondling" each other into "a fever of sexual hunger," until "Diana mounts Max" and "the screen is filled with the voluptuous writhings of love" as "Diana cries out with increasing exultancy." Then, finally: "She screams in consummation, sighs a long, deliciously shuddering sigh, and sinks softly down into Max's embrace. For a moment, she rests her head on Max's chest, eyes closed in feline contentment."

Dunaway would later say that her fundamental concern with the sequence was not its explicit sexuality, but the vigorous rush of verbiage it required her to deliver. "There is not a second of it when the dialogue stops," she said. "The speed of it parallels the rhythm of their lovemaking." Compared to the nearly silent scene she shared with Steve McQueen in *The Thomas Crown Affair*, where their characters seduce each other with gestures (and the provocative fondling of some chess pieces), the motel rendezvous in *Network* is driven almost entirely by her dialogue. "I could not afford to stumble on a single word; it would have killed the momentum of the scene," Dunaway said. "It was the exact opposite of 'sex as chess,' five minutes of quiet seduction."

But this was not how Dunaway presented her apprehensions to Lumet and Gottfried. As the New York shoot commenced, starting with a few uncomplicated moments in the Beale and Schumacher apartments, Gottfried recalled, "She says to Sidney, 'I'm not going to do that scene. I don't have to do it.'"

Dunaway was right in this respect: according to long-standing rules of the Screen Actors Guild, the participation of a performer in a nude scene required her agreement with the scene and her written consent. She could not be forced to appear naked on-screen. Furthermore, Dunaway was uncomfortable with the idea of acting out an orgasm, as the scene required. (She would also later say that it was Holden, not she, who "came very close to not doing the love scene": "There were long talks about it. He had a strongly held belief that making love was a private thing that should not be exposed by film.")

The *Network* creative team was thoroughly baffled, as much by Dunaway's refusal as by her sudden display of modesty: she had, after all, been seen wearing just as little or less in films such as *Bonnie and Clyde* and *Chinatown*. Lumet had tried to make the case to her that the nudity in the scene was not prurient or gratuitous, but necessary to convey its reality, and would be handled in a tasteful way. Where he failed, Chayefsky attempted to convince Dunaway that the sequence was comedic; it was funny—after all, he had written it—and it was necessary to establish Diana as a woman who derives her pleasure primarily from her professional success. (At the recommendation of MGM executive Daniel Melnick, Chayefsky had already deleted a scene in which Diana, on a visit to Los Angeles, surreptitiously slips into a gay bar and hires a bisexual "stud hustler" to service her in her hotel room. That sequence would have culminated in another sex act and, for Diana, "an unhappy climax": "tears are streaming down her cheeks. She cries a short little GRUNT of consummation, sighs deeply, closes her eyes." In his notes to Chayefsky, Melnick described it tersely but accurately as a "tough scene.")

Even so, Gottfried said, "She wouldn't budge." He, too, made a visit to Dunaway in her *Network* trailer, where he planned to reiterate the arguments that Lumet and Chayefsky had already laid out. Only this time, Gottfried said, "Her lawyer was there. And he said, 'Look, she doesn't want to do it.'"

Presented with this startling ultimatum, Gottfried and his partners were forced to consider two equally unappealing courses of action: they could cut the motel sequence or they could cut Dunaway. "There's no sense in kidding yourself," Gottfried said. "We had already shot ten days of the movie, and that costs money, and she was in a lot of it. To threaten to fire her—which we were going to do; we were not going to put up with that—could be quite foolhardy. You could say, 'Look, I'm firing you,' and the studio's saying, 'Bullshit, you're firing her—to hell with the *scene*.'"

The only person left who might be able to talk Dunaway down

from the ledge was her agent, Sue Mengers. And the only way Mengers would appreciate the gravity of the situation, Gottfried believed, was if she felt there was a genuine possibility that Dunaway would be dropped from the film if she did not perform the scene. "Sure, it's a threat," Gottfried said. "If you knew Paddy, that scene was going to be in the movie. Believe me, this was not a bluff." Girding himself for battle, Gottfried first spoke with Frank E. Rosenfelt, the MGM president and chief executive, and received his blessing to tell Mengers that Dunaway's role was on the line. ("If Sue calls you," Gottfried told Rosenfelt, "back me up on it and say that the studio will go along with that. I was not going to call Sue Mengers and give her a line of crap.") Then, if circumstances required, Gottfried said he also had the studio's permission to fire Dunaway.

By the end of the day, Gottfried's message to Mengers and her subsequent discussion with Dunaway had defused the standoff and restored order to the *Network* set. The truce was codified in a February 2 letter from Gottfried to Dunaway.

> Dear Faye Dunaway:
>
> Sidney Lumet has informed me that you and he have thoroughly discussed the scenes between Diana and Max during which Diana and Max make love, and Diana has a sexual climax. He also tells me the scenes were rehearsed during the rehearsal period and you all agreed and consented to the way in which they were to be performed. Although Diana will have a sexual climax in the scene, the film will not show complete nudity and, in fact, there will be no exposure of the unclothed female breast below and including the nipple, or of any sexual organs, or their pubic area.
>
> Your signature at the end of this note, where instructed, will signify your concurrence with its contents.
>
> Very truly yours, Howard Gottfried

Dunaway signed the letter as directed, formally acknowledging that she would perform the love scene. Then, beneath her signature, she added a further statement in sharp capital lettering: "IT IS MY UNDERSTANDING THAT PRIOR TO PHOTOGRAPHY SIDNEY LUMET WILL CONSULT WITH ME CONCERNING CAMERA ANGLES AND HE WILL GIVE REASONABLE CONSIDERATION TO MY VIEWPOINTS."

By comparison, an emotional face-off between Max and Louise Schumacher was completed with relative ease, epitomizing Lumet's brisk directorial pace on a typical day of filming *Network*. The scene in which Max candidly tells his wife he has been seeing Diana for nearly a month and cannot be sure when his infatuation with her will end, and Louise orders him to move out, ruefully warning him that he's "in for some dreadful grief," was shot in a single day, on Wednesday, February 4, at Apartment 9F of the Apthorp building at 390 West End Avenue.

Scene 127, as it is called in the *Network* shooting script—Max and Louise argue as they move throughout the apartment, their feelings of love and scorn, and their positions of dominance and subjugation, fluctuating on a moment-to-moment basis—consists of a master shot, filmed in a continuous take, which was performed twice, and twelve coverage shots, filmed from various angles, most of which were performed about two to three times each. The exception is Shot 127E, which required a staggering nine takes, more than Lumet would allow for any other shot in the movie. The portion in question runs about thirty seconds and follows Louise as she crosses from the kitchen to the foyer, the foyer to the living room, and then back to the foyer, while delivering the "great winter passion" portion of her exchange, in which she rebukes Max while "striding around, weeping, like a caged lioness."

> This isn't just some convention weekend with your secretary,
> is it? Or some broad you picked up after three belts of booze.
> This is your great winter romance, isn't it? Your last roar of

passion before you sink into your emeritus years? Is that what's left for me? Is that my share? She gets the great winter passion, and I get the dotage?

The sheer copiousness of Chayefsky's dialogue may have resulted in a take count that very nearly reached double digits, or the unnatural alliteration in these lines ("broad . . . belts . . . booze") may have been Straight's undoing. But whatever on-the-spot suggestions the screenwriter may have had for improving the scene, Lumet was not interested in hearing them. At one point, the director said, "Paddy started toward me with a comment." Lumet, who was then at the tail end of his third marriage, halted Chayefsky: "I held up my hand and said, 'Paddy, please. I know more about divorce than you do.'"

Shot 127E had not yet finished stirring up all the trouble it would cause. That evening, as the editor, Alan Heim, was reviewing the footage shot earlier in the day, a curious line reading by Straight stuck in his ear. In every take of the scene, he heard her ask Holden about his "*e-meh-REE-tus years.*"

"The word, of course, is *emeritus,*" Heim said, using the correct pronunciation. "And the first thing I did was look it up, because I used to keep a dictionary in my cutting room, just for occasions like this." Heim was astounded that Chayefsky, so widely read and keenly attentive, could have missed the mistake: "I sort of blinked and I said to myself, 'It's emeritus.' And I went and looked it up, and the only pronunciation for it is emeritus. So at dailies that evening, I said, 'Paddy, do you know that's the wrong pronunciation of the word *emeritus*?' And he said, 'Really? I never heard it pronounced before.'"

Lumet was not particularly bothered by the error. "Sidney said, 'Well, there's a second pronunciation,' which was always Sidney's solution," Heim recalled. "Sidney was the guy who could not be defeated by a crossword puzzle; he would write over things." And if Chayefsky was a man of letters—if not a man of their correct pronunciation—so be it.

"It struck me that he wrote the word as a poet would," he said, "and when she said it, it just seemed perfectly normal to him. It's not a common word."

The "emeritus" line became one of only a few pieces of dialogue in *Network* that had to be overdubbed before the film was released. At her rerecording session, Straight told Heim that she had never heard the word pronounced before, either.

At one point, the Arthur Jensen scene had a fine actor set to play the industry titan who rails against Howard Beale for having "meddled with the primal forces of nature" and a sterling location to serve as the "overwhelming cathedral" of a conference room that the character compares to Valhalla. Then it had neither. Roberts Blossom, who was originally cast for the role, had been cut loose in early January after Chayefsky and Lumet disagreed over his performance. And the New York Stock Exchange, which was at first amenable to allowing the scene to be filmed in the boardroom of its Wall Street headquarters, withdrew that permission after reviewing the relevant portion of the screenplay, in which Jensen declares there is "no America" and "no democracy" but "only IBM and ITT and AT&T and Dupont, Dow, Union Carbide and Exxon."

"Some PR guy that worked for the stock exchange heard the name Paddy Chayefsky and said, 'You know, you better read this thing,'" recalled production designer Philip Rosenberg. "Before you knew it, a lot of pressure was put on the president of the Exchange, a lot of the corporations mentioned in that, they eventually asked for the script, and Mr. Jensen's speech did not appeal to them."

Finding a new location for the scene, which was to be filmed on Tuesday, February 10, was inconvenient if ultimately serendipitous. Having been denied the New York Stock Exchange, the production was instead given access to the Beaux-Arts boardroom of the New York Public Library, and to the library's majestic lobby, which would stand in as the entrance to CCA. Though the lobby would be instantly recognizable to New Yorkers, Rosenberg said, "Anybody outside of the city, in the rest of the country, wouldn't exactly know where that is." Finding an actor to perform the scene was slightly more down to the wire.

During their time in Toronto, the *Network* cast and crew had overlapped with Robert Altman and his team, who were working on his Western-cum-showbiz satire *Buffalo Bill and the Indians, or Sitting Bull's History Lesson.* (Among its leads was Paul Newman, whom Chayefsky had sought unsuccessfully for *Network.*) Chayefsky and Altman knew each other, and during their shoptalk Altman recommended to Chayefsky an actor he had worked with named Ned Beatty, a husky, hot-blooded Kentuckian who had just played the good-ol'-boy husband of Lily Tomlin's gospel singer in Altman's film *Nashville.* The endorsement was good enough for Chayefsky, who called the actor in for a meeting when *Network* returned to New York, barely a week before the Jensen scene was scheduled to go in front of the cameras.

Whether or not Chayefsky remembered it, Beatty had previously performed in a 1968 revival of his play *The Tenth Man*, at Arena Stage in Washington, D.C. The comedy-drama, about the congregation of a Long Island synagogue attempting to exorcise a dybbuk from a possessed young woman, had provided Beatty with some of his earliest introductions to the customs of Judaism—he was delighted to learn to play the shofar for the role—as well as to the play's gruff author. Beatty would later affectionately describe Chayefsky as "that little guy who smiled every three or four years or so."

Coming into his meeting with Chayefsky, Lumet, and Gottfried, Beatty was intimidated by the length of Jensen's speech, but excited by the character and the film—and, like any good actor, hungry for work. Like Jensen, Beatty's father had worked as a salesman, as had Beatty himself (who had briefly peddled floor sweepers and baby furniture in leaner times), and in that lineage he thought he saw a way to win himself the part.

Salesmanship, said Beatty, "was all about learning to close the deal.

The three of them are sitting there, and I thought: Do I really have the *cojones* for this one? I could tell they didn't want to make up their minds." So the actor delivered a pitch of his own, one not to be found on any page of Chayefsky's script.

As Beatty recalled, "I said, 'I know this is difficult. Everybody's talking about this part, and they're saying you've got to do a speech that's three minutes long, for heaven's sakes. I know there's a lot of people that want to play this part, but look, I've got another offer, and it's for more money. I'm going to walk out of here and I'm going to make a call to my agent. I'm going to say, "Hold on just a little while. I'll let you know if I want to do that," and when I come back through the door, I've got to know.'"

The threat of the competing offer was a total flimflam. "I was lying like a snake," Beatty said gleefully. "I think they liked the fact that I was at least trying to be sly. I was doing something that maybe might be in their lexicon." When he returned to the room from his nonexistent conversation with his agent, he was told that the *Network* role was his.

Beatty, who had missed the rehearsal process for the film, said he was given only a brief explanation by Lumet on how he wanted the scene to be played. "He said, 'I've been an actor too,'" Beatty recalled. "'And I know what you want to do: you want to do this whole speech from the top to the bottom, as just a piece and you know the piece, and I know you know the piece and you can do it that way. But I know exactly how I want to film it.'"

Lumet wanted the scene broken up into smaller, more easily digestible pieces: Beale and Jensen's entrance into the boardroom; various pans across its table and angles of increasing closeness on Jensen as he hails the coming of "that perfect world without war and famine, oppression and brutality—one vast and ecumenical holding company, for whom all men will work to serve a common profit"; and reaction shots from Beale as he watches aghast and asks, "Why me?" ("Because," Jensen responds, "you're on television, dummy.")

In his screenplay Chayefsky described with precision and specificity how the sequence should look on-screen. After inviting Beale into his office, Jensen was to push a button making "the voluminous drapes slowly fall, slicing away layers of light until the vast room is utterly dark." Then: "The pinspots at each of the desks, including the one where Howard sits, pop on, lit by an unseen hand and creating a miniature Milky Way effect. A shaft of white LIGHT shoots out from the rear of the room, spotting Jensen at the podium, a sun in its own little galaxy."

But the severe restrictions imposed on the *Network* crew by the New York Public Library—which would allow no elaborate riggings or external lights to be brought into the room, other than the banker's lamps and candelabra that were already there—made this almost impossible to realize. "You'd have to put smoke in the room, and backlight the smoke to give the rays of light," said Owen Roizman, the director of photography. "And I couldn't do any of those things. They wouldn't allow us to use smoke or anything like that." To achieve the signature look of the scene, in which Jensen begins his speech in an apparent spotlight then disappears into darkness as he journeys around the table, Roizman said, "I basically begged to hang one light on a post at the far end of the table to light Beatty at the other end. It's one of the only scenes where I wasn't crazy about what I did with that. The light was okay, but I think I overexposed it just a little too much."

Amid the somber atmospherics and Beatty's vaudevillian performance, Finch—who was called upon to do little more than sit in a chair and watch the theatrics—had to find ways to keep himself engaged between takes. Separating Finch from the only other performer on hand was the monolithic boardroom table, which became a stage for his animalistic antics. "At one time," said Beatty, "I turned away from him for a second. And I turned back, and he's standing on top of this table. He's come out of his chair and he's standing on top of the table. And he's doing an ape. But very well." Watching Finch strut and amble capably on all fours (and give the occasional satisfied shriek), Beatty suspected he had practiced this routine before. "He's not just doing any ape," Beatty said. "He's doing *his* ape."

When shooting wrapped, Beatty, who had spent the day throwing himself into a taxing character and his histrionic orations, piled out of the boardroom and into an antechamber. There, he encountered Chayefsky and excitedly asked him how he thought the shoot had gone. There was a pause, Beatty said, and then "without moving a single muscle, anywhere on his body," the author gave his answer: "It's okay."

At the end of a day's shooting, as the arctic chill that had swept through the city was at last beginning to thaw, the camera operator Tom Priestley Jr. saw Chayefsky come bounding over to Lumet to pay him a compliment.

"Sidney," Chayefsky said, "how perspicacious of you to facilitate this scene."

Priestley, who had been taking a home vocabulary course and had only recently been introduced to the adjective *perspicacious* ("having great mental insight and vision"), could not resist injecting himself into the conversation. "I don't know what happened," he recalled. "I just said to Paddy and Sidney, '*Perspicacious!* What a great word!' And Sidney looked at me, not expecting me to know this word, and he says to Paddy, 'We better get out of here—the gorillas are getting educated.'"

As swiftly as the flu virus that was winding its way through the *Network* cast and crew, a spirit of camaraderie was uniting them as they hurried from one Manhattan location to the next—a feeling that the film they were making was important and was going to matter somehow. There were, of course, the occasional blowups and breakdowns, usually emanating from one particular source. On the windy day of a lengthy exterior tracking shot that followed Holden and Dunaway along a stretch of Central Park West, Kay Chapin noted in her diary that "Faye was nervous about the scene and very short with wardrobe people. She flubs a lot and had a hard time getting through a long speech but looks terrific." Conditions were considerably less glamorous behind the camera that day, where Chapin said she and her peers were "knee deep in dog shit along the park wall" with "lots of soot flying around."

There was also plenty of gallows humor and unexpected bonding over the considerable ground that needed to be covered over the next month. At the start of February the production moved into a vacant retail space on Forty-Fourth Street and Sixth Avenue, where sets had been constructed for the UBS newsroom (including its time- and space-warping spiral staircase, which originated in Toronto and terminated in New York) and the adjoining offices, packed with pulsating ticker-tape and Teletype machines, microfilm readers, carbon paper duplicators, refrigerator-size photocopiers, and all the latest technology a news-gathering organization could want. Filming there was scheduled for three days, but Lumet, moving at his usual clip, finished it in a day and a half, including the two-part tracking shot that the opening credits of *Network* would play over, where Beale and his UBS colleagues use their top-of-the-line tools (pencils, paper, and a steady supply of cigarettes and coffee) to map out the precise timing of the evening's news broadcast.

Lumet could be blindingly efficient but he could have his temper tantrums, too. During the office shoots, he was seen losing his patience and threatening to fire an actor who asked what a scene was about. (The besieged performer had just one line in the scene and had been provided only the page of the script with his portion of dialogue on it; Lumet's contention, somewhat misdirected, was that all actors should receive complete scripts so they know exactly where they fit in.) But this was a rare lapse in the famously charming demeanor of the director, who more commonly addressed his actors and coworkers as "angel" or "pussycat" or "heart," and deemed every take to be "ravishing" or "first-rate," even when it was terrible.

He had special nicknames for his director of photography, Owen Roizman, whom he addressed as "Oven," and his first assistant director, Alan Hopkins, who became "*Ay*-lan." They in turn learned to understand his special lexicon of pet expressions, in which "gnatz" (accompanied by a flicking of the fingers) meant to move the camera slightly in a certain direction and "woof" (with a downturned palm) meant to stop.

At a night shoot on February 11, along Sixth Avenue and in a bar near Radio City Music Hall, Finch and Holden filmed the bittersweet *Network* prologue, where Schumacher tells Beale, the "grand old man of news," that he has been fired, effective in two weeks, and after the two old friends get "properly pissed," Beale begins to conjure up his plan to kill himself on the air. Speaking more to himself than to Beale, Schumacher offers a sarcastic-sounding response that is pure, unadulterated, and sincere Chayefsky: "Hell, why limit ourselves? . . . I love it. Suicides. Assassinations. Mad bombers. Mafia hit men. Automobile smash-ups. *The Death Hour*. Great Sunday night show for the whole family. We'll wipe that fucking Disney right off the air." Holden was gently and affectionately teased by the crew for his dialogue gaffes—he seemed either to have trouble remembering his lines or not to have studied them all that carefully—but somewhere along the way, he lost the further exhortations in this speech to "watch somebody get guillotined, hung, electrocuted, gassed" and to see "murder in the barbershop" and "human sacrifices in witches' covens."

Two days of filming the gala meeting of the UBS network affiliates followed at the Grand Ballroom of the Plaza Hotel; then a day spent on Holden and Dunaway's windswept walk along Central Park West; and then three days at the duplex apartment that was supposed to belong to Diana Christensen. The first of these days, on Friday, February 20, was devoted primarily to scenes of Dunaway in bed: one where she is attempting to watch Howard Beale's press conference declaration that he can no longer be the "dispassionate pundit, reporting with seemly detachment the daily parade of lunacies that constitute the news," all while a naked stud is "fondling, fingering, noodling and nuzzling Diana with the clear intention of mounting her"; the other depicted her in a postcoital moment with Schumacher, "lying naked on a maelstrom of sheets, both still puffing from what must have been an ebullient bout in the sack."

After a weekend's break, shooting resumed at the apartment on Monday, February 23, where Dunaway and Holden filmed the scenes in which Schumacher brings his affair with Diana to a bitter conclusion. One day was needed for the prelude to the breakup, located primarily in Diana's kitchen, where Schumacher makes his desperate "primal doubts" speech; and the following day, February 24, was used for the conclusive moment, set in Diana's foyer, where a defiant Schumacher declares her to be "virulent madness" and, perhaps the greater insult, "television incarnate": "All of life is reduced to the common rubble of banality. War, murder, death are all the same to you as bottles of beer. The daily business of life is a corrupt comedy."

The prelude scene was the one that had bothered Lumet in rehearsals, when he noticed that Holden would not make eye contact with Dunaway. Now the director's careful scrutiny and note taking from that preparatory phase would pay off with a single instruction to the actor. "On the day we shot it," Lumet recalled, "I said, 'Bill, I want you to do just one thing. Latch on to her eyes and don't ever look away from her.' And this world of emotion came pouring out." To Dunaway, Lumet said, "I gave her the same direction: 'Don't take your eyes away from him. But just try to understand what he's talking about.' She doesn't know what he's talking about. Just try to get it. And thank God the phone rings just in time."

Following from the instant that Schumacher angrily kicks over the pages of his unfinished memoir—his "dumb damn goddam book about the early days of television"—the scene ends on a series of close-ups, and each one is startling in how candidly it presents the film's leading performers: Holden looking haggard and depleted, his wrinkles unconcealed and his tousled hair a mixture of dyed chestnut and authentic gray, while his hangdog eyes emit alternating currents of despair and rage; Dunaway, beneath her flawless face, immaculate grooming, and pursed red lips, exuding an almost childlike naïveté and a seemingly total lack of comprehension. Despite his preliminary warning to Dunaway not to play the character with any vulnerability, Lumet later said, "That's as close a moment as she gets."

Dunaway, of course, knew exactly what she was doing in the scene, and would later describe Diana's gaze of doe-eyed blankness as "the quintessential expression" of the character. What Diana confirmed in that instant, Dunaway said, is that she "isn't connected as a woman, doesn't feel like a woman. With just those few seconds on the screen, you knew that she was completely unable to love."

The impact of these performances may have been enough to distract from some technical errors in these scenes. As Alan Heim said of Lumet, "Sidney was not a great believer in doing an extra take for safety," and this raised a possible problem as he reviewed footage of Holden. "Something happened in the focusing process," Heim said, "and they focused on the stair rail behind him instead of on his face. And it's a big close-up and he's a little soft. I called in the morning when I saw it, and I said, 'Sidney, maybe you want to look at it at lunchtime. You're still on the set and it is a little soft.' And he said, 'Aw, come on. How bad is it?' I said, 'Ehhh, it's pretty bad.' And we went and we looked at it, and he threw his arm around my shoulder and he said, 'Don't worry about it, *boychik*.' And that's it."

For the next two weeks, from February 25 until March 11, the *Network* team would be encamped at 1350 Avenue of the Americas, a thirty-five-story complex at Fifty-Fifth Street that was the New York headquarters of Metro-Goldwyn-Mayer, and that, in an act of convenience and expediency rather than satirical commentary, would now double as the offices of UBS. The empty upper floors of the tower, going unused by the studio that was coproducing *Network*, offered nothing but an overhead grid from which a drop ceiling could be hung, but to the production designer, Philip Rosenberg, the building's many wide windows, with their sweeping views down the avenue and across the island of Manhattan, suggested the perfect steep perch from which Schumacher would tumble, and where corporate cronies such as Frank Hackett would build their nests.

For Robert Duvall, who played Hackett, it was also the ideal vantage point from which to antagonize passersby on the streets below. As one person who worked on the film recalled, after the MGM office shoot began, "He opened up the window and screamed out the window, this very absurd primal scream out there." And then, this person said, Duvall lowered his pants and thrust his bare buttocks through the window frame. "We're on the twenty-second floor or whatever, and he's like, 'I mooned this guy down on Sixth Avenue.' I went to Sidney and said, 'You know, your actor's going a little over the top in your camera room.' I didn't elaborate on it. I think that's the way he got into character."

For Roizman, the location posed a unique lighting challenge: any scene shot during daylight hours had to be finished before the sun had visibly shifted, and any scene shot at night had to contend with the cumulative glow coming from every other window of every nearby office and apartment. "Remember that this was not a set and those were not backings, but actual Manhattan buildings with lights in the windows," said Roizman, who found it all but impossible to illuminate these shots with traditional external lights. "Every time I would think of putting a light somewhere, I would look in the glass, and there it was. I couldn't avoid my own lights." Fortunately, the film's gaffer, Norman Leigh, had been experimenting with "gimmick lights" he created by purchasing large quantities of aerosol deodorants, spraying their contents until the cans were empty, then cutting them open, painting them black, and attaching them to his lighting units so they wouldn't be visible onscreen.

For Gottfried, the MGM building was the site of an unusual query he received from Peter Finch. "When you have an office set," the producer explained, "obviously you have a lot of extras: people at typewriters, people running around doing nothing. Some of the extras are black. And some of them are women." This arithmetic, Gottfried said, added up to Finch's bid for the following favor: "He said, 'Don't let me be near one of the black secretaries if my wife is around, because she will kill me. No, really.'"

And for Chayefsky, this latest setting for his film came with new and unforeseen details to complain about—even the specifications for the set design of Schumacher's office. "When he saw a big window being installed in the office," Rosenberg recalled, "he came over and said, 'In all my years in television, I never saw, ever, a news department [head] have a window in his office.' Not to get into any kind of a battle with him, I would steer him to Sidney, who could convince him that he had staging involved, where the entire office had to be privy to what was going on in the office later on. And finally he was able to convince Paddy about it. I'm not sure I would have been able to, so it worked very well for me."

When a reporter from the *Sunday News* came to visit the *Network* set in early March, she was taken with the obsessive screenwriter, whom she described as "a bearded teddy bear of a man who sat in on each scene, quietly smoking a cigar." Lumet had just wrapped the scene where Hackett boasts of his "big, fat, big-titted hit" and the attendant media coverage it has generated—even "an editorial in the holy god-dam *New York Times*"—and informs Schumacher he is fired; the director, having told Dunaway that her reading was "divine," had settled in for his lunchtime nap. Chayefsky, on the other hand, was by his own admission "a bundle of nerves." "I'll have to try to figure out something to get unhappy about, but I'm having trouble," he told the reporter between puffs of his cigar. "I don't trust it when things are going this well. I don't have to do the lighting. All I have to do is watch, and I don't even have to do that."

Finch, who had become the latest member of the ensemble to succumb to the flu and was presently having his facial reactions filmed while tucked into a bed that had been propped up on its side, vouched for Chayefsky between takes. "He has a very strict rhythm, like George Bernard Shaw, and you can never break that rhythm," Finch said of the screenwriter. "He's one of the few writers in film who has a rhythmic quality all his own."

Holden, when he was not poring over the latest issue of *Popular Mechanics*, compared the making of *Network* to his time on the 1954 MGM ensemble drama *Executive Suite*—he meant this as a favorable parallel—and suggested that Chayefsky was a willing if wily collaborator when it came to changes in the screenplay. "I asked Paddy's permission and he said that it was all right," Holden claimed. "Four weeks later you suddenly find out your changes are no good. And you go to him again, and tell him you want to go back to the original script and he says, 'I was waiting for you.'"

Chayefsky's counterresponse to the reporter politely implied that Holden's account had simply been a bit of well-intentioned public relations. "All the rewrites were done in advance," he said. "There's enough hysteria-making in films without that."

"If there's anything worse than a bullying director," Chayefsky acknowledged, "it's a defensive writer. A writer should be available to make improvements all the time." And yet he had to admit that things on this picture were generally going right; for all the stress he placed upon himself, trying to prepare for every possible mistake or complication, perhaps the greater anxiety was realizing that he wasn't truly needed here. "A couple of the scenes in the film play better than they were written," he said. "In the end that is what's up there—it's the actor and the audience and the actor has to feel comfortable. We have a helluva cast—a beautiful company."

Chayefsky had never spent time among the radical groups that flourished in the 1960s and '70s and, for all he knew, had now staked out a permanent place in the national political discourse. There was no discernible difference, as far as he was concerned, between an organization such as Students for a Democratic Society and a group such as the Symbionese Liberation Army. Whatever their stated goals, all that interested these groups was the destabilization of the country, the sowing of discord, and the spreading of violence. Whereas the SLA had been operating from safe houses dotted across the San Francisco Bay Area, he set the command center of his fictitious Ecumenical Liberation Army in the sleepy suburb of Encino and, in his acerbic stage directions, described it as a "shambles of cartons, crates, scraps of food and litter"; in its dining room, "tattered sleeping bags and newspapers cover the floor, and the walls are bare except for various militant posters of the likes of Mao and Marlon Brando."

Lumet did not go even as far as the West Coast; on Monday, March 15, for the second time in nearly two months, he brought the *Network* shoot to Rockland County, New York. There, on about seventy acres of apple orchards and vegetable gardens in the northern hamlet of Congers, his production designer, Philip Rosenberg, had found the Dr. Davies Farm, the site of a 140-year-old farmhouse that, in 1891, became the home of Arthur B. Davies and his wife, Dr. Lucy Virginia Meriwether Davies. He was the president of the Association of American Painters and Sculptors, which organized the controversial 1913 Armory Show that introduced America to avant-garde modern art; she was one of the nation's first female doctors, a relative of the explorer Meriwether Lewis, and a cousin of Mildred and Patty Hill, the composers of "Happy Birthday to You." Now their estate would provide the unlikely home for an opportunistic gang that fought the "increasingly desperate, imperialist ruling clique" and "the entire apparatus of the bourgeois-democratic state."

The farmhouse shoot was among the rare production days that did not involve Holden, Dunaway, Finch, or any of the other principal members of the cast, and instead focused on the business negotiations between the Ecumenicals and various representatives of ICM and the William Morris Agency. Prior to filming, Chayefsky had substantially reduced the role of a character named Heywood, described in drafts of the *Network* screenplay as "an old union lawyer, given to peroration," and who, on behalf of the Ecumenicals, was supposed to have told Diana, "Well, we're not going to sell out, baby! You can take your fascist teevee and shove it right up your paramilitary ass!" (In his notes on the script, Daniel Melnick of MGM wrote simply, "This scene should come out," and it did.) That left only a handful of supporting players, including Kathy Cronkite, who was playing the group's resident heiress, Mary Ann Gifford ("a fire-eating militant with a bandolier of cartridges across her torn shirt"); Marlene Warfield as Laureen Hobbs, a fictionalized version of radicals such as Angela Davis; and Arthur Burghardt as the Great Ahmed Kahn, Chayefsky's big, brooding gloss on latter-day revolutionaries such as the SLA's Field Marshal Cinque—and who, the script said, is first seen wearing "a hussar's shako and the crescent moon of the Midianites hangs around his neck."

By now, Cronkite had reconciled herself to the possibility that her being cast in *Network* had less to do with any particular acting talent than the lifelong friendship between Lumet and her father. Still, the role epitomized a personal struggle that she had been waging, at least since she had moved to Los Angeles to pursue an acting career, to establish an identity that was separate from her father's name; that struggle was now reignited as she found herself once again living under her parents' roof while she worked on the film. "It was a time of my life when there was so much challenge to my individuality from Dad," Cronkite said. "Just going out to L.A., it was hard to be my own person, with everybody assuming that every part I got was because of Dad."

It did not help matters that the fictional circumstances of Mary Ann Gifford so closely resembled events in the life of Patty Hearst, offering Cronkite an unpleasant reminder that her own connections to wealth, fame, power, and the platform of the media put her at risk, too. "I had friends joking about kidnapping me, and it was so not funny, and scary," she said. "Because Patty Hearst got kidnapped, I could be kidnapped. These were slightly unsavory friends, and I think the reason it was so scary was that I didn't really know how much they were kidding."

Cronkite's big moment at the farmhouse occurred as the radicals and the agents were battling over the contractual details of *The Mao Tse Tung Hour*, during which Gifford was to come charging down a rickety flight of stairs, bellowing about the value of her contribution to the show. Her line, as given in the screenplay, is "Fugginfascist! Have you seen the movies we took at the San Marino jail break-out demonstrating the rising up of a seminal prisoner-class infrastructure?!"

Like so many of her costars before her, Cronkite found it trying to say even this much. "I'm coming down the stairs screaming this line of propaganda that was so rich in politics and so convoluted, and not that accessible to me," she recalled. "This is not something that I identify with or empathize with. Particularly when I'm coming in with that passion. All I really want to say is, 'F you, F you!' I don't want to be spouting multisyllabic propaganda. And it was very difficult to get the words out."

Where the youthful and inexperienced actress differed from nearly everyone else was in boldly asking Chayefsky if her line could be altered to something more manageable. "I remember saying to Paddy, 'Look, can we just say this instead?'" she said, laughing at the memory of her innocent blunder, adding that she will be haunted "for the rest of my life—'How dare you, how dare you turn to Paddy Chayefsky and ask him to dumb down one of his lines?' It's just astonishing to me. My face is red as I'm even thinking it. It's just astonishing that I would have the gall to do something like that. And naïveté. It didn't occur to me that that wasn't done, you know?"

Not that Chayefsky was offended by her request. "Oh, he was lovely, he and Sidney both," said Cronkite. "They just said, 'Well, no.' But they didn't make me feel dumb or embarrassed or out of line. They just basically said, 'Well, let's try it again the way it is.' Sidney had an amazing way of saying, 'You screwed up,' so that you felt you were the greatest thing in the world. He had this amazing way of saying, 'Oh my God, that was fabulous. How about if we try it again, and just tweak it a little?'"

A few days earlier, Marlene Warfield had filmed a scene with Dunaway where their characters were introduced to each other at what was supposed to be a UBS network conference room in Los Angeles (actually an office building in Melville, Long Island): Diana Christensen announced herself as "a racist lackey of the imperialist ruling circles," and Laureen Hobbs identified in kind as "a bad-ass Commie nigger." For Warfield, who had already played numerous roles in Manhattan theater, on Broadway, on television, and in film, this language was blunt but hardly bothersome to her.

"It tasted very good," Warfield later said of the line. "And it was satirical. But there's a lot of facts, there's a lot of truth to it. It's throwing it back in the faces of people who looked down on it, and who misunderstood what it really meant." In appropriating this racial slur, Warfield said Chayefsky and Lumet "didn't mean to harm anyone. They just wanted to show the hypocrisy of the way people interpret things, when they hear something that they know is true."

Lumet, in particular, helped Warfield understand this exchange in a way that Chayefsky probably never could have. Lumet told Warfield to think about it as similar to *The Blacks*, an avant-garde satire by Jean Genet whose traditionally all-black cast of characters includes a royal court and a queen dressed in white masks or whiteface makeup. Recalling the director's instructions to her, Warfield said, " 'You are the black queen, and there is the white queen.' He hit it, man, he hit it right on the button when he said that's what this is about. And from then on, we did the scene. That's all he had to say. Whoa!"

It was never clear to Warfield whether Lumet knew she was one of the actors who had performed in *The Blacks* during an East Village run in the 1960s. "I'm saying, 'Damn, did you see me in that, too?' " she said. "I guess he did. It was on my résumé. But that was a stroke of genius, to cough that up."

But not all her costars at the farmhouse felt the same way. At the bottom of its staircase, seated against decrepit curtains and decaying window blinds and surrounded by a phalanx of actors playing agents, managers, and lawyers, was Burghardt, in sunglasses and his ceremonial military dress, a prop pistol concealed at his side. To him, the decision to play the Great Ahmed Kahn was a perilous bargain that had to be weighed against the political battle for which he had sacrificed much of his adult life.

Only two years earlier, on February 15, 1974, at the age of twenty-six, Burghardt—then known as Arthur Banks—had been released from a federal penitentiary in Sandstone, Minnesota, after serving almost twenty-eight months of a five-year sentence for draft evasion. This was the third such institution where he had been incarcerated after his conviction, having started his term in 1971 at a medium-security prison in Danbury, Connecticut. The next year, he was transferred to a maximum-security prison in Terre Haute, Indiana, where he was involved in a peaceful protest for which he was sprayed with mace and brutalized in his cell, then placed in solitary confinement for the next fifteen months. In December 1972 he was charged with having assaulted an officer during the protest, and an Indiana judge ruled that his lawyer, William Kunstler, could not represent him in the case because of public statements of support Kunstler had made that violated court rules. The U.S. Supreme Court was about to review the case when the actor was released on a $10,000 bond.

When Burghardt read the role of the Great Ahmed Kahn in Chayefsky's screenplay, he saw the character as "a tyrant, a punk, a criminal"— and a cartoonish reduction of a far more complicated political spectrum that he knew firsthand. "I knew that black people were far more relevant to the world, and there were more important black leaders than these cowards, punks, and petty dictators who emerged out of the back eddies of the civil rights movement," Burghardt said.

But the larger message of Network—about a man who is severely punished for enunciating some necessary and uncomfortable truths— was one that the actor could not walk away from. "I realized that this was a black comedy," he said, "and I had to be part of it." The question, Burghardt said with a sardonic laugh, was whether his own community would punish him for accepting a part he knew to be a caricature— "whether or not I was going to be considered a traitor."

If his character had to be an archetype, Burghardt said, "I decided I'd play the archetype to the hilt." Earlier that day at the farmhouse, he had filmed a scene with Cronkite and Warfield in which Kahn is surprised by the news that his group is being considered for a television show. By his own decision, Burghardt said, "I wanted my mouth to be filled with fried chicken and shit. There had been a bucket of Kentucky Fried Chicken there. And in one take, I said, 'What the fuck are you talking about?' And some chicken came out and it got Kathy on the side of the head. Lumet said he liked it. I was very embarrassed. I said, 'Tell you what, we're getting low on fried chicken. Give me some toilet paper and I'll stuff my jaw full of toilet paper.' I smeared some of the chicken grease over my mouth."

When it came time for him, as Kahn, to interrupt the bickering of the Hollywood power brokers and chic radicals by firing his gun into the air and announcing, "Man, give her the fucking overhead clause," Burghardt said, "I realized I had to go deep inside of me to be somebody that I did not want to be, whom I actually loathed inside. Yes, there was a part of me that didn't want to do this. There was another major part of me that realized that I had to do it, and I had to tell myself, literally, shut up. Be in the moment."

"All I had to do was sit there and not bemoan the loss of my vaunted, wonderful career in doing this," Burghardt said, fully expecting that there would be future consequences for the choice he had made. "'Oh, yeah,' I thought, 'I'll probably never work again. A lot of black people won't like me doing this role. People on television won't want me *in* television.'"

The festive assignment on St. Patrick's Day, March 17, was to caravan out of the city to the Sea Spray Inn, a small hotel and a cluster of cottages on Ocean Avenue in East Hampton. There, Holden and Dunaway shot most of the scenes that occur during Max and Diana's Long Island getaway: their frolicking on the beach, their secluded dinner at an Italian restaurant, their tense, excited moments as they enter the motel room where the principal activity of the evening is about to occur. But once the actors passed through the door to their boudoir, their work was done: all their most intimate activities had already been filmed the previous day.

As part of the arrangement to pacify the recalcitrant Dunaway, the interior of the bedroom at the Sea Spray Inn was re-created in a small studio on West Forty-Eighth Street in Manhattan, where only essential personnel were allowed. Despite the semi-seclusion these accommodations offered her, Dunaway remained nervous about the sequence. "I'm never at ease in love scenes, and actually feel quite shy about them," she said. "But this was a scene I was terrified to do. It seemed so outrageous, and I felt foolish astride Bill and babbling away about ratings in between gasps. It is one thing when the camera is shooting two people in bed, mostly hidden by sheets and blankets, with a shoulder exposed here, a leg there. It is quite another when you know that the camera is spending a lot of time shooting close-ups of your face as you try to enact this incredibly intimate moment."

In a further measure of consideration, Lumet spoke with Dunaway in advance and, without mincing words, described exactly how he planned to shoot the scene. "We would open with a high shot of the two in bed, then the camera would dolly in behind her," he said. "I assured her that the bedsheet would be high enough that we would see no crack of the ass. As we moved in closer, her arm would be at such an angle it would cover her breast. And during filming we stuck to that agreement. I would not violate it, because among other things, Faye had to play the scene. It wouldn't have been good, much less funny, if there was so much tension she couldn't act."

The official filming log from that day is consistent with the pre-shoot strategy Lumet laid out. The scene begins with a wide shot of

Max and Diana, the camera dollying in as they kiss and she removes her boots. In a second shot, they remove their shirts, and Diana is fleetingly seen topless before she dives underneath the bedsheets. In the third shot, Diana lifts up the sheet to allow Max into the bed, and in the fourth she has her orgasm, "screams climactically and collapses," according to the shooting script. The last remaining shot is a close-up of Diana in climax; the accompanying notes say she was either "clean" or "clear" as she "drops down out of frame." "For all the Sturm und Drang that went on about it," said Philip Rosenberg, one of the few crew members permitted on the closed set, "it was a very uneventful shoot that day. It was all very controlled and very quick."

As Dunaway later recalled the experience, the key ingredient that allowed her and Holden to complete the sequence was "a huge measure of good humor." "Bill could not make it through a scene without dissolving into laughter at some point along the way," she said. "And Lumet was great, he just went zooming about on his invisible roller skates as if this scene was like all the others."

Without quite revealing what had transpired off camera, Lumet would later say that his sympathies during the love scene were with Holden, who in this circumstance was "an actor being used." "To be one of the biggest stars, and let the other person have all of the fun, the whole speech, and you have to lie there, faking that you're pumping into her, and not allowed any reaction that's going to interfere with the comedy"—to put up with all that, Lumet said, was "noble of him."

One more step remained before this material could be used in the film. Under her agreement to perform the love scene, Dunaway was also permitted to join Lumet, Chayefsky, Gottfried, and their editor, Alan Heim, when they watched the raw footage from the shoot, and accounts vary as to how she reacted when the day's results were presented to her at Heim's editing suite. According to Gottfried, the actress was unimpressed with what she saw and, after having fought so vigorously to keep herself covered up on-screen, looked at the takes and said, "You could have shown a little more." "She complained because they were so unsexy," Gottfried said. "That's the funny thing about her. I mean, really."

Heim had a different recollection of how the review with Dunaway proceeded. Far from responding with apathy and nonchalance, Heim said, the actress noticed that in one of the takes her nipples were briefly but clearly visible at the bottom of the frame—a direct violation of the written agreement between her and Gottfried—and she exploded in anger at the men, who outnumbered her in the room, demanding to know what had happened.

As Heim hurriedly explained to Dunaway, her inadvertent exposure was the accidental result of how the scene had been shot and how the footage was being played back to her, but this mistake would not show up in the completed film. When Dunaway was performing the love scene, Heim said, "She was wearing a sheet for the most part. Sometimes, though, when she moved, the sheet would expose a little bit of her nipple. When we screened that scene for Faye—and they screened it in the screening room, and unfortunately the projectionist put in the mask that was not the proper mask for the film. With that mask in the way it was, you could see a little bit of her nipples. She was furious. And I had to reassure her—we all did—that this was an anomaly. It's on the film frame, it was never intended to be, and if you look at it in the movie, it's not there. When it's projected properly, you don't see it. Sidney would not have done that; it's not his kind of prurience."

Even so, Heim and his cohorts could not understand what all the fuss was about. "She did have to be seminude in that scene, otherwise it wouldn't have played," he said. "I hate love scenes where women are wearing bras and men are wearing shorts. Give me a break."

With this hurdle cleared, only two days of filming with the principal cast remained, all minor scenes set within the UBS offices. On Sunday, March 21, the cast and crew gathered at Sardi's to celebrate the completion of their work—and the fact that Lumet had finished a week ahead of schedule, at a savings of $400,000—and to bid one another farewell. The party was formally hosted by Gottfried and Chayefsky, who were both in attendance, as were William Holden, Sidney and Gail Lumet, and Peter and Eletha Finch. As parting gifts, Kay Chapin, the script supervisor, received a lion's tooth from Holden and a Gucci checkbook wallet from Finch. Marlene Warfield, who had been too shy throughout filming to engage her more illustrious colleagues, finally found the courage to approach Chayefsky at his table and ask him for his secrets to being a successful writer.

"You have to be disciplined," he told her. "You have to get up early in the morning, every morning, and just sit in front of the page until something comes out. Write one word, if that's all you can do in one day. And just keep doing it until things start pouring out."

But not everyone was in such a generous mood, and amid the array of festive celebrity caricatures that decorated the walls of Sardi's, one famous face was noticeably absent from the gathering of partygoers. As *New York Post* columnist Earl Wilson described the occasion, "Faye Dunaway ducked the 'wrap-up' party of the film *Network* at Sardi's and the others were a little hurt."

Even after good-byes had been said by those who wished to exchange them, one substantial portion of the film remained: the crescendo of impressionable television viewers running to their windows, at Howard Beale's urging, to stick their heads out and yell that they, too, were mad as hell and not going to take this anymore. As Chayefsky's screenplay had described this impromptu "Nuremberg rally," the scene was to unfold on a stormy evening starting at the apartment of the Schumachers, as their daughter, Caroline, looks out onto "the rain-swept streets of the Upper East Side, the bulking, anonymous apartment houses and occasional brownstones." Max then joins his daughter to gaze upon "the erratic landscape of Manhattan," seeing "silhouetted HEADS in windows—here, there, and then out of nowhere everywhere, SHOUTING out into the slashing black RAIN." There would be "a terrifying THUNDERCLAP, followed by a FULGURATION of LIGHTNING" that "punctuates the gathering CHORUS coming from the huddled, black border of the city's SCREAMING people, an indistinguishable tidal roar of human RAGE."

Chayefsky's stage directions spelled out a clear vision for the scene, but they did not discourage Lumet from imagining an alternate presentation. As Gottfried recalled, "One day when we were talking about it, Sidney comes in with an idea. He thought it would be funnier, and perhaps even more effective, if, once the scene started with Peter, that people start shouting it in different areas. Like sitting in a taxi, they'd stick out their heads and shout, 'I'm mad as hell and I'm not going to take it anymore.' People coming from different places, coming from a taxi, coming from people walking in the street or something like that. I thought the original scene as Paddy wrote it would be far more powerful, and ultimately Sidney agreed. I know he did. That was basically changing the script, which certainly Paddy wouldn't go in for."

Lumet's simpler approach may have been born of expediency—a preemptive expectation that shooting a sequence like this in cash-strapped, resource-starved New York would be expensive and impractical. As his camera operator Fred Schuler later said, "In California, because they always had all the money in motion pictures available, everything was, 'You want a crane? Sure, no problem, you got a crane. What else you want?' In New York you had to fight for everything, because it was not instantly available; it had to be made or you had to make a compromise."

Once the commitment was made to Chayefsky's version of the scene, it became "the biggest shooting of the picture," according to director of photography Owen Roizman. The sequence required three nights of filming, from March 23 through 25, and more gear and equipment than had been used at any point in the New York production, including "fire trucks with water hoses to wet down the buildings, so that we could get a little sheen from the water dripping off the windowsills," Roizman said, and "huge cherry pickers with lightning machines on them to light each building. . . . You could practically melt the generator with all the current that it draws."

In one respect, the declining fortunes of New York City were beneficial to the scene and the real estate it required: urban flight had opened up an entire block's worth of vacant residential buildings in the West Fifties, some that were being prepared for demolition and others that were simply lying dormant, that could be easily populated with the angry acolytes of Howard Beale. These apartments, however, provided nothing more than the physical space in which the shouting extras were to stand and scream—beyond that, the production had to supply its own curtains, blinds, and other window treatments; its own interior decorations; and even its own power. "There was no electricity and no elevator," Roizman said, "so the electrical crew had to carry lights and cable all the way up to the top floor and spread out and get in there and put up lights in the rooms. Then there were these huge lightning machines which we mounted either on a cherry picker or on a roof across the street. We would shoot a section and then jump to another area and maybe do two or three a night."

At 10:15 P.M. on Thursday, March 25, 1976, the final cries of the "mad as hell" chorus were heard, and the filming of *Network* was complete.

By sticking faithfully to Chayefsky's script, working quickly, and delivering a minimum number of options for each scene, Lumet had made it easy for editor Alan Heim to assemble a rough cut of *Network* while the film was still being shot. The studios backing the movie had already been shown portions of it before principal photography was completed and were pleased with what they saw. On March 20, MGM's Daniel Melnick wrote to Chayefsky:

Dear Paddy,

You are a man of your word and of your words. The picture looks great and we thank you for it.

Love,
Dan

With much of this heavy lifting already out of the way, what remained for Heim to finish his cut were mostly odds and ends, such as excising most of the short but nonvital scenes that showed characters walking from one office to another in the UBS building. "I knew they were going to go immediately," Heim said, "and we took pretty much all of them out if they didn't further the story in some way. Paddy had wanted those in, and he never said a word about taking them out, once we took them out. We just sat there, we looked at it, and I think I said, 'Why don't we get rid of all the shots between stuff that's happening? Between the important stuff.' We got rid of that."

But at least one crucial decision was reached in the editing stage, a choice that, if it had been made otherwise, might have eliminated Beatrice Straight's performance from the film almost entirely. As Chayefsky had originally called for in his screenplay, Louise Schumacher's devastated dismantling of Max was supposed to come before the motel liaison between Max and Diana. But when Heim played the film for Chayefsky, Gottfried, and Lumet, the transition between these two sequences seemed wrong somehow; the consensus among his collaborators was that Louise's diatribe was slowing things down and needed to be eliminated, but Heim said he made a last-ditch plea to preserve it by having the motel love scene come first.

"It didn't play," Heim said. "I remember saying to Paddy and Howard and Sidney, 'Look, let me just take this scene. I'll move it here. Take a look at it and see how it plays.' And Sidney said, 'No, it's not going to work. We have to drop this'—the scene being the Beatrice Straight scene. And I didn't want that scene taken out of the picture. I would have lain across the doorway and fought with my life to keep that scene in the picture."

A final ruling from MGM's Melnick ensured that the editor would never have to make such a spirited display of his loyalty. "We showed the film to Dan Melnick; he flew in on a Friday," Heim recalled. "Sunday night, I got a call from Howard Gottfried. And he sang my name. He said, '*Aaaa-laaan.*' And if you've been a Jewish son, you know when somebody sings your name, some kind of confession or attack is coming. And he said, '*Aaaa-laaan*, you know, Danny'—that is, Dan Melnick—'Danny came up with this great idea for the movie.' And he then proceeded to feed me back the idea I had been asking him to do for two weeks. And I said, 'You know, Howard, I'm going to do that.' He said, 'Do that, and when we come in, we'll look at it.'"

As much as Heim wanted to remind the producer that this was what he had been recommending all along, he knew it would be a violation of protocol. "You don't do this as an editor," Heim said. "You don't say, 'Listen, I've been after you to do that for a month. Why haven't you done it?' You just wait for it to happen or not. But in this case I said, 'Howard, I've been telling you guys that this was a good idea, and you wouldn't even look at it.' And he said, '*Boychik*, does it matter where an idea came from, as long as it works?' And I took that to be a lesson for the rest of my career. Because it doesn't."

As he and Lumet wound down their work, Heim found himself in a wistful, appreciative mood. He had now worked with the director for twelve years of what was already a two-decade-long feature-filmmaking career and was in awe of his perseverance, despite a résumé on which not every movie was a bona fide hit. "He was a journeyman, but he was a brilliant journeyman," Heim said of Lumet. "Like those baseball stars that played for thirty years, he made three films every two years when I started working for him. Nobody does that anymore. Nobody could do that. He had some down times, but if he had the right material, he'd do a great, great job."

Unsure of how audiences were going to receive the movie they had just completed, Heim summoned the courage to ask Lumet how he approached his own work. "I said, 'You know, you've got an enormous career, more than anybody will ever do again,'" Heim recalled. "And I said, 'How do you pick your projects?'"

In response, Lumet extended a hand. "You do five movies," the director said, sticking out his thumb, "one is going to be very good. . . . And one," he said, extending his pinky, "is going to be bad." He unfolded his three other fingers. "And the other ones are going to be average. The important thing is to keep working."

5

A STORM OF HUMANITY

For a few months it may have seemed that *Network* was a true collaboration, the result of a cast and crew, a director and a screenwriter, working in tandem, if not always in harmony. But once the film was shot, edited, and in the can, the actors, artisans, and crew members moved on to their next projects and their next paychecks. And when all the moviemaking apparatus was stripped away, there remained one man who would receive the praise and bear the blame for the film, who had fought from its inception to make sure the final product was his vision and that all who saw it knew it was his creation. As the opening-credit sequence for *Network* declared, after announcing the names of its lead performers, its own title, and the studios that made it, but before acknowledging its director, producer, or any other contributor, this was a film *by* Paddy Chayefsky.

In the spring of 1976, with several months still to go before *Network* was released in theaters, the time had come to start pulling back the curtain on a movie whose true intentions were largely mysterious to the people who had helped make it and to the media that had begun to cover it, and to decide how it should be positioned in the public eye. And the angle that was seized upon in promoting *Network* was controversy. As a poster for the film prominently warned audiences, "Prepare yourself for a perfectly outrageous motion picture," adding that "Television will never be the same again." The poster's design was the handiwork of Stephen Frankfurt, the former Young and Rubicam advertising executive who had created enduring marketing campaigns for *Rosemary's Baby* ("Pray for Rosemary's baby") and Lay's Potato Chips ("Betcha can't eat just one"), and the stark and deceptively childlike opening title sequence of *To Kill a Mockingbird*. The central image of his *Network* campaign, evoking the rainstorm that rages as Howard Beale makes his "Mad as hell" speech, was a jagged bolt of lightning descending from a cloud and striking the letter *W* in the film's title.

Similarly ominous images were swirling in the imagination of Paddy Chayefsky, for whom *Network* had thus far been only a phenomenon observed at point-blank range—words in his mind and on a page, and scenes acted out for him where he sat—but who quickly seemed to grasp how this promotional strategy was going to reflect on the film and on him. As he wrote around this time to his friend Calder Willingham, the author and screenwriter, "I know I am in for a storm of humanity."

MGM and United Artists scheduled the release of *Network* in the final weeks of the year, seeking to capitalize on any political fervor that remained after the 1976 presidential election. The studios committed to a marketing campaign budgeted at nearly $3 million, almost as much as the cost of the film itself, and hired Howard Newman, a veteran New York publicist who had worked on films such as *West Side Story*, *The Godfather*, and *The Exorcist*, to assist with the promotion. One of the earliest dispatches to come from his office was a set of production notes dated April 12 that trumpeted "the provocative theme of Paddy Chayefsky's NETWORK and the calibre of its collaborative creators," which combined to make it "one of the most important films of the year," and describing it as "a frightening story told in comedic terms."

Chayefsky's name was always listed in these materials ahead of those of Sidney Lumet, Faye Dunaway, William Holden, Peter Finch, and Robert Duvall. If the ultimate goal of such a document or the campaign in which it was being deployed was at all ambiguous, the production notes made clear in their second paragraph that "virtually everyone connected with NETWORK has won the esteem of their peers by Academy nominations or awards," including Chayefsky, who "carried away the coveted little golden statuette for his screenplay *Marty* in 1955 and *The Hospital* in 1971."

This compilation of personal biographies, cast and crew rosters, and character summaries would be distributed to any reporter, critic, feature writer, or broadcaster with an inclination to say anything about *Network*, and it was not shy about indulging in histrionics. Dunaway's character of Diana Christensen, it said, "should lay to rest the prevailing cliche that 'good roles aren't written for women anymore,'" breathlessly adding that Diana was "undoubtedly the strongest role written for an actress since Tennessee Williams created Blanche DuBois." Its description of anchorman Howard Beale compared the character to Walter Cronkite, John Chancellor, and Eric Sevareid, while declaring that Finch "emanates the very aura of dignified authority, articulate, well-educated, completely informed on everything from the inner politics of the Arab Emirate to kitty litter. Even the agonies of his disintegration are overlaid with respectful admiration for a giant brought down by an unkind destiny."

These words, of course, were not Chayefsky's, and where the author offered his feedback on the *Network* publicity materials, his comments were limited to remarks such as "Note: I never won an Emmy" and "!!! NOTE—DO NOT EVER refer to this film NETWORK as a 'black' comedy !!! I can't think of anything less likely to induce people to see it." But where he felt fully invested in matters that were even tangentially related to the presentation of the movie, Chayefsky remained fiercely protective of his intellectual property.

Among the ancillary projects prepared to coincide with the release of *Network* was a paperback novelization of the movie, written by Burton Wohl, the screenwriter of films such as *Rio Lobo*, and published by the Pocket Books imprint of Simon and Schuster. But in a letter offering his thanks for the assignment, Wohl did not endear himself to Chayefsky. Addressing his words to "Dear Mr. Chayevsky [*sic*]," Wohl wrote that he found *Network* to be "an intelligent, literate and highly dramatic script." Nonetheless, he added, "I hope you'll indulge my need to change a bit of your dialogue from time to time, dialogue which I found uniformly excellent but which, for the purposes of the novel, is sometimes insufficient. I haven't embroidered much, only now and then . . . most of the stuff is yours and it worked beautifully."

Taking no chances, Chayefsky laid out a series of strict guidelines in a letter to Pocket Books editor Agnes Birnbaum, and which he expected to be obeyed completely. To begin with, he said:

> The adaptor must remain entirely outside the telling of the story, invisible and as inaudible as possible. That means, the adaptor (storyteller, author, novelizer, whatever) must never introduce his own comments, insights, impressions, opinions. He simply tells the story, adding only what is desperately necessary to let the audience see and hear what is happening. The storyteller in our instance is simply that, and no more—a storyteller; and his attitude is that of a man telling a story that might seem occasionally hard to believe but did in fact actually happen.

In his further, increasingly rigid decrees, Chayefsky added that the author should never say "what the characters are thinking, remembering, reflecting upon, speculating about, mentally associating with or subconsciously imagining," but simply "what the characters say and do"; that this writer's prose style is to be "spare, lean and economical" and should avoid similes and metaphors. ("If somebody's hair is green, you have to say it is green, but you do not have to say it is as green as grass. Green hair is a sufficiently startling image in itself.") Finally, Chayefsky suggested, "The adaptor should not try to be funny. Writers who try to be funny are not funny. On the other hand, he shouldn't try to be sad either. He shouldn't try to be anything except the teller of the story."

When the edited pages of the *Network* novelization were delivered to him, Chayefsky was unmistakably disappointed with the results and ruthless in his notes back to the publisher. Across its very first page, he left untouched only its opening sentence—"This story is about Howard Beale, network news anchorman on UBS-TV"—and slashed away entire paragraphs that described the character as "dignified without being pompous, serious without being solemn, humorous without being silly" and a lengthy discourse about the difference between being a "hero" and being "heroic." In the right-hand margin, a perplexed Chayefsky wrote, "What's this shit got to do with anything?"

In another edit, Chayefsky struck out a passage that said Beale had been giving "more and more of himself to booze and casual cooze until his prostate grew to the size and texture of a hummingbird's nest and his audience rating dropped to 8." (His note on this particular embellishment was "rubbish.") His additional comments on the manuscript included "shit and not funny"; "how to butcher a joke"; "neither of these men is a dirty old goat, which is what we've got here"; "are these banal interpolations being presented as necessary novelistic improvements?"; "what is this shit?"; "no comment"; and "not everybody spends every waking moment thinking about getting fucked."

When the *Network* novel was published, its author was given as Sam Hedrin, a pseudonym that evoked the word *Sanhedrin*, the title given to the council of judges that governed ancient Israel and that, among other duties, passed judgment on Jesus before turning him over to Pontius Pilate.

The July 29 edition of *Women's Wear Daily* recorded the enthusiastic reaction to a sneak preview of *Network*, held at the Regent Theatre in the well-to-do Westwood neighborhood of Los Angeles and attended by such VIPs as Dustin Hoffman, David Geffen, and his girlfriend Marlo Thomas. The screening, it said, was "frequently interrupted by sustained bursts of applause," with the most spirited approval coming after "Bill Holden's impassioned speech to Faye Dunaway about the prurient nature of TV itself." "On the way out," the article said, "Hoffman was slapping MGM's Dan Melnick on the back, and Geffen was cheering, 'It's dynamite.'"

But a full-color press circular sent out by the studios a few weeks later emphasized a different strain of reactions that *Network* was starting to elicit. This promotional material focused less on the positive passions the film was stirring up and more on the ways in which it seemed to be indicting the television industry, the corporations that controlled the American media conglomerates, and the men who sat atop those corporations. Opening on the lightning bolt image from the movie poster and the assurance that "the excitement builds for a perfectly outrageous motion picture," the circular reprinted portions of two recent news articles, the first one also from *Women's Wear Daily*, but not as welcoming as that publication's earlier report on the film.

"*Network*, Sidney Lumet's new movie," this latest article said, "is the bitterest attack yet on television. The Bluhdorns and Paleys of this world might well run for cover when they see news commentator Peter Finch, programmer Faye Dunaway and news director William Holden (all superb) acting it out in the TV jungle. The writer of the *Network* script, Paddy Chayefsky, is telling us TV is a menacing monster and together with the business world 'they' are trying to control all. No wonder ABC-CBS-NBC would not let Lumet's cameras near their studios. Instead, Lumet filmed inside TV newsrooms in Canada." In a comparison that was both fortuitous and portentous, it continued that *Network*, "to be released in November, is as big a shock, and as powerful entertainment, as *All the President's Men.*"

A second article in the press circular, from *Newsday*, drew heavily from the *Women's Wear Daily* story; it reported that "advance word on the yet-unfinished *Network* touts it as the most controversial movie ever made about television," and noted that "a gossip columnist for *Women's Wear Daily* called it 'the bitterest attack yet on television' and claimed that the U.S. TV networks had refused to cooperate because they were so angered by the script." Howard Gottfried countered that *Network* was really about "the destruction of the individual and traditional American ideals through a system dedicated to conformity, standardization and the least common denominator," and made the preliminary claim that the studio segments of the movie were filmed in Toronto simply because it offered "superior facilities to anything available in New York." Chayefsky added that while critics had treated his movie *The Hospital* as if it were an exposé, it was embraced by the medical profession. "I think the same sort of thing will happen to *Network*," he said. "I basically write stories about institutions as a microcosm of human behavior."

Also on the record about *Network* for the first time was *CBS Evening News* anchor Walter Cronkite, who had been an ally to Chayefsky and Lumet in the making of the film. Asked to account for his daughter Kathy's appearance in a movie that satirized his profession, Cronkite responded: "The two things don't impinge on each other. I'm just delighted she's got work." He acknowledged he had not seen *Network* yet.

In the fall, Chayefsky began receiving letters of congratulations from industry colleagues who had been shown the movie at preliminary screenings. Mark Goodson, one of the prolific television producers behind game shows such as *I've Got a Secret* and *The Price Is Right*, wrote to say that he had reacted to *Network* as follows:

1. Whimpered and pouted a lot because I hadn't been invited to a screening by you.
2. Ground my teeth in rage as I once again suffered the experience

of realizing how brilliantly you create—harnessing tight discipline and wild imagination.

3. Had one of the best nights of my life—laughing, gasping, recognizing, appreciating.

Phil Gersh, the Hollywood agent whose clients included Arthur Hiller, the director of *The Hospital*, said in an otherwise complimentary letter to Chayefsky, "I only have one regret and that is that Arthur Hiller wasn't involved." On his personal stationery, Peter Bogdanovich, the in-demand director of *Paper Moon* and *The Last Picture Show*, wrote to Chayefsky that he thought *Network* was "absolutely terrific, as I'm sure you know." He added: "It's as if you've been rehearsing all your life to write it. That script is the only one in memory I wish had been offered to me, though I can't imagine it having been done better."

A few weeks later, Chayefsky replied to Bogdanovich to thank him for his compliments, but also to register his hurt feelings that he had been abandoned by many of the people with whom he had made *Network*. "Of all people," he wrote, "you must have some idea of the hysteria attendant on the opening of a film, and I have been right in the middle of it. Sidney Lumet was up in Toronto shooting EQUUS, Faye Dunaway simply refused to do any public relations at all; so the whole burden of the East Coast nonsense fell on me." Once this flow of admiration had passed, Chayefsky anticipated that a larger and more menacing wave was looming.

MGM sent out its invitations to preliminary screenings of *Network* in October, billing the film as "a penetrating look at the complex machinery of television," and announced that its official premiere would be held at the Sutton Theater in New York on November 14, prior to a national run that would begin the following month.

Well before most ticket-buying audiences knew what *Network* was, they were being told by the news media how their own industry members felt about the film and what they thought it was saying about them, beginning with an October 24 feature by Tom Shales in the

Washington Post that was evocatively titled " 'Network': Hating TV Can Be Fun." The article noted that the movie "won't open in New York until mid-November (and in Washington until mid-December) but already dozens of broadcasting people and critics have seen the picture in Los Angeles and New York advance screenings." "Whatever critics eventually decide about the film's cinematic worth," it continued, "it is already a guaranteed hot potato. One network producer became 'physically ill' during the picture, says one of the man's colleagues. Two weeks later—though it could only be coincidence—he had a heart attack."

"People in broadcasting," Shales wrote, "are calling it 'preposterous.' " And they were happy to line up to do so, by name and on the record, in his article. Paul Friedman, who had newly been appointed the producer of NBC's *Today Show*, said *Network* was "heavy-handed" and "outrageous," adding that "it would be a shame if it were a big hit," because it presented a distorted picture of the people who work in television.

"It's so unfair," Friedman said of the film. "It's simply not true. Television is not as powerful as Paddy Chayefsky thinks it is. 'Indifferent to suffering?' Come on. We do lots of things that deal with joy, too. We had something on the *Today Show*, just this morning—scenes from *Porgy and Bess*. People were crying in the studio, it was so beautiful.

"Of course it's an attack," he continued. "What makes me mad is that magazine and newspaper writers will be rubbing their hands with glee over it. There's an incredible inferiority and hate complex on the part of people in the print media who write about TV, and they'll just take this and run with it."

Richard Salant, the president of CBS News, said that he had not yet seen *Network* but, the *Post* wrote, "he has read the script and does he ever hate it!" It was "awful," Salant said, "just such a caricature. It simply couldn't happen. Will I go see it? Oh yeah. I'll see it because it's something about us."

William Sheehan, the president of ABC News, had not seen *Network*, either, but that did not prevent him from characterizing the film as "an unflattering portrait of the business we're in." Even so, he said he would "definitely" see the movie, "even if I have to pay to get in."

Meanwhile, the newsmen who had assisted Chayefsky in research-ing his screenplay did not provide many ringing endorsements. John Chancellor, the anchor of the *NBC Nightly News*, could only vaguely remember reading the script for *Network* ("I think I'm in it," he said) and seemed to recall it was about "an anchorman who goes crazy," while also containing what he thought was "a marvelous scene where the woman programming executive sort of rapes the head of the news division." Well, Chancellor concluded with an all-but-audible shrug, "Paddy said he was going to write something funny."

At CBS, Walter Cronkite had now changed his tune. He dismissed *Network* as a "fantasy burlesque" and said, "I really don't find any great significance in it." Asked if he had been irritated by the film, televi-sion's most trusted newsman replied, "Oh—no, I don't think so. I might be irritated by those who find it important, however. I just thought it was a rather amusing little entertainment." He added: "I laughed, quite a bit in fact. I think I laughed at some of the wrong places."

Chayefsky, for his part, seemed baffled by these hostile responses, and unsure why anyone would read *Network* as his personal payback against the television business. "Nothing bad happened to me in televi-sion," he told the *Post*. "All the people in television I've talked to love the picture. Of course, unless it's a big kiss on the you-know-what, some people will take offense at anything."

On Election Day, as Jimmy Carter defeated Gerald Ford and ensured that the last vestiges of Richard M. Nixon's administration would be swept from the White House in January, an outwardly joyous Chayefsky was in the Milton Berle Room of the New York Friars Club, toasting the successes of the president-elect, the soon-to-be-released *Network*, and what he called "the best chef salad in town."

Yet even as the screenwriter was celebrating, he was that same day being pummeled by a second barrage of disapproving and disgruntled newsmen who were angry at how *Network* portrayed their line of work.

An article in the *Christian Science Monitor*, which said the film was "seen as a searing but unfair indictment of television morality," once again turned to CBS's Richard Salant, who said that reading the screenplay had made him "sick." "It is an all-out attack on TV news, and I have no intention of seeing it," Salant said. "It is a distorted fantasy and simply could never happen." To the chorus of censorious voices was added that of esteemed NBC journalist Edwin Newman, who in September had moderated the first presidential debate between Ford and Carter, and who said of *Network*, "I didn't understand it to be a black satire—I couldn't tell which parts were supposed to be taken literally and which parts were supposedly exaggerated. There are valid things to be said about TV news, but this movie didn't say them." M. S. Rukeyser Jr., an NBC executive who held the title of vice president of public information, added that the film was "very boring," having "nothing to do with our business," and was "written by somebody who doesn't know how network television operates."

And in another salvo from Walter Cronkite, the CBS anchor incorrectly observed, "They cut my daughter's part down to almost nothing."

Edwin Newman expanded on his remarks in *W* magazine, telling the publication that *Network* "was such an incompetent movie, such a poor job, that any point it tried to make was lost. I've rarely seen a drunk scene worse than the one that opened the movie. That experienced actors could wobble around that way in front of the camera surprises me." He added that real-life TV producers would never stoop so low for the sake of ratings. "There's evidence that the opposite is true," Newman said. "You ignore ratings at your risk, but you don't base everything on them. Any news operation is a compromise—but I don't like to use that word. When I do a program I do my best to interest people—I try to make my writing interesting, catchy, amusing—you can't be in the news business and just employ stenographers to repeat what people in public office or sports figures tell them. It's more complicated than that.

"As a representation of network news," he repeated, "it was incompetent, and as a movie it was incompetent. I don't even want to talk about it seriously."

Cronkite, criticizing the premise of the film for a third time, agreed. "The record of network management has proved highly responsible in regard to news," he said. "Since the birth of television, all of us have known how we could hype our ratings almost instantly through the methods of the penny press, but you don't see any hint of things like that.

"But," he added, "I enjoyed it. It's a fun movie."

Privately, Chayefsky fumed at the accumulated battering he and the movie were receiving and started drafting a response aimed at the entire television industry. In this open letter (which he characterized as a "first revolt against bullshitism"), the author declared, "Television people should stop worrying about whether their image is being tarnished and start examining their responsibilities to the public—Stop making so much money. Out of self respect, give the people a lot more beauty, commitment and reality, even if those shows lose money. So you don't make a hundred and fifty million dollars profit."

Following a string of disconnected maxims—"TV destroys evil along with the good," "TV coarsens human life, reduces the complex uncertainties of common rubble"—Chayefsky defended *Network* as "a condemnation of the corporate way of life in which human life is no more than just another factor in corporate decisions." "I think that fact is one of the basic paranoias of our contemporary way of life," he continued. "I don't think it is just my personal paranoia. I think it is a deeply-embedded paranoia in most Americans. I think many Americans feel they have lost the individual value of their lives." The letter was never published.

For perhaps the only time in his career, Chayefsky began to feel regret for having hurt the industry peers he respected, and fear that he had betrayed the trust of people who had risked their reputations and the esteem of their profession to help him get his movie made. If these nagging and uneasy emotions were unfamiliar to him, so, too, was the action he took as a result, which was to apologize directly to those he may have wronged. On November 4 he composed a letter to an addressee identified as Walter—the recipient could only have been Cronkite—offering his genuine contrition. "Dear Walter," it began:

> I'm just beginning to get some negative feedback on my movie, "Network," from some television people which, I must say, surprised me. I thought television people would like it. It is, after all, the sort of jokes television people make among themselves. But the purpose of this note is to let you know that—if this movie or I have put you in any kind of awkward spot within the industry—then I am truly sorry, and if there is ever anything I can do to make amends, please let me know. Sidney told me that, after you read the script, you said that it wasn't about television at all; it was about our whole society and its fabric. Well, that's gospel true, Walter. I never meant this film to be an attack on television as an institution in itself, but only as a metaphor for the rest of the times. I'm sorry, Walter, if we've caused you any personal inconvenience or professional discomfort. We would never have asked you to allow us to use your newscast if we had dreamed it might embarrass you. Or maybe I'm making too much out of the whole thing. I hope so.

Its closing read, "My very best."

That same day, Chayefsky wrote a similar letter to a recipient named John—almost certainly the NBC anchor John Chancellor, whom he did not know as intimately, but whom he felt was owed an apology.

> I read a piece in the Washington Post which indicates my movie "Network" has aroused resentment among some people in television. Has this caused you any embarrassment or

professional discomfort? If so, John, please know I never dreamed television people would be angry about the film. I figured there were always a few stuffed shirts in every business, but that most television people would love the film. In fact, all the television people I've spoken to loved it. Anyway, I would never have asked you for help if I had thought the net result would embarrass you. If you have been put in an awkward spot, please let me know if there is anything I can do to make amends.

Whether or not Chayefsky realized it, *Network* **was having an** impact at the highest echelons of the television news industry, affecting the lives of people he had never known or encountered. For Barbara Walters, the film's release was the culmination of several deeply uncomfortable months in her career—an annus horribilis that began when she was named coanchor of ABC's *Evening News* and became the first woman ever to hold a network anchor position.

For the fifteen years prior, Walters had been a staff member at NBC's *Today Show*, where she had been named cohost in 1974 only after exploiting a loophole in her contract when the program's longtime host, Frank McGee, died unexpectedly. Two years later, she was recruited by William Sheehan, the president of ABC News, to join Harry Reasoner at the anchor desk of the network's national evening news broadcast; eager to make history and fulfill her potential, Walters readily accepted the offer. It was only years later, reflecting on this decision, that she said, "I should have had my head examined. Because the whole attitude was still so very anti-female."

Walters's troubles began at the moment the terms of her deal with ABC were announced, on April 23, 1976. The *New York Times*, in the very first sentence of its front-page story, revealed that she was to be paid $1 million a year over the next five years for her employment. It hardly mattered that half her annual salary represented the actual amount she would be paid for her *Evening News* anchor duties, and the other half would pay for the four hour-long entertainment news specials she would host each year. The total sum was far more than any of her male counterparts, at ABC or elsewhere, was currently being paid, and it set tongues clucking.

That was strike one against Walters; strike two was ABC's announcement, simultaneous with her hiring, that the network would expand its national newscast from thirty minutes to forty-five, and that its local affiliates were expected to do the same with their regional news broadcasts, thus creating a ninety-minute block of news each night. Instead, the affiliate stations, which did not want to yield lucrative airtime when they could be selling commercials for syndicated sitcoms, dramas, or game shows, rebelled against this plan and it was never implemented.

Then, strike three: NBC, which still had Walters under contract until September of that year, would not release her to its competitor, and for the entire summer of 1976 she was exiled from TV screens, unable to report on major news events such as the U.S. bicentennial or the presidential conventions. Even the date when she finally took her coanchor post at ABC proved inauspicious. "I went on the night of Yom Kippur," Walters later said, "and I felt that God never forgave me."

At ABC, Walters found herself frozen out by Reasoner, her coanchor, who resented the fact that he had to share his program with anyone—let alone a woman, and let alone a woman whose background was solely in broadcast journalism, rather than print. In the wider world, she was excoriated for not having an impact on the ratings of *Evening News* commensurate with her substantial salary. Crossing paths at a party with Clay Felker, the editor of *New York* magazine, which had recently rendered its judgment on Walters in an article titled "She's a Flop," Walters recalled, "I said, 'That was so hurtful.' And he looked me in the eye and said, 'Well, you are a flop.'"

Into this volatile mix of professional rivalries, personal animus, and gender politics came *Network*, which had presciently placed a bold female character in the highest ranks of its fictional hierarchy and made sure hers was always the loudest voice in the room. (In the words of one feminist critic, Diana Christensen was the "Great American Bitch," who had "moved out of the house and into the corporate structure" and who "embodies not only the fabled bloodlessness of TV executives but also the frightening impersonality of the medium itself.") Already burdened with battling the prejudices being directed against her personally, Walters now found it her weary and unwanted responsibility to have to answer for the satirical and stereotypical portrait of a working woman that the movie put forth.

"What troubled me," she told the *Washington Post* soon after seeing the film, "is that it gives such an exaggerated picture of television news. Obviously it's the result of Paddy Chayefsky's bitterness toward what happened to him in television. . . . People will think they're getting the inside story, and they're not."

In the *Christian Science Monitor*, Walters said that *Network* was ultimately "very good" as "an entertainment," and that "there is some truth in it—for instance, the holier-than-thou atmosphere that network news executives take at the same time that all they are worrying about is ratings." But in its overall depiction of television news, Walters worried that it was misleading. "If people accept the film as reality," she said, "it will be dreadful because it is an unfair, exaggerated portrayal."

Walters said later that *Network* "was not on the top of my list of things to worry about in those days." The film imagined that in order for a woman to succeed in TV news, she said, "you had to be tough as nails. That's changed—you don't, any more than a man has to be tough as nails. But the leading woman had to be a bitch. And that was typecasting of a woman working." The problem she faced at ABC was simpler and more insidious: "Not that I was considered tough as nails, but 'You don't belong. You're not one of us.'" Whether she was hard or soft, stubborn or accommodating, there was no right way for a woman to present herself, she said, "not at that point."

Richard Wald, the NBC News president who had given Chayef-
sky access to his department while he researched the *Network* screenplay, said his corporate superiors had a blunt reaction to the film: "They
hated it. Oh my God. And I got flak later because I had allowed him free
rein of the news division. The news division is a tiny part of the movie,
but it was the only one they could really nail to me." Wald himself took
no offense at the film or how Chayefsky had used his access at NBC; he
did not know the author personally and had only been acting on the
recommendation of NBC's entertainment division when he served as
the author's chaperone that past spring. "But," he said, "I got a call
from the entertainment department, and they knew him. Apparently
they felt bitten by this thing. Not apparently—they felt bitten by this
thing."

Wald did not see Chayefsky again after the scriptwriter's preliminary visits to NBC, but the author had promised to send Wald a copy
of the screenplay if he used his name in it, and he made good on this
vow. "Ultimately," Wald said, "I got two pages of a script, and I was all
excited: William Holden is fired, he goes downstairs, and he says to his
secretary, 'Get me Dick Wald; he'll know what to do.' And oh boy, big
deal." When Wald and his wife were invited to an early screening of
Network in New York, Wald said he was looking forward to his nomi-
nal film debut: "We dress up and we go to the New York premiere, and
William Holden gets fired and we're watching the movie and I'm waiting for my big moment. And nothing! Absolutely nothing." Dismayed,
Wald contacted Chayefsky after the screening to ask why he hadn't
been mentioned. "I sent him a note and I said, 'Hey, where am I?'" he
recalled. "And the answer came back: 'Welcome to Hollywood. You're
on the cutting room floor.' And that's the last I ever had anything to do
with Paddy Chayefsky."

Chayefsky emerged in November to give his first interviews on
Network, sounding somewhat chastened by the criticism the film had

taken from the broadcasting industry, even as he pushed back against it. Speaking alongside Gottfried to the *New York Post*, Chayefsky said he was "upset to hell" that so many prominent television personalities thought the movie was attacking them. As Earl Wilson recounted the scene in his It Happened Last Night column, a "very innocent" Chayefsky declared *Network* to be "a fond, affectionate satire." Then, "smiling mischievously," he added: "I'm not the only one who thinks so."

Gottfried was quick to contradict his partner. "It's not affectionate," he said. "It says basically that TV tends to corrupt the people in it to get ratings."

Chayefsky, puffing on a small cigar, replied, "If we were in charge of a network, we wouldn't be different."

"Then," Gottfried observed, "we'd be equally corrupted."

Addressing an audience of high school and college students attending a preview screening of *Network* at the Sutton Theater, Chayefsky said that the film "was not written out of rancor." "My rage isn't against television," he said. "It is a rage against the dehumanization of people." Nor, he said, was the character of Diana Christensen, or Dunaway's portrayal of her, a commentary on women in the business: "That part is me. She is a man." The film, he said, was about Marshall McLuhan and "the illusion we sell as truth. It's about how to protect ourselves. We have to avoid the bullshit."

But over several more minutes of sustained inquiry, Chayefsky gradually reverted to a familiar, cynical form, holding forth on the evils of foreign investments in the U.S. economy ("The Saudis have bought $200 million worth of AT&T stock. That's what I mean by too much. There is so much information in the movie, you can get a headache"); the inferiority of TV news to its print counterpart ("You put a camera in front of a cop and suddenly the crook becomes a perpetrator—a newspaper reporter can just go over and ask what the fuck happened"); Gene Shalit of the *Today Show* ("The man is a professional clown"); and why he had generally given up watching television journalism in favor of Knicks games. Speculating on how *Network* was going to be received by critics, Chayefsky said, "We're going to get murdered," as Gottfried and an MGM publicity executive winced at the remarks.

Chayefsky (who was described by *Women's Wear Daily* as possessing "the look of a satyr who has retired from active duty") sounded prematurely defeated, in one breath dismissing television as "an industry built on hysteria," while complaining in the next that cinema was "not a writer's medium." "Most films are too tidy," he said. "They're predictable little packages." Were it up to MGM, he said with some overdramatization, *Network* would have concluded at the moment Schumacher breaks up with Diana and returns to his wife—had he not stuck up for the version of the screenplay he had written: "That's the picture, I told them."

In an interview with the *New York Times*, Chayefsky struck his most contrarian note, stating, "Television is democracy at its ugliest."

"The conception of *Network* is a farce," he said, "but once the idea is there, it's all real, every bit. I don't attack; I just tell the truth. Television will do anything for a rating. Anything!"

This article concluded by noting that Chayefsky and Gottfried had broken up their friendly poker games some time ago, as Gottfried now preferred to go to Vegas and Chayefsky preferred to stay home. Rather than waste his time on the contemporary TV programs he so clearly despised, Chayefsky said he had recently watched an old kinescope of "Catch My Boy on Sunday," a teleplay he wrote for *The Philco-Goodyear Television Playhouse* in 1954, and decided that it had held up well in the years since it was broadcast.

The day before *Network*'s official New York premiere, the principal members of its creative team gathered for a 10:00 A.M. press conference at Shepheard's, the small downstairs nightclub of the Drake Hotel on Park Avenue, and everyone was in character: Sidney Lumet waxed philosophical, asserting that the aim of the film "is to stretch realism past its limit, but never to violate the truth," and repeated his familiar credo that while he, Chayefsky, and Gottfried all had their professional origins in television, "we never left it—it left us." William Holden reminisced about having been a classmate of Jackie Robinson's when the two attended Pasadena City College in the late 1930s. ("I would have failed biology class if it hadn't been for Jackie Robinson. I sat and cribbed from his notes.") Peter Finch, attending with his wife, Eletha, touted the new home he had recently purchased in Beverly Hills and hailed *Network* as "a cautionary tale about our lives today—we're becoming computerized, deodorized, whiter-than-white lambs." Faye Dunaway arrived an hour late and dismissed the notion that any feminist ideals had influenced her portrayal of a character that Lumet described as "a ruthless, remorseless killer." "Lady Macbeth will do," she replied through a smile.

Chayefsky made one more attempt to plead his case that *Network* actually treated the television news business with respect: "There are many people in television, especially in the various news departments, that I consider incorruptible," he said. "Many of these people are my friends and have been since the early days of television. I consider them decent, respectable, sensitive people. I'm not talking about these people in my film. I'm talking about the executives who run the industry, those decision makers who are part of a larger corporation. I'm talking about what happens to a network when it's taken over, made into a cash-flow industry and becomes part of a larger corporation, which is exactly what is happening to networks in America right now."

In a similar spirit, he argued that *Network* was in fact a satirical send-up of what could someday be, not a criticism of things as they were. "The American tradition of journalism is objectivity," Chayefsky said. "We have an editorial page. We have a comic page. There is nothing valuable about a journalist—or anybody for that matter—getting up and comicalizing the news. The news should not—must not—become part of the entertainment scheduling. To make a gag out of the news is disreputable and extremely destructive."

The first major review of *Network* to see print was published in the *New York Times* on November 15, one day after the film's premiere. It was a rave. Tweaking its sensationalized promotional campaign, Vincent Canby wrote that the film was, "as its ads proclaim, outrageous. It's also brilliantly, cruelly funny, a topical American comedy that confirms Paddy Chayefsky's position as a major new American satirist. Paddy Chayefsky? Major? New? A satirist? Exactly."

As astounded as he expected his audience to be that the observant dramatist and common-man champion of *Marty* had matured into the withering ironist of *The Hospital* and now *Network*, Canby wrote of Chayefsky, "His humor is not gentle or generous. It's about as stern and apocalyptic as it's possible to be without alienating the very audience for which it was intended." But to dismiss the absurdities of *Network* as scenarios that could never happen was to miss the point: "These wickedly distorted views of the way television looks, sounds and, indeed, is, are the satirist's cardiogram of the hidden heart, not just of television but also of the society that supports it and is, in turn, supported." Praising the performances of Finch, Holden, and Dunaway (who was "touching and funny" as "a woman of psychopathic ambition and lack of feeling"), the supporting turns of Duvall and Beatty, and the direction of Lumet, Canby concluded, "As the crazy prophet within the film says of himself, *Network* is vivid and flashing. It's connected into life."

In the *Saturday Review*, Judith Crist declared *Network* "a ruthless exploration of the 'aesthetics' and 'art' of television that goes beyond its present-day realities to forecast the brave new world of the medium's tomorrow, let alone some innovations of this very season," adding that "Chayefsky's drama is rooted in the realities of life in those Sixth Avenue monoliths that house the networks, its near-roman à clef personalities identifiable to anyone familiar with the industry." The *Daily News* gave it two thumbs-up as well, with film critic Rex Reed deeming *Network* "a blazing, blistering indictment of television by the brilliant probing mind of Paddy Chayefsky," while television editor Kay Gardella wrote that it "sustains an artistic perception of network television that is both outrageously funny and, with a good stretch of the imagination, quite believable."

A few days later, Canby was back in the pages of the *New York Times* praising *Network* in a follow-up essay as "a satiric send-up of commercial television that contains only one decent, upstanding, honorable, moral fellow of recognizable strength in the cast of characters—that is, Chayefsky, who doesn't appear on the screen at all but is the dominant presence in the film."

"Though Sidney Lumet has directed it as if we were there and it was happening now," Canby wrote, "*Network* is not meant to be realistic, a movie-à-clef. It's a roller coaster ride through Chayefsky's fantasies as he imagines what television might do if given the opportunity." This, he realized, was not going to be everyone's cup of tea.

> I understand people simply not finding this sort of thing as funny as I do. It's a bit masochistic, like sitting on the stern of the Titanic and giggling all the way until you finally slide under the water. But to be morally outraged by Chayefsky's moral outrage, on the grounds that Chayefsky (1) offers no solutions, (2) finds no redeeming factors, or (3) sets himself up as judge and jury, seems to me to be missing the point of satire, which is to be as sweepingly stern as an Old Testament prophet, intelligently concerned and bitterly comic. Satirists have no obligation to be fair to the enemy, or especially accurate. . . . It would be reassuring if we could piously blame TV's ills on a few isolated people. It might also be the same as blaming Patty Hearst for having had the poor form to allow herself to be kidnapped.

By this point *Network* was in need of a few ardent defenders. Reviewing the film for *New York* magazine, John Simon wrote that *Network* "inherits the Glib Piety Award direct from the hands of *The*

Front, the previous winner. When it comes to sanctimonious smugness and holier-than-thou sententiousness, the new laureate is even more deserving of the unsavory prize. *Network*, moreover, is a further lap in Paddy Chayefsky's, the scenarist's, fascinating race against decrepitude and impotence. . . . The onscreen result is worse than a three-ring circus, however: verbal and intellectual Grand Guignol." While impressed by Lumet's direction and the work of the acting ensemble (though Holden, "alas, has not aged well"), Simon concluded that "this crude film really panders to whatever is smug and pseudosophisticated in an audience of self-appointed insiders; their smart-alecky laughter was not an inspiriting thing to hear."

At the *Nation*, Robert Hatch asked rhetorically, "So this is a slashing comment on network television and therefore exceedingly bold? Not by a country mile. There is plenty wrong with television, plenty to satirize. But *Network* prudently misses the point, dishing up an outrageous razzle-dazzle stew that will ruffle no network feathers and delight a popular audience that enjoys being titillated by improbable threats."

And in the *New York Post*, a young film critic named Frank Rich dismissed *Network* as "a mess of a movie" that "is drastically out of control—dramatically, cinematically and intellectually—and it treats its audience with more contempt than any other serious American movie this year." With some economy and restraint, Rich wrote, Chayefsky "might have had a classic 15-minute sketch for *Saturday Night Live*." Instead:

> We begin to feel that Chayefsky is a cranky paranoid who's overstacked his polemical deck, and we stop believing in his message. Since the script treats the mass public that watches TV as morons, too, *Network* at times seems to be saying that we deserve the TV we get—and that neutralizes the film's point even further. . . . You begin to suspect that Chayefsky wrote *Network* not so much to attack TV as to attack a generation of American kids who frighten and baffle him.

Overall, Rich said that *Network* "contains so much extraneous material that it's hard to believe Chayefsky ever wrote a second draft." And he lambasted Dunaway's performance (playing "the meanest woman to be seen in an American film since the Wicked Witch of the West") as a living embodiment of the film's flaws: "She's so busy trying to outrage us that she doesn't even notice that she's drowning in her own bile." But then again, he wrote, "In *Network*, everybody stinks—except Chayefsky."

Perhaps the most scathing response to the film came as a one-two punch published in the December 6 issue of the *New Yorker*. Pauline Kael, in a film review unpromisingly entitled "Hot Air," wrote, "In *Network*, Paddy Chayefsky blitzes you with one idea after another. The ideas don't go together, but who knows which of them he believes, anyway? He's like a Village crazy bellowing at you: blacks are taking over, revolutionaries are taking over, women are taking over. He's got the New York City hatreds, and ranting makes him feel alive."

Though the story of Howard Beale's breakdown might contain "a fanciful, Frank Capra nuttiness that could be appealing," and Finch's "fuzzy mildness is likable," Kael wrote that "Chayefsky is such a manic bard that I'm not sure if he ever decided whether Howard Beale's epiphanies were the result of a nervous breakdown or were actually inspired by God." And while Dunaway brings to her performance "a certain heaviness . . . that has made some people think her Garbo-esque," her character ultimately isn't "a woman with a drive to power, she's just a dirty Mary Tyler Moore."

Kael wrote that, for all of *Network*'s flaws, blame rested squarely on its author, for whom the film is "a ventriloquial harangue" that he spends thrashing around "in messianic God-love booziness, driving each scene to an emotional peak."

What happened to his once much-vaunted gift for the vernacular? Nothing exposes his claims to be defending the older values so much as the way he uses four-letter words for chortles. It's so cheap you may never want to say **** again. Chayefsky doesn't come right out and tell us why he thinks TV is so goyish, but it must have something to do with his notion that all feeling is Jewish.

Elsewhere in that same issue, Michael J. Arlen, the magazine's television critic, provided his own epitaph for the film. "As entertainment, it's probably fair to say that *Network* is lively, slick, and highly professional, and combines the attention to background detail and the avoidance of interior complexity which more or less define the show-business ethos it was attempting to criticize," he wrote. "As satire or as serious comment, the movie seemed oddly pious and heavy-handed. In other words, it was another typically overmounted, modishly topical, over obvious popular entertainment—good for a few laughs, and something to do after dinner."

The polarizing responses to *Network* played right into the campaign devised for it by MGM and United Artists, which were busy producing thousands of buttons and bumper stickers that read, I'M MAD AS HELL AND I'M NOT GOING TO TAKE IT ANYMORE. The controversy surrounding the film merely suggested to audiences that it was something they needed to see for themselves and form an opinion about; and the harder it was attacked, the more bulletproof it became.

Propelled by some of the reviews that described *Network* as a roman à clef, an idea had taken hold in the media that each character in the film was an analog for a real-world figure who had somehow wronged or offended Chayefsky, and the screenplay was his mocking revenge on him. An item in *New York* magazine straightforwardly declared that Max Schumacher was based on Edward R. Murrow; that the UBS executives played by William Prince and Wesley Addy were William S. Paley and Frank Stanton of CBS; and Laureen Hobbs was Angela Davis. There was wide consensus, too, that Diana Christensen was a gloss on NBC's female vice president of daytime programming,

Lin Bolen, who had spoken briefly by phone with Dunaway while she was preparing for the role. "'Tis said Lin axed some of Paddy's pet TV projects," the gossip columnist Liz Smith wrote. Had anyone sought to confirm these claims with the author, he would have handily dismissed them.

As the year drew to a close, *Time* magazine published its own battlefield update from the ongoing skirmishes that continued to be waged around *Network*. Dubbing it "The Movie TV Hates and Loves," the newsweekly reported that Lumet had recently been barred from a screening at NBC because of the film, while quoting an anonymous NBC vice president who said of the movie, "It's a piece of crap. It had nothing to do with our business." The article also cited supporters such as Norman Lear, who called it "a brilliant film," and Gore Vidal, who said, "I've heard every line from that film in real life."

In a sidebar to the *Time* article, Chayefsky did not address his supporters or attack his detractors, but took aim directly at the medium of television. In a treatise that could have come right from his *Network* screenplay, he wrote, "I think the American people deserve some truth—at least as much truth as we can give them—instead of pure entertainment or pure addiction."

"Let's at least show the country to ourselves for what it really is," Chayefsky wrote.

> It includes more than pimps, hustlers, junkies, murderers and hit men. All family life is not as coarse and brutalized as it is presented to us on TV. There is a substantial thing called America with a very complicated, pluralistic society that is worth honest presentation. . . . Television coarsens all the complexities of human relationships, brutalizes them, makes them insensitive. The point about violence is not so much that it breeds violence—though that is probably true— but that it totally desensitizes viciousness, brutality, murder, death so that we no longer actively feel the pains of the victim

or suffer for the mourners or feel their grief. . . . We have
become desensitized to things that are usually part of the
human condition. This is the basic problem of television.
We've lost our sense of shock, our sense of humanity.

Desperate as these words sounded, Chayefsky had not yet given up
entirely on his fellow man. Amid the furious back-and-forth over the
release of *Network*, he had received an unexpected note of support
from an ABC employee named Barbara Gallagher, the assistant to the
president of the network's entertainment division, who sent him an
appreciative fan letter. "Wow! What a movie!" Gallagher wrote. "I was
caught up in 'Network' . . . I can't tell you what an impact it had on me.
It's a classic, + absolutely the best picture I've seen in years. Bravo!" Then,
beneath her signature, she informed him: "P.S. I'm quitting my job . . ."

Chayefsky gently mimicked Gallagher in his reply, writing, "Wow!
What a note! You are terrific. You are also very sweet and kind to have
taken the trouble to write me."

He added: "Don't quit yet. On the whole, ABC has been very kind
to me."

6

PRIMAL FORCES AND PHANTASMAGORIA

By the time 1976 drew to a close, American movie theaters had offered eager audiences countless forms of paranoia and despair to choose from. A cinematic calendar of futility, confrontation, and retribution had opened in the winter with the release of *Taxi Driver* and Travis Bickle's vow that "someday a real rain will come and wash all this scum off the streets." By the spring, this message came clad in a more polished wardrobe, with *All the President's Men* and its stylized, Redford-eyed treatment of the *Washington Post*'s investigations into Watergate; and it spent the summer dressed in the genre garb of Westerns such as *The Outlaw Josey Wales* and horror movies such as *The Omen*. The cycle reached its zenith in the fall, when screens were spattered with the blood and sweat of *Marathon Man* and *Carrie*, and the air was choked with the expended lead and urban decay of *King Kong*, *Assault on Precinct 13*, and *The Enforcer*, the latest trigger-pulling escapade of

Clint Eastwood's "Dirty Harry" Callahan. You want inspiration and uplift? Go watch Rocky Balboa beat up a side of beef.

The "cheapjack cynicism" that *Network* satirized, Vincent Canby wrote in a *New York Times* essay proclaiming the arrival of the new "cynical cinema," "is now almost the entire point of what virtually amounts to a whole new subcategory of contemporary suspense melodrama—the film that deals with a dread, unnamed and unnameable conspiracy that the film's hero-victim goes through the picture like someone who has awakened to find himself in a public place without his pants. It's a bad dream but it's all true."

Network, which began its wide release in December, fit perfectly into this motion picture landscape of helplessness and mistrust. Attuned to a national mood that seemed to be turning increasingly hostile, the movie put forward a wide array of institutions and organizations to vilify, and a unique prescription to this plague of frustration. It said the answer to your problems wasn't in government or in the media, in dogged newspaper reporters or rogue cops, but in you, the viewer. You didn't need to raise a fist or draw a gun to subdue your enemies; you just had to get mad. The teachings of *Network* resounded not in bullet wounds or spent shell casings but in the loud and articulate language of its characters. The film was hardly bloodless, but with the exception of a couple of key scenes, at least it kept its vital fluids on the insides of its characters.

Network was also a financial success, on its way to grossing more than $20 million in its original theatrical release and becoming one of the most lucrative movies of the year. Paddy Chayefsky's film was a widely mentioned candidate for Academy Awards and other end-of-the-year honors, but securing its nominations and victories meant keeping the movie and its stars in the public eye, and that in turn meant more promotion.

Barely one month after the movie's premiere in New York, the number of key players who could be counted on to support *Network* in the press had dwindled. Chayefsky himself would rise to service whenever he was called upon, but one never knew what he was going to say or whom he was going to offend. So, too, would William Holden, but his interviews yielded similarly mixed results: one reporter might catch him reminiscing about "nights when the networks came through with footage showing the tragedy of Danang, with the blood of civilians flowing in the streets," while another observed him as he "rambles authoritatively," ending on the "ever so slight a suggestion of a harrumph" that signals "he's decided any possible answer he could provide is going to be more interesting than any question likely to be brought up."

Sidney Lumet moved on to his next film, *Equus*, and Faye Dunaway was rarely much help to *Network*. Among the few appearances she deigned to make for the film's release was a joint interview with Holden in the upscale pages of *W* magazine, accompanied by photographs of the costars on a carefree autumn walk through Central Park. In that article, Dunaway embraced her industry nickname, Runaway Dunaway, and noted that she had seen eight different psychoanalysts in the decade since *Bonnie and Clyde* was released. ("In each case I was looking for some compassion behind the professional detachment," she said. "For the most part I found them wanting.") With a smile on her face, she attempted to pass off Holden as the source of difficulty on their love scene ("Whenever we got into bed Bill couldn't stop laughing," she claimed), and he gladly took the fall. "I just feel there are certain things that require privacy," Holden said. "We don't just urinate on the streets."

Supporting players such as Ned Beatty and Beatrice Straight pitched in on publicity duties, too, with Straight telling the *Sunday News* that her work in the film was too brief to merit rewards or trophies. "If you blink, you miss it, but it is a lucky break," she said. "It's just a contrast in the film." But more firepower was going to be needed from the bigger guns of *Network*, and Peter Finch was happy to supply the artillery.

In the months after he finished shooting *Network*, Finch, now sixty, had recommitted himself to his craft and to the possibility of having an acting career in Hollywood. He gave up his self-imposed semi-exile in

Jamaica and relocated with Eletha and their children to Los Angeles, where they lived in an apartment on West Hollywood's Sunset Strip while renovations were made to a house he had purchased in Beverly Hills. The move, he said, was partly to escape political turmoil in the Caribbean and partly to enhance his career. "This is the place where all the deals are made," he said of his new habitat. "When you get to be my age, producers are never sure what you're going to look like. If you're not here for them to see they may be afraid you've suddenly gone over the hill." In that spirit, he had also cut out the copious drinking he was famous for when he still caroused with the likes of Errol Flynn and Trevor Howard. Since then, Finch said cheerfully, "Death has gotten one of us and our livers got the rest of us."

The work was starting to come steadily again: he was filming a lead role as Yitzhak Rabin in NBC's TV film *Raid on Entebbe*, and he had been cast in Warren Beatty and Buck Henry's film version of *Heaven Can Wait*. For the first time in several years, Finch hired a personal publicist to help manage the many requests he was receiving for interviews and personal appearances, and he wholeheartedly embraced the increased demands on his time—wanting as much to ensure that *Network* was seen as to make certain he was nominated alongside Holden as a leading actor and not relegated to the category of supporting actor. "We're all so dreadfully egocentric in this business," he told *Women's Wear Daily*. "The nomination lets people know you're there—for a moment at least."

Having been a long-shot Oscar nominee in 1972 for *Sunday Bloody Sunday*, Finch sought to ensure that this time he would go all the way. "Peter wanted to win that Oscar," Finch's personal publicist, Michael Maslansky, later said. "It was an obsession with him." In the months following *Network*'s release, Maslansky estimated, "Peter must have done three hundred interviews with foreign and domestic media—radio, television, the works. Nobody, but *nobody* was missed. And there was no one Peter refused to talk to."

While his campaign was under way, it became Finch's custom each morning to practice reciting an Academy Award acceptance speech he had been preparing, performing it to himself in his bathroom mirror or to Eletha as she brushed her teeth. As his daughter Diana would later recall, "He would turn to my mom and he would say, 'If I should win, darling, this is a huge, huge honor. I want to thank my peers . . .' Every actor, in their lifetime, whether you're a starting actor or you've had a career for many, many years, you always have an Oscar speech, regardless of whether you win or not, you always have that. Because you never know."

Then Finch, who did not hold an American driver's license and preferred to walk four or five miles a day, would stroll over to the Beverly Hills Hotel and its Polo Lounge, which had become the sort of haunt where he could show up without a cent in his pocket. "He always knew somebody—because he was Peter Finch—would buy him breakfast," said his manager, Barry Krost. From whichever table he had affixed himself to, he would conduct his day's press assignments, whether praising the underlying message of *Network* to the *Christian Science Monitor* ("The problems and the potential power of TV exist everywhere in the world") while decrying its liberal use of four-letter words ("I'm a little sad we put so many in"); or musing to the *Advocate* about the many hours he and Chayefsky spent talking through the psychology of the Howard Beale character. "There had to be a suggestion that he was eminently sane underneath the madness and that he did, in fact, have a kind of revelation," Finch said. "That's a very thin edge to play." He had lately been reflecting on his vagabond upbringing, the many people it had taken to raise him, and places where he had come of age, and he was thinking of writing a book about his experiences, which he planned to call *Chutzpah*. As Finch explained, "There is a lot of phantasmagoria in my life."

On the last day of the year, Sidney Lumet shared an anecdote with the *New York Times* about Paddy Chayefsky and the screenwriter's trusted companions Herb Gardner and Bob Fosse. As Lumet told the story, Chayefsky (whom Lumet described as a "Jewish Shaw" who's "always funny but he's always serious") and Gardner had gone to the hospital to visit Fosse, who was slated to have heart surgery the next day. Fearing the worst, Fosse had drawn up a will that he asked his friends to witness, and Gardner signed it right away. Chayefsky, however, explained that he never signed anything without reading it and reviewed the document slowly, in silence, page by page. Upon reaching the end, he angrily looked up and said to Fosse, "You didn't leave anything for me in it."

"Bob was pretty upset," Lumet said, "and he began to explain that he had to take care of his family, didn't have that much money, and so on."

The possibility that death might soon claim someone so close to him did not inhibit Chayefsky's morbid sense of humor. He threw the will at Fosse in his hospital bed and said, "Damn you, live."

Fosse did as he was instructed, and as 1977 commenced, the prospects for *Network* seemed to brighten considerably. On January 4 the New York Film Critics Circle named Chayefsky the author of the year's best screenplay. The Los Angeles Film Critics Association also chose *Network* as best screenplay and cited Lumet as best director, and the film tied with *Rocky* for best picture. When nominations for the Golden Globes were announced, *Network* found itself vying for five major awards: best dramatic film; best director, for Lumet; best screenplay, for Chayefsky; best actress in a drama, for Faye Dunaway; and, in the category of best actor in a drama, Peter Finch.

With new wind in his sails, Finch was booked to appear on *The Tonight Show* on January 13, returning to Johnny Carson's couch after an absence of nearly a decade. If the fact that Finch was scheduled as the first guest of the night—ahead of George Carlin, Joanie Sommers, and Ruth Gordon—was not sufficient indication of the esteem Carson had for the actor and his performance in *Network*, the host lavished him with praise almost from the moment he sat down next to Carson's desk. "Paddy Chayefsky, when he gets his dander up on something, he really goes at it," Carson said with equal parts glee and envy. "It's really

Paddy Chayefsky in 1954 on a New York street during the filming of the motion picture *Marty*, for which he would win his first Academy Award. (Credit: Jack Stager/ Globe Photos/ZUMApress.com)

Paddy Chayefsky working on the screenplay of *Network* in 1976. Having won a second Oscar for *The Hospital*, he found himself frustrated when his scripts were not executed according to his precise wishes. He channeled his disappointments, personal fears, political paranoia, and inside industry knowledge into his new project. (Credit: Photograph by Michael Ginsburg)

Director Sidney Lumet on the set of *Network* in Toronto. Lumet, the celebrated director of *12 Angry Men*, *Serpico*, and *Dog Day Afternoon*, had moved in a career path parallel to Chayefsky's and had gone into films after starting in television's Golden Age. Lumet's TV experience would prove crucial to *Network*, which simulated the production of several live broadcasts.
(Credit: Photograph by Michael Ginsburg)

Lumet shows the actor Peter Finch how to execute a nervous breakdown he would perform in the role of Howard Beale, the mentally unstable anchorman of *Network*. A British-born actor who grew up in Australia, Finch was living in Jamaica and considered himself semi-retired before he was hired to play Howard Beale, after the part had been turned down by several top Hollywood stars, including Paul Newman and George C. Scott. (Credit: Photograph by Michael Ginsburg)

The producer Howard Gottfried on the set of *Network* with Paddy Chayefsky in Toronto. Gottfried had worked as a producer of Off-Broadway theater and television before he started producing Chayefsky's motion pictures. Gottfried was genial and accommodating; he could fight the battles Chayefsky wasn't equipped for and put out the fires his partner started.
(Credit: Photograph by Michael Ginsburg)

The star-studded principal cast of *Network* was rounded out by Robert Duvall, who played the belligerent executive Frank Hackett; Faye Dunaway, the glamorous leading lady of *Chinatown* and *Bonnie and Clyde*, as the ratings-obsessed TV executive Diana Christensen; and the former marquee idol William Holden as Max Schumacher, the defeated news-division president who falls under Diana's spell.
(Credit: MGM Studios/Getty Images)

Chayefsky's primary concern during the filming of *Network* was to ensure that every line of dialogue was performed exactly as he had written it. And to best observe the actors' work, he felt it was necessary to situate himself as close as possible to their performances. To accommodate him (and prevent him from appearing in their shots), the *Network* crew created a light where he could stand and called it "the Paddy light." (Credit: Photograph by Michael Ginsburg)

The actors seen here as members of the radical Ecumenical Liberation Army include Kathy Cronkite (center, with prop gun pointed at Chayefsky), as Mary Ann Gifford, a kidnapped heiress in the mold of Patty Hearst, and Arthur Burghardt (right), as its leader, the Great Ahmed Kahn. Cronkite, the daughter of the CBS news anchor Walter Cronkite, was struggling to define her identity, while Burghardt had recently served twenty-eight months in prison for draft evasion.

(Credit: Photograph by Michael Ginsburg)

Dunaway brought her tantalizing and intimidating exterior, curious intellect, boundless passion, and mercurial mood to the part of Diana Christensen. Her strong ideas and even stronger will would nearly cost her the role, but she believed the character was worth fighting for. "If you wanted to succeed as a woman in a man's world, you had to beat them at their own game," she said. "Diana, I knew, would end up right in the middle of that debate." (Credit: MGM Studios/Getty Images)

Beatrice Straight, a member of one of New York society's most prominent families, believed that her role as Louise Schumacher, the loyal wife devastated by the infidelity of her husband, Max, was too small to merit attention for awards. "If you blink, you miss it, but it is a lucky break," she said. "It's just a contrast in the film." (Credit: Photograph by Michael Ginsburg)

Peter Finch became synonymous with *Network* for his searing delivery of a monologue in which the increasingly unhinged Howard Beale announces to his TV audience, "I'm as mad as hell, and I'm not going to take this anymore!" He was only able to perform the scene once in its entirety during the filming of the movie. During Take 2, Lumet said, "He stopped halfway through. He said, 'Sidney, I can't do any more.'" That was as much the director was willing to ask of Finch.
(Credit: MGM Studios/Getty Images)

"You have meddled with the primal forces of nature, Mr. Beale, and I won't have it!" Ned Beatty, who played Arthur Jensen, the explosive tycoon who converts Howard Beale to his "corporate cosmology," was a late addition to the cast, replacing the character actor Roberts Blossom. After auditioning for Chayefsky, Lumet, and Gottfried, Beatty told them he had a competing offer from another film. But Beatty later admitted, "I was lying like a snake."
(Credit: MGM Studios/Getty Images)

The poster for the original theatrical release of *Network*, designed by Stephen Frankfurt, an advertising executive who had also created campaigns for *Rosemary's Baby* and Lay's potato chips, promised controversy and outrage. And while the movie was a commercial and critical success, receiving ten Academy Award nominations including best picture, it also provoked angry reactions from reviewers and the TV news business, with much of that indignation directed squarely at Chayefsky.
(Credit: MGM Media Licensing)

Peter Finch died of a heart attack on January 14, 1977, one month before his portrayal of Howard Beale earned him an Academy Award nomination for best actor. When Finch won the award that March, Chayefsky —who had just received his own Oscar for the *Network* screenplay—invited the actor's widow, Eletha Finch, onto the stage to pick up the trophy for her late husband.
(Credit: Bettmann/CORBIS)

The morning after she won the Oscar for best actress, Faye Dunaway allowed Terry O'Neill to photograph her at the pool of the Beverly Hills Hotel, surrounded by strewn newspapers as she contemplated her statuette with uncertainty. O'Neill said the image depicted Dunaway in a "really reflective" moment, while the actress said it showed that "success is a solitary place to be. In my life, it has been the same. . . . Or, as Peggy Lee sang, 'Is that all there is?' " (Credit: Terry O'Neill/Getty Images)

an outrageous, crazy look at the corporate structure of the networks without naming the networks—and they offended pretty much all the networks, I guess."

Finch, dressed in a gray suit that could have come right from Howard Beale's wardrobe and speaking naturally in his London-by-way-of-Sydney accent, proudly defended the film's satirical sensibility. He observed that what Chayefsky was really attacking was "the diminishing liberty in our individual lives. And every one of us feel, even subconsciously, that computers and bureaucracy and numbers are encroaching on our lives. And my character rails against it suddenly, and says, 'Beware, look out, what's happening to us?'"

Carson was particularly taken with Finch's performance of the "Mad as hell" monologue, misquoting its crucial line as "I'm mad as hell and I'm not going to put up with this anymore," but declaring with confidence that it was "going to become a standard, probably, from motion pictures."

"There are certain lines from motion pictures that you always remember," Carson told him. "That's the one."

"Well, I'm—I'm very lucky, I suppose," Finch started to answer, "because people go around quoting it. And if an actor's associated with one of those lines, it gives you a lot of—"

Before he could finish the thought, Carson interrupted: "And everybody feels like that once in a while," he said. "They say, 'I don't want to put up with it anymore.'"

A pair of clips from *Network* were shown, including a portion of the "Mad as hell" scene, after which Carson and Finch led the *Tonight Show* audience in an exuberant (and, this time, correctly quoted) chorus of "I'm mad as hell and I'm not going to take this anymore."

"This group," Carson observed, "is ready to follow you anyplace, Peter. Right into the waters."

The next guest of the night was Carlin, the irreverent, long-haired comedian, who began his stand-up set by informing the audience, "You know you're all going to die, aren't you? All of you." Once the laughter had subsided, the comic delivered a routine focused entirely on death: its inevitability ("You'll all die in different ways, different places. Unless you all walk out together in front of the same bus tonight"); its mystery ("My religion believes you go to a coin return in Buffalo"); its finality ("You get really popular when you die. You do, you get more flowers than you ever got when you were alive. They'll all arrive at once—too late"). Then, invited over to Carson's desk, Carlin continued to speculate on the subject, hypothesizing that in our final moments we might see a flashback of our lives in the form of a movie.

Using the example of a drowning man, Carlin said, "But okay, you're out there, and you see the movie of your life, and you get toward the end of it, and that includes arriving at the beach, going in the water, and starting to see the movie again. So according to the movie, we can never die."

"That's comforting," Carson replied.

As Finch was being driven home from the *Tonight Show* studios in Burbank, his publicist, Michael Maslansky, would later recall, the actor reflected on Carlin's morbid routine, which he had enjoyed. "Peter talked about death," said Maslansky, "saying how fitting and funny a subject it could be for a comic monologue because death was, in the ceremonies and incidents surrounding it, 'a hilarious thing.' That is what he said. 'A hilarious thing.' That's a direct quote."

The following morning, as was his routine, Finch walked the mile and a half of twisted, turning, hilly road from his new house (his family had moved in on New Year's Eve) to the Beverly Hills Hotel, where he sat in the lobby and waited for Sidney Lumet to join him for a battery of appearances on the morning talk shows. Just as the director arrived, he saw Finch slump over in his chair. "I was walking down the staircase toward him," Lumet later said. "Peter was sitting on the banquette, and I saw him go right over. I ran over and started to give him mouth-to-mouth resuscitation." He did not know what had afflicted the actor, "but it was clear he was in deep trouble." Paramedics were summoned to the scene, and when they could not revive Finch, he was taken unconscious in an ambulance to the intensive care unit of the UCLA Medical Center. There, he was pronounced dead of a heart attack.

Barry Krost, the actor's manager, was alerted to the news before he was able to leave his house for work that morning. "I had four phone lines at home," Krost recalled, "and the first phone went, and then all the lines lit up at the same time." It was now his "strange, difficult" duty to contact Eletha and bring her to the hospital before the information reached her in some other manner. Krost said of a man who had always relied on the kindness of strangers, "I think when he died he had two quarters and a couple of dimes in his pocket. That's all."

Once Finch's wife had been notified, MGM issued a solemn press release that afternoon, confirming the actor's death. "The sudden and untimely passing of Peter Finch has come as a blow to all of us who knew, respected and loved him," the studio's president and chief executive, Frank E. Rosenfelt, said in the statement. "Everyone here at M-G-M who was privileged to know this gifted artist and warm and gentle human being is deeply saddened beyond words by the news. Our sympathy goes out to his wife and children."

That night the handful of *Network* collaborators making the promotional rounds in Los Angeles assembled at the Palm restaurant to pay an impromptu tribute to Finch; the group included Chayefsky, Holden, Gottfried, and David Tebet, a longtime NBC talent executive and supporter of Chayefsky's. As Tebet later described the gathering, the mood was understandably mournful, until Chayefsky declared that Finch would have wanted them to remember him "in merriment rather than sadness." "And before you knew it," Tebet said, "our talk turned into a vicious tirade against the film business and how it could kill a man like Finchy. But Paddy Chayefsky said, 'You can't blame the business. It's what we do to ourselves. We're all impulsive and neurotic.'" In his own spirit of levity, Chayefsky added, "But you know something, in spite of all that, it's better than threading pipe."

The loss of Finch, at a moment when his career was in resurgence and at an age when most former leading men would have been consigned to the scrap heap, was a bitter blow to the acting community, particularly in his native Britain. Memorializing Finch in the *Guardian*, the journalist and broadcaster Russell Davies wrote, "If the film industry told the truth, it would admit that deceased 60-year-old actors are seldom really 'much-missed,' for they are too easily replaced from an embarrassment of survivors." But Finch, he continued, was that rare actor for whom no suitable surrogate existed.

> He was aging into a more credible authority than any of his English-speaking contemporaries; the troubles behind his face seemed to become more interesting and deep with every film. . . . The leathery, hard-drinking Australian maleness which kept the Finch of the 1950s shuttling to and fro between war fields and the Outback might easily have qualified him for a middle age of pipe-smoking paternalism in conservative roles; but his obvious masculinity, coupled with an increasing talent for freezing his face into a marbled facade, covering anything from utter shame to contempt, made him paradoxically available for a new sort of part, the grizzled failure.

An official memorial service for Finch, held in Beverly Hills on January 18, drew more than 220 of his friends and colleagues, including Chayefsky, who eulogized his *Network* star as being "in that very select circle of great actors. He dignified his parts."

It was during this same period that Chayefsky made a private visit to Finch's widow and children at the house on San Ysidro Drive they had moved into hardly two weeks earlier. To the bereaved Finches, Chayefsky was a tremendously admired figure—the author of the part that had reconnected Peter to his talents and returned him to the limelight—and his condolence call was a gesture the family received with great pride. Finch himself had held Chayefsky in such high regard that he had painted a portrait of the screenwriter and placed it on the mantel of his new Beverly Hills home. As the actor's daughter Diana later described the painting, "I remember it to this day: it was in a little black frame, a black-and-white painting with pen and ink, of this man that had glasses and this intense, serious look on his face. My dad didn't really paint portraits of people. So that will tell you how much of an impact Paddy had on him."

When Chayefsky came to pay his respect to the Finches, Eletha and the seven-year-old Diana were excited to show the portrait to its subject, and to point out the venerated position it had been given in their household. "We took him over and we revealed this painting to him," Diana Finch-Braley said, "and we said, look, Paddy, look at this painting. It looks just like you. I remember this look that he had. He was such a serious person. At least, this is what I perceived as a child. He didn't break out into this huge smile. He was just really, really serious. And then he cracked just a little, tiny, almost—you couldn't even notice that it was a smile—and he nodded his head. He didn't say anything. He wasn't overcome with emotion because I don't think he was that kind of person."

On January 29, *Network* won four of the five Golden Globe Awards it had been nominated for, with trophies going to Chayefsky, Dunaway, Lumet, and, posthumously, to Finch. Its lone defeat came in the category of best dramatic film, which it lost to *Rocky*.

Two weeks later, on February 10, *Network* received ten Academy Award nominations, tying with *Rocky* for the most received by any film of the preceding year. *Network* was nominated for best picture, Chayefsky for best original screenplay, Lumet for best director, Owen Roizman for best cinematography, and Alan Heim for best editing. Dunaway, never in doubt as a contender for best actress, received a nomination; so, too, did Ned Beatty, for best supporting actor, and Beatrice Straight, for best supporting actress. And in the category of best actor, *Network* received two nominations: one for William Holden and one for Peter Finch.

Once the initial wave of elation wore off, the creators of *Network* and the Academy of Motion Picture Arts and Sciences, which bestows the Oscars, were presented with an unusual and sensitive situation. If Finch were named the winner of his award, who would accept it for him? Such a possibility had last occurred in an acting category in 1968, when Spencer Tracy, who died shortly after the filming of *Guess Who's Coming to Dinner*, earned a best actor nomination for that film. The award that year went to Rod Steiger for *In the Heat of the Night*, and no precedent was established, as no actor had ever won an Academy Award posthumously.

As preparations began in March for the Academy Awards, Gottfried was contacted by William Friedkin, the no-nonsense director of *The French Connection* and *The Exorcist*, who was producing the Oscars ceremony. As Gottfried recalled, "Bill Friedkin called me and said, 'Look, Howard, I'm not going to put up on this show with any high jinks.'" Friedkin was referring to two recent incidents in Oscars history that had turned the presentation of the best actor prize into something of a circus: one in 1971, when George C. Scott declined his award for *Patton* and refused to attend the ceremony, writing off the "offensive, barbarous and innately corrupt" proceedings as "a two-hour meat parade, a public display with contrived suspense for economic reasons"; and the other in 1973, when Marlon Brando sent the Apache actress Sacheen Littlefeather to turn down his trophy for *The Godfather*, citing "the treatment of American Indians today by the film industry and on television in movie reruns, and also with recent happenings at Wounded Knee."

The directive Gottfried said he received from Friedkin was "I don't want any nonsense on my show. If you haven't decided who's going to accept, I want it to be either Paddy or Bill Holden." ("Even though Bill was a nominee in his own right," Gottfried added, "he thought Bill could accept for Peter—or Paddy, of course, who would be logical.") To which Gottfried suggested, "How about Peter's wife? She was very,

very, very concerned about his career, all his life." To which Friedkin answered, "Absolutely not."

When Gottfried delivered this news to Chayefsky, he said the screenwriter's response was "Where does he get off telling us who?"

The resistance to Eletha Finch could have been a simple issue of propriety: she was not formally involved with *Network*, and allowing her to accept the award over someone who worked on the film could, in future instances, open the door to all kinds of unsuitable proxies. Eletha was also known for her outspoken nature, and there was some question as to whether, if put before an audience, she would stick to a script. As Gottfried described her, "She was one piece of work, let me tell you. Don't you dare mess with Peter Finch while she's around. And then of course, if you're a woman, watch out."

The standoff between Friedkin and the *Network* team spilled over into the tabloids and gossip columns. Liz Smith later reported that the source of Friedkin's opposition was a dislike of "sentimentality," and that he told colleagues in pre-Oscar planning meetings, "It's not going to be that kind of TV show." In response, Chayefsky said he thought sentimentality and emotion were the basis of the movie business, pointing to moments such as Louise Fletcher's use of sign language to thank her deaf parents when she won her Academy Award for *One Flew Over the Cuckoo's Nest* the preceding year. "If sentimentality is inappropriate," he asked, "how does one account for the fact that the greatest moment in *A Star Is Born* is when Esther Blodgett says, 'Ladies and gentlemen, this is Mrs. Norman Maine!'"

Friedkin, for his part, would later say that the decision about who would receive the Oscar was not his to make. "It was made by the board of governors of the Academy," he said. "As the producer of the show, you have nothing to say about who accepts the award."

But as the issue continued to simmer, some uglier speculation began to rear its head, that the Academy did not want Eletha Finch, a black woman, receiving an Oscar on behalf of Peter Finch, a white man, because home television viewers, or the organization itself, were made uncomfortable by such an image. Such a scene could also be an unwanted reminder that, to date, only three black people had won the Academy Award outright. A more insidious whisper campaign at the time suggested that Eletha, who was Jamaican, had remained in the United States illegally after Peter Finch's death and should not be allowed to represent her husband because she risked deportation.

Alan Heim, the *Network* editor, said he would "hate to think" that racism in any way played a role in the Academy's reluctance to let Eletha Finch participate. "I knew that she had a reputation as a bit of a loose cannon," he said. "But I never thought she'd do anything strange. I hate to think that there would have been racism at that point. We had already had Sidney Poitier and other people winning the award."

Still others were not prepared to give the Academy or polite society that much credit. "Back then, they would get upset about the most silly things," said Marlene Warfield. "And it really doesn't matter. People were going to change, and they just didn't know it."

The harder the Academy pushed back against Eletha Finch, the more determined Chayefsky became to see her represent her late husband at the Oscars. In a private meeting among Chayefsky, Gottfried, Eletha Finch, and Barry Krost, the group decided that it would resort to subterfuge. When they were asked whom they were designating to receive a possible award on Peter Finch's behalf, Gottfried said, "We agreed that I would tell Friedkin and whoever else was involved that Paddy was accepting it." Krost would attend the ceremony with Eletha Finch as his date, and if Peter Finch were named best actor, Chayefsky would take the stage first and invite up Eletha from there. "This was all done before it happened," Gottfried explained, "because obviously it only happens when it happens. This was all *if* it happens."

As an item in the *New York Post* quietly reported one week before the Academy Awards: "Peter Finch's widow, Eletha, will attend Oscar ceremonies in case her late husband wins for 'Network.' She and daughter Diana have settled in a Beverly Hills residence. Mrs. Finch has no immigration problems as had been reported."

On March 28, the evening of the Forty-Ninth Annual Academy Awards, the players took their places at the Dorothy Chandler Pavilion, where Chayefsky sat in Box 13, Row F, Seat 46. His wife, Susan, who had been his date on a night very much like this one twenty-one years earlier, when he won his first Oscar, for *Marty*, and the whole world seemed to open up for him, did not attend this ceremony. He was instead accompanied by his lawyer, Maurice Spanbock.

Leading up to the Oscars, *People* published a cover story on Dunaway, in which the magazine unsubtly asked, "Faye Dunaway Has a Surging Career Plus an Unusual Marriage—Now Will She Win the Big O?" Portraits taken by the celebrity photographer Terry O'Neill showed the actress in repose with her husband, Peter Wolf, while in the accompanying article she spoke of how their marriage had brought her a new sense of stability and inner strength. "As the feelings well up," Dunaway explained, "I feel somehow bigger. I want to play bigger people now. Large, vital, mainstream characters who live on a lot of levels at once and are going through dramatic changes, just as I feel I am."

When Dunaway, an odds-on favorite over Liv Ullmann in the best actress race, was asked if she wanted an Oscar, she answered, "Yes, I'd like to win. It would be a nice present. But my life doesn't depend on it."

At the outset of the Oscars show, whose panel of hosts consisted of Jane Fonda, Warren Beatty, Ellen Burstyn, and Richard Pryor, *Network* did not look like an immediate winner. In one of the first categories announced, Ned Beatty lost the competition for best supporting actor to Jason Robards, who played *Washington Post* editor Ben Bradlee in *All the President's Men*. Despite the ferocity of his performance as *Network*'s Arthur Jensen, Beatty (who also appeared in *All the President's Men*, as the investigator Martin Dardis) was gracious about his defeat and the speed with which it had occurred. As he would later joke, "They gave the best supporting actor thing right off the bat, I think before they turned the camera on or anything."

More than an hour elapsed before *Network* claimed its startling first prize. Following a playful routine in which Sylvester Stallone and Muhammad Ali swatted each other around the stage, the two pugilists announced that the Oscar for best supporting actress went to Beatrice Straight. The genuinely shocked actress, whose fellow nominees included Jodie Foster in *Taxi Driver* and Piper Laurie in *Carrie*, sat open-mouthed in her seat for a moment and ran a hand through her hair before making her way to the podium. "It's very heavy," Straight said, picking up her statuette, "and I'm the dark horse." Adding that her victory was "very unexpected," she said, "I should have known that when I had someone like Paddy Chayefsky writing and saying things that we all feel but can't express, and when we have someone like Sidney Lumet, who makes one want to act forever, and a producer like Howard Gottfried, then how can I miss?" Her complete acceptance speech ran one minute and thirty-two seconds, roughly a third as long as her *Network* showdown with Holden, which ran four minutes and forty-five seconds.

Neither Alan Heim nor Owen Roizman prevailed in their technical categories, and as the author Norman Mailer prepared to announce the screenwriting prizes, he punctuated his remarks with a favorite proverb: "Once a philosopher, twice a pervert." (The line is attributed to Voltaire, who is said to have uttered the phrase by way of explaining that, though he had enjoyed a recent visit to a gay brothel, he would not be returning to the establishment.) Then Mailer opened his first envelope and announced that the Academy Award for best original screenplay would go to Paddy Chayefsky, for *Network*.

Chayefsky, dressed in square-framed glasses, a tuxedo he wore like a cloak, and a drooping bow tie, started his speech with a nod to Mailer's off-color anecdote: "In the name of all us perverts," he said as he received his trophy. In an earlier draft of the remarks he planned to make, should the occasion befall him, Chayefsky was going to confess his dislike of "modest acceptance speeches in which the acceptor thanks a host of other people for his own achievement" and then go on to give such a speech, one that thanked Lumet, Gottfried, Roizman, and Heim by name, and the film's "practically flawless cast," and conclude with an apology "for this—believe me—uncharacteristic display of sincerity."

Instead, Chayefsky deviated from this plan, and the man who wrote some of the most incensed and rancorous dialogue ever recited on a movie screen shared what was, for him, a tender and difficult sentiment. "I don't as a rule—in fact, I don't ever before remember making public acknowledgment of private and very personal feelings," Chayefsky said, "but I think it's time that I acknowledge two people whom I can never really thank properly or enough. I would like to thank my wife, Sue, and my son, Dan, for their indestructible support and enthusiasm, for their ideas, their discussions, their stimulation, and for their very presence. My gratitude and my love. Thank you."

Dunaway made her own attempt at graciousness when, a short while later, she received the Oscar for best actress that nearly everyone anticipated she would win. "Well," Dunaway said, "I didn't expect this to happen quite yet, but I do thank you very much and I'm very grateful." Between audible and excited breaths, she continued: "I would like especially to thank Sidney Lumet, Paddy Chayefsky, Howard Gottfried, Danny Melnick, and the great generosity of a rare group of actors— company of actors—in particular William Holden, Robert Duvall, and Peter Finch." She concluded with a special thank-you to her "friends in the back room," Susan Germaine, who had been her hair stylist on *Network*, and her makeup artist, Lee Harman.

The backdrop behind presenter Liv Ullmann dimmed to a dark blue as she announced the five nominees for best actor, observing that such a performer may be measured by "his willingness not to conceal himself, but to show himself in all his humanity, and to expose both the light and the darker sides of his nature, openly and truly." The live audience seemed to applaud just a shade more enthusiastically for Peter Finch than for the other nominees. William Holden, shown on a split screen just beneath a photograph of his deceased costar, could be seen sighing in relief as Ullmann opened her envelope and read Finch's name. Over a triumphant orchestra fanfare, an announcer stated, "Accepting the award for the late Peter Finch, Mr. Paddy Chayefsky."

Chayefsky rushed out from the stage-left wing and kissed Ullmann's extended hand as he approached the Oscar already waiting on the lectern, preparing to give what most expected would be the formal acceptance speech for Finch's award. But he delivered a different set of remarks, his voice growing more resolute as his true intentions became clear. "For some obscure reason I'm up here accepting an award for Peter Finch, or Finchy, as everybody who knew him called him," Chayefsky said. "There's no reason for me to be here—there's only one person who should be up here accepting this award, and that's the person who Finch wanted up here accepting his award: Mrs. Peter Finch. Are you in the house, Eletha? Come up and get your award."

It took a few moments for the cameras to find Eletha Finch, making her way through the rows of applauding industry peers with Krost lending her a guiding hand. ("She was panic-struck," Krost would later recall. "I saw her to the end of the row, just to help her get onstage.") Clutching her fur coat to her dress with one hand and, with the other, struggling mightily to hold on to her purse and corsage, Eletha Finch received a kiss from Chayefsky and another from Ullmann. With tentative steps, she approached the microphones and attempted to recite to the 250 million people watching the ceremony around the world a version of the speech she had heard her husband give so many times before.

"I want to say thanks to members of the Academy," she said amid tears, her trembling voice a mixture of her gentle Caribbean lilt and her late spouse's regal enunciation. "And my husband, I wish he was here tonight, to be with us all. But since he isn't here, I'll always cherish this for him. And before he died he said to me, 'Darling, if I win I want to say thanks to my fellow actors who have given me encouragement over the years.' And thanks to Paddy Chayefsky, who have given him the part. And thanks to Barry, who have tell us to come from Jamaica, to come and do this part. And he says, 'Most of all, thanks to you, dar-ling, for sending the right vibes the right way.' And thanks, the mem-bers of the Academy Award. Thank you all." With her husband's Oscar in hand and Ullmann's arm around her shoulder, Eletha Finch exited the stage.

Neither the title of *Network* nor the names of any other artists involved with the film were announced as winners for any more Acad-emy Awards that evening. Lumet, vying for best director honors for the third time in his career, would be denied a victory yet again; this time the prize would go to John G. Avildsen, the director of *Rocky*, who prevailed over contenders Lumet, Alan J. Pakula, Ingmar Bergman, and Lina Wertmüller, the first woman to be nominated in the category. At the conclusion of the ceremony, which ran nearly four hours, *Rocky* ful-filled its own underdog, out-of-nowhere prophecy by claiming the Oscar for best picture, its feel-good spirit prevailing over less sunny and more psychologically complicated rivals such as *Network*, *Taxi Driver*, and *All the President's Men*.

A cascade of similarly challenging emotions washed over the *Net-work* crew. The film had won four Oscars in total, tying *All the Presi-dent's Men* for the most of any motion picture that night. But one of their comrades had paid the ultimate price for his award, and still other top prizes had eluded the production. Now, even as they celebrated their hard-earned victories, there was a palpable sense that their work together was truly over and that nothing bound them together anymore. Heim and Roizman, who had been unlucky nominees but nominees none-theless, arrived at the Governors Ball, the star-studded post-Oscars banquet, to find that they had been situated nowhere near their more illustrious *Network* colleagues.

"We were sitting with a bunch of executives—accountants, really—from MGM," Heim said. "And we were sitting with these people, and Owen and I were the only ones buying extra wine for the table. And we were so far away." It was a slight that Heim would chalk up "to Howard

Gottfried's cheapness." At a later hour, Heim saw Avildsen, the newly decorated director of *Rocky*, with his Academy Award in tow, and could not help but think of Lumet. "He was not going to let that go for any-body," Heim said of Avildsen. "And I felt terrible for Sidney. I felt Sidney really deserved it."

Dunaway spent most of her night with the photographer Terry O'Neill, searching without success for a distinctive location where he could capture her with her Academy Award. During his initial assignment to shoot the actress for *People*, O'Neill would later recall, he had approached Dunaway with a proposition: "I said to her, 'I've got this idea for a picture that I wanted to do of an Oscar winner, because I've seen plenty of Oscar winners, and I can't stand that picture afterwards—you know, the one where they're standing there, holding it up smiling and all that.' I didn't feel that it told any story. I knew the fact that the next day, they're sort of stunned. They've now won the Oscar and they're dazed the next day, when they realize that their money's going to double or triple and they're going to get offered every top part."

Finding insufficient inspiration on the after-party circuit, O'Neill sent Dunaway back to the Beverly Hills Hotel, where she and the rest of the *Network* team were staying, and told her to meet him at the hotel pool at 6:30 the following morning. There, the photographer documented a weary Dunaway, dressed in her nightgown and a pair of high-heeled sandals, as she leaned back in a beach chair and struck a pensive pose. In the background was the placid, shimmering pool, lit by the rising sun, and rows of unoccupied patio furniture and cabanas; in the foreground was Dunaway's breakfast table, ornamented with unconsumed food and beverages, a cigarette lighter, and an Oscar statuette that the actress appeared to be contemplating only partially as she gazed into an unseen distance. Strewn on the table and the ground beneath her were various periodicals and newspapers that O'Neill had obtained before the shoot, including a copy of that morning's *Los Angeles Times*, lying at the foot of Dunaway's chair, whose front-page headline clearly read POSTHUMOUS OSCAR FOR FINCH.

To O'Neill, this indelible image, published a few days later in *Time*, depicted Dunaway in a "really reflective" moment. "First of all," he said, "she's had three hours' sleep. That was one thing. And also, it was suddenly dawning on her, the enormity of winning the Oscar. That was when it dawned on her, this was going to be a new beginning for her career." He added, however, that "different people see different meanings in it." As Dunaway herself described the photograph, "In Terry's picture, success is a solitary place to be. In my life, it has been the same. . . . Or as Peggy Lee sang, 'Is that all there is?'" But others saw it as a moment of supreme apathy—apathy to the enormity of her own accomplishment, and to the sanctity of a place where a colleague and fellow honoree had breathed what might have been his last breaths.

On the morning of March 30, the Beverly Hills Hotel sent a note to the room of Paddy Chayefsky, congratulating him on winning his latest Oscar and thanking him for his stay during the Academy Awards. But the screenwriter had checked out the previous day and was already headed back to New York. Los Angeles did not really suit his temperament; neither did awards ceremonies, nor did fawning attention. While he made the journey home, the latest addition to his trophy case would for the time being stay behind in Hollywood, in the possession of Howard and Mary Lynn Gottfried, who would make arrangements for the pristine memento to be engraved with Chayefsky's name. Until then, the couple kept it on display in their hotel room, where the occasional bellman or housekeeper would ask to hold it to feel its weight or just to gaze in awe at the unetched and anonymous statuette.

7

CORRUPT AND LUNATIC ENERGIES

On April 3, 1978, almost a year to the day after he won his Oscar for the screenplay of *Network*, Paddy Chayefsky returned to the Dorothy Chandler Pavilion in Los Angeles, as a presenter at the Fiftieth Annual Academy Awards. That evening's milestone program opened with Debbie Reynolds performing a song-and-dance salute to the maturity of Hollywood and the progress that American cinema had made in the last half century. "Look how we've matured!" she crowed. "Look how self-assured! We've been through pranksters and monsters and gangsters, and look how we endure!" But Chayefsky was in no mood for backslapping congratulations.

As the celebratory telecast ticked toward its third hour, a glittering backdrop on the theater's stage rose to reveal Chayefsky ambling down a flight of stairs, dressed in a tuxedo and bow tie nearly identical to those he had worn at the previous year's ceremony, as he headed toward the lectern to announce the winners of the screenplay awards. His mind, however, was not on his assigned duties but on an acceptance speech made earlier in the night by Vanessa Redgrave, who, in receiving her Oscar for best supporting actress in *Julia*, had used her own time at the microphone to decry the "small bunch of Zionist hoodlums" who had protested *The Palestinian*, a documentary she had produced in support of the Palestine Liberation Organization. Those remarks had drawn some jeers from the audience, mixed within an equal smattering of approving applause, but had otherwise gone unacknowledged in a show that had nonetheless made time for the banter of R2-D2 and C-3PO, the chirpy robot sidekicks of *Star Wars*, and a performance by Aretha Franklin of "Nobody Does It Better," the theme song of *The Spy Who Loved Me*, accompanied by a cadre of neon leotard–clad dancers who could have stepped right off the cover of a David Bowie album.

With the passing of each interminable minute yielding no other champion to rise and confront Redgrave on comments that Chayefsky felt were clearly outrageous and anti-Semitic, the author decided he would do so himself. He weighed in his mind the words he should use and the mood he should strike, sensing the potential of the moment that would soon be upon him. But he could hardly have expected that the words he was about to speak, considered for a matter of minutes and uttered in the span of just a few more, would come to define him as completely as any lines of dialogue he had labored over in his decades-long career as a dramatist. Nor could he have known that, for many thousands seated in the theater and millions more watching him on television that night, they were likely to be the last words they would ever hear him say.

In the months since *Network* was released, the film had woven its way into the fabric of the national culture—if not the entire movie, then one discrete and memorable moment from it. As Richard Kahn, MGM's vice president of advertising and publicity, wrote to Chayefsky in a memo in early 1977, "There must be no greater reward for a writer than to be able to penetrate the general consciousness of the public."

Attached to the letter was a packet of recent news clippings that all, in some form or another, referenced Howard Beale's combustible catchphrase. The headline of a *Los Angeles Times Magazine* article introducing its readers to alternative and overlooked candidates in an upcoming election cycle read, "WE'RE MAD AS HELL AND WE'RE NOT GOING TO TAKE IT ANY MORE . . ." A letter to the editor of the *Los Angeles Times*, responding to a report that Barbara Walters would soon be leaving her coanchor's chair at ABC News after an irreconcilable falling-out with Harry Reasoner, began, " 'I'm as mad as hell! And I'm not going to take it anymore!' No truer words can be uttered. This is the way I feel when I read articles on such people as Harry Reasoner versus Barbara Walters." When that same newspaper wanted to editorialize on the plight of American agriculture, it published a cartoon depicting a farmer in his fields using a tractor to carve out the start of a message that read, I'M MAD AS HELL AND I'M NOT GONNA TAKE IT A. And when *Time* recounted the story of Anthony Kiritsis, a failed businessman who had held his mortgage broker hostage at gunpoint for sixty-three hours, the magazine described this thwarted kidnapper as a man who "was mad as hell, and he decided not to take it any more."

To Chayefsky, these accumulated citations were hardly validating. Instead they represented a gross oversimplification of the themes of *Network*—encroaching technology, malleable media, and the battle to maintain individuality in a complex world—reducing them to an easily digestible slogan, a caricature. There was even a *Mad* magazine parody of the movie, titled "Nutwork," in which a news anchor named Harrowed Bile instructs his viewers to "go to your windows and open them and yell, 'I'M MAD AS HELL, AND YOU AIN'T GETTING A LOUSY PIZZA! WITH OR WITHOUT EXTRA CHEESE AND PEPPERONI!' " In a manner similar to its source material, the satire ends with the character's assassination—not by the Great Ahmed Kahn, but by pistol-packing cartoons of Harry Reasoner, Walter Cronkite, John Chancellor, and Barbara Walters.

Back in New York, viewers could turn on their television sets and see a commercial for a local banking chain lampooning the Beale speech by showing enraged citizens running to their windows and screaming for free checking. Though this would-be tribute displeased Chayefsky, he concluded he could not stand in its way. "They shouldn't have appropriated my idea," he groused. "It just isn't right. The most I could do, however, is seek an injunction."

Asked later how he had hit upon the "Mad as hell" monologue when he was writing *Network*, Chayefsky showed no particular preference or affinity for the scene. "I just made it up," he explained. "That's one of those things you count on from impetus."

If this fetishization of Beale's angry motto mystified its author, equally mystifying to his audience was why such bleak signals should be emanating from Chayefsky, who, having earned his reputation for being so closely attuned to the plights and frustrations of the common man, now seemed to be picking up his transmissions from some darker and more despairing place. In one of the author's rare daytime TV talk show appearances, the usually ebullient Dinah Shore told him, in a soft and conciliatory tone, "You're the fellow who wrote those lovely, delicate, tender, sensitive characterization pieces—*Marty* and *The Middle of the Night*, and now you come out with a scorcher."

With uncommon gentleness, Chayefsky replied, "It's not me. I'm still writing tender, delicate pieces. It's the world that's gone nuts."

There was no imminent pressure on Chayefsky to produce a follow-up to *Network*, and for once in his career he could patiently consider his next move. He walked away from a $500,000 offer to write a screenplay about the Israel Defense Forces' successful rescue mission at Entebbe Airport in Uganda (the NBC television version of this story, *Raid on Entebbe*, had been Peter Finch's unexpected swan song), and declined an NBC project called *The War Against the Jews*. Though the network would find success with a similar production, called *Holocaust*, an Emmy Award–winning miniseries starring Fritz Weaver, Meryl Streep, and James Woods, Chayefsky concluded that "the subject was simply too painful for me to write about." More to the point, he said, the network was "going to cut it any way they want to cut it. They're not going to give me the final control."

During the theatrical release of *Network*, the eminent science-fiction author Ray Bradbury had written a tongue-in-cheek essay suggesting that the film should not have ended with Beale's death; instead, Bradbury said, Beale should have been given a stately funeral that would have driven the ratings at UBS even higher, and buried in a "grandiose tomb" with "an immense sculptured rock in front." After three days, the rock would have been rolled away and the tomb would have been found empty, setting the stage for Beale's Second Coming. "The assassination, of course, was a fraud," Bradbury wrote. "Finch, struck by soft bullets that anesthetized rather than killed, has been kept on ice in some Florida rest home against the day when it is time for his ecclesiastical rebirth."

Sidney Lumet, who had been sent a copy of the essay by Bradbury, wrote back to say that he loved the idea and would forward it to Chayefsky, adding, "Among other things, it gives us a chance for NETWORK two." "Also," Lumet continued, "with the reality of television, it would allow them an on-going series because each time he is shot and the stone rolled back and he reappears, it could be the beginning of a new series." The resurrected Beale, the director suggested, "could come back each time in the guise of whatever is in fashion: i.e., a black militant, Bella Abzug, an esoteric film director, or, what have you. Who knows, he could even come back as a fashion designer."

As he promised, Lumet sent the offbeat proposal to Chayefsky, where it went no further.

In this same period, Chayefsky made slightly more progress on a screenplay treatment for *Reds*, Warren Beatty's motion picture about John Reed, the American journalist and author of *Ten Days That Shook the World*, who was a firsthand witness to the Bolshevik Revolution. After reading biographies of Reed, Chayefsky began to sketch out the acts of a story that would follow the journalist over a period of five years, on a journey from Portland, Oregon; to Greenwich Village; to

Petrograd. (Beatty would later say that he was asking Chayefsky only to provide his informal advice on *Reds*, not to write the screenplay. "I was not asking him to work on it," Beatty said. "I was mooching on his opinion.") But Chayefsky agonized over how he would make a hero out of Reed, who not only had been an ardent supporter of communism—a system Chayefsky fervently believed was inferior to capitalism and destined for failure—but had given his life for an inherently flawed and ultimately wrongheaded movement.

Seeing no parallels with and feeling no sympathy for his would-be protagonist, Chayefsky wrote in his treatment, "We've got a guy who falls in love with his role in history—which is all he ever really wanted. . . . He is world-famous, admired, respected and influential—and all that has no more meaningfulness to it than anything else—The resolution seems to be it's all shit, no matter what you do." When Reed died, Chayefsky wrote, "He didn't want to live because the great ultimate truth he had fallen in love with and given his life to—(the betterment of the world)—turned out to be as full of shit as everything else." The overall story that Reed's life suggested to Chayefsky was "that a man can live without love, but he can't live without his illusions. (Something in that as a theme, maybe.)" Even for Chayefsky, it felt too nihilistic.

Forgoing other people's pitches and suggestions, Chayefsky pursued the modernized Jekyll-and-Hyde story he had first begun to sketch out while he wrote *Network*. In his telling, the central character—first named Edward Jekyll, then rechristened Eddie Jessup—would be "an associate professor in behavioral psychology" who has for years "experimented with hallucinogenic drugs, isolation chambers, sense-deprivation tanks, hypnotic and induced trances, Eastern mysticism and Western gestalts," and who, via an unknown mushroom compound he encounters at a tribal ceremony in Mexico, hits upon what he believes is life's "Ultimate Force" and "Final Truth," but is instead turned temporarily into "a small, finely furred, erect, bipedal, protohuman creature."

In the afterglow of *Network*, Chayefsky was as committed to the project as to the target price he expected for it. "Paddy decided he wanted a million bucks," Howard Gottfried recalled. "That's it. He wanted a million dollars. You don't want to pay? Forget it."

As he had done on *Network* and *The Hospital*, Chayefsky immersed himself in field research for the project, traveling to hospitals and universities and meeting with scientific experts up and down the East Coast, at Harvard and at Duke and throughout New York, at Columbia, Hofstra, Fordham, Lehman College, and the State University of New York at Stony Brook. He familiarized himself with the writings of Aldous Huxley, Carlos Castaneda, Timothy Leary, and Dr. John C. Lilly, whose studies of human consciousness had combined the use of isolation chambers and psychedelic drugs. And on a visit to Stockton State College in California, Chayefsky tried a sensory-deprivation tank for himself, describing the experience as "a warm return to your mother's womb."

With the help of Sam Cohn, the powerful talent agent from ICM, Chayefsky sold, as a novel, a short, incomplete treatment of his proposed film about "the subject of laboratory experiments involving man's primal instincts and his ability to revert to them." Chayefsky had never written a novel before and was wary of this arrangement, but he agreed that it would help create awareness and stir interest for the eventual movie. Together with Gottfried and Daniel Melnick, the former MGM executive who had helped guide *Network* and who was now an independent producer, he then brought the new project to Columbia Pictures.

The studio was eager for its own science-fiction thriller, laden with makeup and special effects, to keep pace with the latest Hollywood vogue created by the runaway box-office grosses of *Star Wars*, which had opened in May 1977. But Columbia's president and chief executive, David Begelman, had one lingering question about how its narrative would be resolved.

As Gottfried would later recall the meeting, "We reached the point where Paddy really has nothing else to say. And Begelman says, 'What happens then?' Paddy hesitates and says, 'I don't know.' Begelman says, 'What do you mean you don't know?' He says, 'Well, we'll work on it.'"

Chayefsky nonetheless had his million-dollar deal, and it was as lucrative, as intense, and as stressful a bargain as he had ever struck. He immersed himself in the project, but that summer, as he labored over the manuscript of the novel and tormented himself to devise an ending for the story—should Jessup die, or should some other unknown fate befall him?—Chayefsky suffered a heart attack. As the author, now fifty-four years old, told his son, Dan, during a visit with him in the hospital, "At least this proves I'm mortal."

For the key players who had once been associated with *Network*, it was a season of transition and tumult. Sidney Lumet was putting the finishing touches on his film adaptation of *Equus* and would soon be moving on to his first musical, *The Wiz*, a modernized, soul music retelling of *The Wizard of Oz* based on a hit Broadway show, for which his all-star cast included Diana Ross, Michael Jackson, and the director's mother-in-law, Lena Horne.

In Los Angeles, Peter Finch's widow, Eletha, had been struggling since her husband's death. "I've got two children to raise and I need income," she explained in a gossip item in the *New York Post* that reported that she had started renting out the family's Beverly Hills home to tenants while she and her children moved to a more modest three-bedroom apartment; she had also lost twenty-five pounds and begun taking acting lessons in preparation for a small on-screen role in an episode of TV's *Police Woman*, arranged for her by its star, Angie Dickinson. Her summer was spent in court, fighting for her share of the estate of her late husband, who had not written a will since 1965 and had never named Eletha as a beneficiary. The value of that estate, accumulated by an actor who in his lifetime had appeared in more than fifty motion pictures, was placed at $115,000.

Faye Dunaway, whose life had always been treated as an open book by the news media, had split from her husband, Peter Wolf, by that summer. She had begun an affair with Terry O'Neill, the photographer who had shot her *People* cover story as well as her unforgettable post-Oscars portrait, and within months it was a matter of public record. These modest scandals had no measurable impact on Dunaway's career; the actress was paid a reported $1 million to star in Irvin Kershner's thriller *Eyes of Laura Mars*, and $750,000 to appear opposite Jon Voight in a remake of the boxing drama *The Champ*. But any goodwill she might have won with her victory on Oscar night seemed to have evaporated in the morning mist rising from the pool at the Beverly Hills Hotel.

Dunaway's relationship with Sue Mengers, the talent agent who helped persuade her to take *Network* and then ensured that she was not fired from it, had deteriorated, and the two were no longer working together. "She just didn't like me," Mengers would later say, "and I didn't like her." In the press, she was a villainess again, and for every minor misstep or embarrassment—say, a beauty magazine paying $2,000 to retouch the crow's-feet, laugh lines, and facial puffiness in the portrait of Dunaway that ran on its cover—there was an enthusiastic audience waiting to hear about it.

William Holden, meanwhile, was trying a different tack with his personal life. In an article in the *New York Times* (which described him as once possessing a "smiling, unlined face" that "served as a safe map of American aspirations and triumph," but now being "58 and, finally, looking it"), he came clean about his relationship with the actress Stefanie Powers, who at thirty-four was about as far apart in age from Holden as Diana Christensen was from Max Schumacher. The off-screen couple had been introduced in 1973 at a celebrity tennis match. "I was fortunate to find a compatible female human being as curious as I am about the world and the effects of progress," said Holden. "We didn't gravitate toward each other because we were eager to jump into bed, although we did that too," said Powers. Now they traveled the world together as Powers assisted Holden in his various projects, such as gathering four hundred pieces of indigenous artwork from the government of Papua New Guinea and selling them at Bloomingdale's. "I have been an actor for 38 years," said Holden, shrugging off his Oscar loss to Peter Finch. "I have been a conservationist in Africa for 18. The danger—the danger is being considered a dilettante both as an actor and a conservationist."

The couple sent Christmas cards to Chayefsky decorated with traditional seasonal imagery and depictions of jungle creatures frolicking underneath rainbows, and inscribed with entreaties to visit them at Holden's palatial home in Palm Springs. But the author—who since his heart attack had been told to avoid caffeine, tobacco, and salt and to exercise more—did not take them up on their invitation. When Chayefsky was feeling well enough to write again, one of the first places where his name appeared was in a *New York Times* advertisement placed by a group calling itself Writers and Artists for Peace in the Middle East. Alongside fellow signatories such as Saul Bellow, Bernard Malamud, Arthur Miller, Leon Uris, and Elie Wiesel, Chayefsky (who also helped compose the letter) urged readers to remember the fifth anniversary of the 1972 Munich Olympics and the eleven Israeli athletes murdered there by a radical Palestinian group. "But we shall not forget," the letter read, "that the P.L.O. says Israel has no right to exist. Would any state in the world be asked to talk to those who say you must die at the end of the conversation?"

In the same film season that she was nominated for an Academy Award for her performance as the title character in *Julia*, the pseudonymous friend and anti-Nazi activist from Lillian Hellman's memoir *Pentimento*, Vanessa Redgrave produced, narrated, and appeared in a documentary called *The Palestinian*, in which she interviewed Palestinian refugees and leaders and the PLO's chairman, Yasir Arafat. Theaters that showed the documentary were widely picketed, and the actress faced protests at public appearances where she did not promote or even mention the film. Dore Schary, the honorary chairman of the Anti-Defamation League, called the film "a terrible piece of work" and described it as "very dull, fortunately," adding that "the only comment you keep hearing is 'Kill the enemy.' They keep saying that Israel is intransigent." Redgrave countered that she had made the documentary "because I believe the Palestinian people have been denied the right to be heard," adding that she had "consistently championed the rights of the Jewish people." "No one can challenge the stand I have taken against fascism and anti-Semitism," she said.

Such remarks did not dissuade members of the Jewish Defense League from turning out at the 1978 Oscars ceremony to demonstrate against Redgrave's appearance, nor did they keep away supporters of the PLO who came to demonstrate against the JDL. And when, near the start of the broadcast, Redgrave won the Oscar for best supporting actress (for a role that Faye Dunaway had turned down), she could hardly avoid weighing in on the continuing controversy. Thanking her *Julia* costar Jane Fonda and the film's director, Fred Zinnemann, Redgrave said they had done "the best work of our life" because "we believe in what we were expressing: two out of millions who gave their lives and were prepared to sacrifice everything in the fight against fascist and racist Nazi Germany.

"And I salute you," Redgrave continued, "and I pay tribute to you, and I think you should be very proud that in the last few weeks you've stood firm, and you have refused to be intimidated by the threats of a small bunch of Zionist hoodlums whose behavior"—she paused to let pass the boos and cries that were drowning out her speech—"whose behavior is an insult to the stature of Jews all over the world and to their great and heroic record of struggle against fascism and oppression." With a concluding expression of gratitude to Hollywood for having dealt "a final blow against that period when Nixon and McCarthy launched a worldwide witch hunt against those who tried to express in their lives and their work," Redgrave hoisted her trophy and pledged to "continue to fight against anti-Semitism and fascism."

Redgrave's comments were followed by a commercial break, and when the Oscars show resumed, neither its host, Bob Hope, nor any of its presenters made further mention of them. But backstage at the ceremony, expectations ran high that a response was imminent, and that it would be coming from Paddy Chayefsky. "Paddy just went nuts after her speech," recalled Mike Medavoy, one of the United Artists executives who had worked with him on *Network*. "He was furious. I remember going to the bathroom and encountering Paddy railing on her outside the restroom." Sherry Lansing, then a junior executive at MGM, said later that "everybody ran to Paddy and wanted to say something." A huddle of people formed around the screenwriter, all of them asking, "What are you going to say, Paddy?" In due time they had their answer.

When his turn to speak came later that night, Chayefsky approached the lectern with a speedy gait and his head bowed slightly, and began: "Before I get onto the writing awards, there's a little matter I'd like to tidy up, at least if I expect to live with myself tomorrow morning. I would like to say, personal opinion of course, that I'm sick and tired of people exploiting the occasion of the Academy Awards for the propagation of their own personal political propaganda." The theater rang with applause and cheering, though a television camera that panned across fretful faces and folded hands in the audience showed that not everyone was supportive of his rebuttal.

Undaunted, Chayefsky continued: "I would like to suggest to Ms. Redgrave that her winning an Academy Award is not a pivotal moment in history, does not require a proclamation, and a simple 'thank you' would have sufficed." As another wave of applause subsided, Chayefsky gave a quick nod, wiped his lips, and attempted to change the subject. "And now, on to much more important matters," he said, picking up an envelope and then letting it slip from his hands as he realized he still had his official presenter's speech to give.

Without any discernible difficulty, Chayefsky shifted his tone from one of quiet condemnation to another that was tender and humbled. "Screenplay writing," he said, "is a much-misunderstood form of writing."

> In the old days, the image of the screenwriter was that of the
> great novelist who had gone derelict in the corrupt tropics of

Hollywood and nowadays I think they think of the screen-writer frequently as somebody who helps out the director with lines of dialogue. But in point of fact, screenwriting is a very special, highly refined discipline. It requires all the standard storytelling talents and it also requires a visual eye as well, because the screenwriter frequently has to tell a story without words, which are, after all, the primary tools of the writer's craft. When it works, a good screenplay is a thing of beauty, a model of precision and clarity and imagery and concept [so saying, he extended his hands as if he were put-ting them around a woman's waist] and mobility, wit, pas-sion. It is something to celebrate and something to honor, so, let's honor them.

Then he picked up the envelope he had earlier dropped on the lectern and started to tear it open, as audience members who had held their tongues throughout the proceedings started shouting at him.

"Oh!" Chayefsky exclaimed. "I forgot to read the nominees." Falling back on his Borscht Belt ways, he jokingly adjusted his glasses, quickly removing them from and returning them to his face, and said to the laughing crowd, "I'm that eager to know, I must say. Every one of these fellas are friends of mine." Then, finally, he read the nominees for best original screenplay.

Chayefsky's oration was instantaneously sensational and instan-taneously divisive, even before he was led off the Oscars stage by Alvin Sargent, who won the Academy Award for best adapted screenplay for *Julia*. (In his own acceptance speech, Sargent said he believed his tro-phy stood for "the free expression of all our good thoughts and feelings and loves, no matter who we are or what we have to say.") While Chayef-sky was still speaking, a camera had caught Shirley MacLaine, a best actress nominee for *The Turning Point*, sitting next to its screenwriter, Arthur Laurents, as he clapped appreciatively and she did not. Their disagreement over the incident and whose side they supported was so vehement, MacLaine later recalled, that after the Oscars, "Arthur didn't speak to me for five years. He just thought that it was terrible that she had said those things about the Jews, and I was saying she had every right to say it, and he was mad at me."

When he returned home to New York, Chayefsky was greeted by numerous appreciative letters and correspondence that applauded him for his rebuke of Redgrave, with supportive messages coming from William F. Buckley Jr. (YOU ARE MY NEW HERO, the *National Review* founder wrote in a telegram, SORRY ABOUT THAT BUT YOU EARNED IT REGARDS), Carol Burnett and Joe Hamilton, Marlo Thomas, Jerry Stiller and Anne Meara, and even Eletha Finch, who in a handwritten note to Chayefsky said, "You were great on the night of Oscar. My husband would be proud of you, you are a 'great man.'" Chayefsky also received a note of praise from the director Frank Capra, who wrote, "You damned near made me cry with your gutsy but courteous put-down of Vanessa Redgrave." Chayefsky replied, "I have to tell you that the response I got after the Academy Awards occasion was larger than the response I have ever received for all of the work that I have ever done put together. It will please you to know that my mail was overwhelmingly disapproving of Miss Redgrave."

This approbation, however, was hardly unanimous. Sean Mitchell, the theater critic for the *Dallas Times Herald*, took the unorthodox step of writing directly to Chayefsky to tell the screenwriter he could not find it within himself to "reconcile my longstanding admiration for your work with your churlish performance" at the Academy Awards show. "How can the same man who wrote 'Marty' and 'Network,'" Mitchell asked, "who clearly understands the indomitable human spirit, so recklessly impugn that spirit as displayed by a colleague? Contrary to your remarks, Miss Redgrave's acceptance speech did not appear as a grandstand play at all, rather, as proof that some actors actually have the convictions of their work. . . . Your soliloquy, on the other hand, seemingly sprang from no irony except that some of Hollywood's best minds habitually soften in the spotlights of this annual pep rally for the industry."

Writing about the confrontation in the *New York Times*, the film critic Vincent Canby condemned Chayefsky for his piousness. Compared to Redgrave's acceptance speech, Canby wrote, "nothing she said came anywhere near the fustian fancies later delivered by Paddy Chayefsky, the self-appointed industry nanny, in what he may have thought to be a rebuttal, though he sounded amazingly like the sort of character that Paddy Chayefsky, the motion picture writer . . . would send up in half a scene. It was not a fine hour—either for him or for the winning writers to whom he was to present Oscars." To a wide swath of observers, Chayefsky's reaction was not courageous and not necessary; it confirmed their perceptions that he was a dyspeptic, intolerant crank.

Chayefsky's cultural standing was not entirely enhanced by the publication of his Jekyll-and-Hyde novel, which was released by Harper and Row in the summer of 1978 and which, after Columbia Pictures tested the project with such names as *The Atavist*, *The Experiment*, and *Exploding Circle*, was given the title *Altered States*. Some critics appreciated the book's lofty philosophical aim of probing more deeply into the kernel of humanity's soul than any of Chayefsky's previous dramatic work. But many were put off by its jargonistic writing—"all the electronic-spin resonance tests," one reviewer wrote, "the metabolites, the fractionating, the images of pyroclastic debris, lapilli, Phlegethon, the excessive VMA and HIAA levels, and the telltale N-methoxy bufatonin in the urine serums"—and the apparent absence of the author's trademark dark humor. Another commentator wrote that *Altered States* "does offer a few passages of spectacularly bad writing, notably in the rendering of crude and quick sexual bouts," and that "Jessup and his companions affect a sometimes annoying locker room vernacular, as if to prove themselves he-men," in an otherwise positive assessment that called the novel "a marvelous and exciting work of the imagination."

Prior to the book's publication and only a few weeks before he appeared on the Oscars, Chayefsky learned that a medical expert who had helped him with the novel was suing him. Dr. Jeffrey Lieberman, the chief psychiatric resident at St. Vincent's Hospital in Manhattan, said that he worked in close consultation with the author on *Altered States* for nearly a year and a half, making what his lawsuit said was "a substantial contribution" to the screenplay that entitled him to half ownership in the property and damages of more than $1.5 million. Chayefsky's lawyer, Maurice Spanbock, countered that while Lieberman had served as a "research assistant in connection with the novel," ultimately "his claims are without merit." But fighting the suit was going to be a long, expensive, and invasive undertaking, requiring Chayefsky to exhaustively inventory every document, draft, and discarded page he had created for the treatment, the novel, and the screenplay, and to rigorously detail his time line and whereabouts throughout the development of the project.

Chayefsky found an ally for *Altered States* at the highest level of Columbia Pictures, where the former MGM executive Daniel Melnick had risen to the studio's presidency. (Reviewing the screenplay a few weeks prior to his official appointment, Melnick had cheekily written to Chayefsky in a telegram, DEAR PADDY: STUNNING, BRILLIANT, BREATHTAKING—BUT WE CAN FIX IT.) The path now seemed clear for a reunion between Chayefsky and Lumet, who was as qualified a candidate to direct *Altered States* as anyone could imagine. But after lengthy negotiations between the two, the writer and director were unable to come to financial terms. When his final deadline to strike a deal elapsed, Lumet informed Chayefsky that he had instead chosen to direct the romantic comedy *Just Tell Me What You Want*, following up with a letter that all but guaranteed an end to their creative partnership.

The five-page handwritten note from Lumet was addressed to "Dearest Paddy & Howard," but it was clear from its opening lines to whom the director was speaking. "I think you know how sad I am that 'Altered States' did not work out," Lumet began. "But, Paddy, in all honesty, it's your own fault. I am not a hustler." Citing his contracts at Universal (where he had a three-picture deal) and Warner Bros. (to whom he owed an additional two films), Lumet said he could not take on *Altered States* for the amount he was being offered "without destroying my credibility at those places."

"But furthermore," Lumet continued, "it's all silly. You know that you've got a 10 to 12 million picture on your hands. What in the hell is the difference in the few hundred thousand that you would have asked me to reduce? You know I'd make it up in the below-the-line, not even mentioning quality!"

Lumet, straining to be diplomatic and gracious for a reader whom no amount of diplomacy or grace would placate, while still sticking up for his own self-worth, wrote to Chayefsky: "No one knows better than I how much intellect, guts & talent goes into your work. But you know how hard I work too. I agree that when a writer is of your caliber, that it's a bit galling to say that to the guy who puts it upon the screen. I am not, as you well know, a believer in 'auteur' bullshit. I serve the script."

> And when it's a script like yours, that's an honor. But the only wise thing Pauline Kael ever said was in an article on Candy Bergen, attacking her for her sloppiness and still being a star. She wrote, "You think it's unfair? Well, life is unfair." If I'm lucky & have earned the right to that dough then I'm going to take it!
>
> I'm doing a wonderful script by Jay Presson Allen. She can write! It's not as good as yours, but very few ever will be. Paddy, you're perhaps one of the five best writers this country has. (I can hear you asking Howard, "Who the hell are the other four?") I wish this had worked because you're going to need a combination of Kubrick's images and my brain & heart. I wish for movies' sake that you have a brilliant picture. Please, pick my brain about another director. You know I'm not a competitive man, no one is irreplaceable, and I want to see this done well.

Lumet concluded, "I love you, love your talent and love working with the two of you. And I'm deeply sorry this didn't work out."

In defeat, Chayefsky and Gottfried turned again to Sam Cohn, who represented Lumet, and were persuaded to hire Arthur Penn, another director on the agent's roster, in May 1978. Penn was an old hand who had known Chayefsky since they worked together on *The Philco-Goodyear Television Playhouse*, and his distinguished résumé of feature films included *The Miracle Worker* and *Bonnie and Clyde*. But he seemed overwhelmed by the complicated effects and design work needed to realize a script that, among other fantastic imagery, called for the depiction of a "flaming cloud of gasses, hydrogen and helium" as it "WHOOSHES across the black screen at 90,000,000 mph" and "a grayish blob" that "folds and slithers into itself to take on other shapes, changing into soft, pulsating globules of matter." Joe Alves, the film's original production designer, would later say that "Arthur really wasn't that positive" about what he wanted "in any visual concept sense. . . . He knew exactly what he wanted from the actors. When it got to the effects things, he sort of stopped. He was sort of waiting for *us* to do something."

That November, during a disagreement with Chayefsky over the size of an isolation tank being built for the movie, Penn discovered he lacked the contractual authority to overrule the screenwriter on this or any other matter. "He had the power to veto everything," said Penn, "and I didn't find that out until we were getting ready to shoot." Knowing that if he quit the production outright he would not be paid for the months of work he had already put in, Penn said, "I went back to the house I had rented in Los Angeles, and I waited for the telegram to come removing me from the film."

October 4, 1978, saw the arrival of a quietly momentous and unexpected occasion: the television debut of *Network*. The film, which once raised concerns that its contemptuous portrayal of broadcasting would prevent it from ever being aired on television, had been licensed in June 1977 to CBS, which paid $5 million for three showings. (That fee was a respectable sum, considering that NBC had spent the same amount in 1976 for one showing of *Gone with the Wind*.) *Network*, whose CBS premiere came three weeks before Lumet's long-in-the-works adaptation of *The Wiz* turned up dead on arrival in movie theaters, would not make its transition to the small screen with all its fury and frankness intact; gone from the TV version was the love scene between Dunaway and Holden and most of the movie's vulgar language. But not all of it: though CBS executives had once contemplated the idea of replacing "bullshit" with "bullsoup," they decided to let stand three of the thirteen instances in which "bullshit" was said in *Network*, once by Dunaway and twice by Peter Finch.

"The use of BS is a focal point of the movie," said Donn O'Brien, CBS's vice president of program practices, censoring himself as he explained the decision. "BS is not obscene. It's gutter slang and can mean many things. We would not allow BS to be used in movies we make ourselves, but *Network* is a movie of renown that won four Oscars." Adding that the movie "was not an easy edit," O'Brien said that he believed CBS had succeeded in delivering its story "without being hit with all that sledgehammer language."

Principal photography for *Altered States* began on March 23, 1979, some ten months after Arthur Penn was let go from the production. In his place now stood Ken Russell, the brave, boastful, and unapologetically confident filmmaker whose previous works of sensory overload included *Women in Love*, *Tommy*, and *Lisztomania*. He had hardly been Chayefsky and Gottfried's first choice as a replacement, and he knew it. "I was the 27th person they offered it to," Russell would later say, exaggerating only slightly. "They had tried just about everybody in town, but for one reason or another, no one panned out." The budget of *Altered States* had risen from about $9 million to more than $12 million, and the film had been dropped by Columbia after another rotation of its executive merry-go-round saw Daniel Melnick replaced by Frank Price, who had no patience for the project's delays and overruns. But Melnick helped get *Altered States* reinstated at Warner Bros. before setting up his own independent production company at 20th Century–Fox.

The first scene to be filmed in *Altered States* was set at an Italian restaurant in Los Angeles (standing in for Boston), as, according to the screenplay, "eight voluble academics gabble away, swilling their wine, stowing their pasta," and Eddie Jessup's wife, Emily, lectures a young medical student on the tool-using abilities of lower primates. Almost immediately, Chayefsky and Russell disagreed on how the moment should be performed.

"We played it one way," said Blair Brown, who played Emily Jessup, "and then Ken wanted me to play it more as if Emily was slightly drunk and starting to find it a little bit hilarious. I know Paddy felt that she would never treat her subjects like that. He had asked me about that just on the side."

Russell, who was not particularly interested in Chayefsky's previous accomplishments or the level of input he expected on his films, was offended by the screenwriter's actions. "While I was busy talking and joking with the crew," the director said, "he took two of the girls in the scene aside and told them they were playing it 'too drunk.' They were very upset with that, and it wasn't until the scene had been shot that I found out what had gone on. That was when I finally said, 'This can't go on,' and requested that Paddy not come to the set anymore."

Richard MacDonald, Russell's newly appointed production designer, remembered the scene slightly differently. "Paddy went out of his head," he said. Filming was halted as Russell ordered Chayefsky to leave the set "or else," at which point the writer exited. "If Paddy wanted a safer approach to the material," said MacDonald, "he should not have chosen Russell in the first place."

Exiled to his bungalow at the Beverly Hills Hotel, a fuming Chayefsky was determined to take his revenge. In a draft of a letter to Ted Ashley, the chairman of Warner Bros., Chayefsky insisted that Russell needed to be deposed from *Altered States*, not because of "pique on my part or personal paranoia," but because every choice the director was making, from line readings to his shot selection—filming with an isolation tank open, for example, when Chayefsky's script called for it to be closed—had pushed the situation to "the point where we have teetered into non-salvageable." He went on:

> If you'd like, I'd be glad to come out and sit through the dailies with you and your people and point out the dozens and dozens of tiny bad moments and false notes and simply bad shit, one after the other, until the overall effect is the loss of reality and credibility and the introduction of overinflated drama and cheap cliche. What I'm telling you now is that you're spending thirteen million bucks on a picture that's going to come out looking not much better than a second-rank horror movie.

"What I'm saying is, he is no longer under control," Chayefsky concluded. "The only thing that ever contained him was the script, and now he's violating the script."

Chayefsky's letters to Gottfried soon devolved into blunt, mechanical recitations of how the author expected the filming of *Altered States* to continue in his absence. "With this advance notice," Chayefsky wrote, "you will be able to forestall a crisis. I will be saved the unpleasant duty of demanding that the scene be re-shot for violating the script—(since, as you know, the film must be photographed in accordance with the screenplay, and no changes can be made in the screenplay without my consent)—and you will be saved the problem of imposing this re-shooting on Russell."

"If the scene is not shot the way it is written and the way I have reaffirmed it to be shot in this letter," Chayefsky added, "I will insist on having the scene re-shot until I am satisfied it is not a violation of the script."

When it became clear even to Chayefsky that his instructions were not going to be followed, he leaned on Gottfried one last time to have Russell dismissed. As Gottfried later recalled, "Paddy said to me, 'Howard, I can't work with him. You've got to fire him. Get rid of him.' I said, 'Paddy, I don't know if I can get rid of him at this point. We've already dismissed Arthur Penn. We are heavily into production. I would have to have somebody else in mind who could come in and take over the movie. And I honestly don't know who that would be.'"

Torn between personal loyalty and professional responsibility, Gottfried saw just one desperate resolution to both problems. "The only way I could do that and get away with it," he said to Chayefsky, "is if I tell them that *you'll* take over the direction of the movie. There's nobody else we could get. I will go up to them and say, 'Paddy really thinks he's the guy to take over the direction of the movie. Consequently, we want to get rid of Ken Russell.' Otherwise, I don't see how I could do that."

But past experience had taught Chayefsky that he was not a director. "He didn't think he should," Gottfried said. "He didn't think he could. And I understand that, he never directed a movie. But at least I could try to sell that. Nobody understood the movie better. Anyhow, he said, 'Well, I can't do that. I won't do that. And if you're not going to do that, I'm going to have to leave the movie.'"

Chayefsky never returned to the set of *Altered States*, and he and Gottfried never worked together again.

One day after what would have been Peter Finch's sixty-third birthday, on September 29, 1979, his widow, Eletha Finch, now forty-one, married Paul Holliman, a twenty-one-year-old actor, in a small ceremony at the Beverly Hills home of Peter's former manager, Barry Krost. "Although the marriage took Hollywood by surprise," *Jet* magazine observed, "the disparity in ages of the newlyweds hardly raised an eyebrow or comment because of the increasing trend of older women who are now taking younger men for marriage mates or live-in lovers." Amid rumblings that her immigration status in the United States was once again in jeopardy, a lawyer for Eletha Finch told reporters that this was no marriage of convenience: "It was the real thing, and since Holliman is an American citizen, there is no longer any danger of Eletha's deportation."

The aspiring actress, now known as Eletha Finch Holliman, acknowledged that she had struggled personally in the two years since Peter Finch's death and that she had even considered suicide. "I started drinking, escaping from reality, ignoring my two kids," she said. "But eventually I fought my way back. If I've learned anything, I've learned how to survive."

The following summer, Chayefsky attempted to send a check for $200 to the Gordonstoun school, a private academy in Britain, indicating that he wanted the amount designated for Christopher Finch, Eletha's son, who was a student there. "I would appreciate your getting this money into the Finch boy's fund as soon as possible," Chayefsky wrote. Within days the check was returned to him, with a letter from an administrator saying that the school could not "accept gifts which are earmarked to a particular individual." "I am sorry about this 'Red Tape' as we would like to help," the letter said, "but we have to be very careful to abide by I.R.S. regulations."

For years William Holden had told the world that, despite the harder-drinking days of his youth, the life he led now was one of quiet and uninteresting sobriety. But as he and those closest to him knew, this was not the truth; in fact, the actor kept an apartment in Malibu, separate from his Palm Springs manor, that he used for his private benders. On a visit to that apartment in November 1981, the actor became so overwhelmed by uncontrollable shakes that he called his personal masseur for help, and when a rubdown failed to calm him, Holden sent the masseur away and began drinking vodka and beer. While intoxicated, he slipped on an antique rug in his bedroom and hit his head on a nightstand with such force that it severed the artery in his forehead. His body was found on November 16, and though some accounts would claim it took several agonizing hours for him to die, his girl-friend, Stefanie Powers, said the coroner told her that Holden had bled out in twenty minutes.

"Bill did more in his life, on and off the screen, than most people do in three lifetimes, and he did it with style and talent," Powers would later say. "*That* is his legacy, not his flaws. Given his lifetime consumption of alcohol, it is almost superhuman that he could have accomplished all he did."

It was with a certain unconcealed joy that the entertainment-industrial complex dutifully reported on the many failures that had befallen Faye Dunaway since she won her Academy Award for *Network*. In the summer of 1979 the *New York Post*'s brutally forthright Page Six gossip column declared, "Faye Dunaway is doing the 'I want to be alone' bit. (Of course, given her latest movies, *The Champ* and *Laura Mars*, leaving her alone may be just what Hollywood plans.) Faye has no projects set and even her agents wonder if she'll work again." A few weeks later, the *Post* said that the actress had been dropped from an upcoming cover of *Los Angeles* magazine because, according to an anonymous "magazine official," she had "simply become too fat to appear on the cover." By the fall, the tabloids were licking their chops at the closure of a troubled clothing store and antiques emporium that Dunaway and her boyfriend Terry O'Neill had opened in Venice, California. The actress, said the *Post*, was in a "deep depression because most of the merchandise is growing old on the shelves instead of selling like the hot cakes she'd hoped."

In June 1980, Dunaway gave birth to a son, Liam Dunaway O'Neill, and after playing Eva Perón in a 1981 NBC TV movie, she made her official return to motion pictures that September playing Joan Crawford in *Mommie Dearest*. The film, adapted from Christina Crawford's memoir about the traumatic upbringing she suffered at the hands of her notoriously abusive, compulsive, wire-hanger-wielding mother, had been a passion project for Dunaway. Terry O'Neill was named one of the film's producers, working alongside the former Paramount Pictures president Frank Yablans, who also served as one of its four credited screenwriters. "She's incredibly demanding," Yablans said of Dunaway, "but I'll take her any day over someone who doesn't care. I would work with her tomorrow and forever." Dunaway, who interviewed such golden-age Hollywood greats as Myrna Loy and George Cukor to prepare for the role, was unapologetic about her assertiveness on the production. "I really like things to be done right," she said. "I'm like Joan in that way."

Variety concisely summed up the public's estimation of *Mommie Dearest.* "Dunaway does not chew scenery," the trade publication wrote. "Dunaway starts neatly at each corner of the set in every scene and swallows it whole, costars and all. Prior to her death, Crawford once commented that Dunaway was among the best of up-and-coming young actresses. Too bad Crawford isn't around to comment now. Too bad Crawford isn't around to comment on the whole endeavor."

Dunaway was apparently more preoccupied with exorcising other ghosts from her past. In 1982 her lawyers sent an ominous letter to MGM and United Artists, charging that a television broadcast of *Network* shown on ITV in Britain "contains footage in which Ms. Dunaway's breasts are exposed" and therefore violates the long-ago agreement she had made to preclude "the use of nudity or semi-nudity and the inclusion of any scene in which Ms. Dunaway's character has a sexual climax or engages in sexual acts without Ms. Dunaway's express written consent." The studios responded that they "have no obligation to make any changes in the film at this time nor are we willing to do so. . . . These scenes have been in the finished motion picture since it was released in the fall of 1976 and shown throughout the world. We have been advised that the version being shown by ITV on television in the United Kingdom is the theatrical version and ITV has added no material to the version delivered to them. Ms. Dunaway has been aware of these scenes since 1976 and has never objected to them."

Speaking to an interviewer at his New York office some months
after he quit *Altered States*, Chayefsky said, "I feel almost totally alienated from what's going on today," adding that he now lived "kind of a
reclusive life almost. I went to dinner last night and the night before,
but I can't tell you how unusual that was. I mean, if I go out to dinner
once in five months it's a big deal. I'm dead tired today, the two days of
dining out are more than I can handle." In that sense, Chayefsky said
he felt like he was "coming back to contact with the American people.
I think perhaps they feel like I do, they really feel unable to cope. Life is
just too much. I take it the American people are becoming as alienated
as I am."

Asked what he thought it was that people were alienated from,
Chayefsky explained that it was essentially everything—"the business
of living." "The problems that face us are beyond any of our conception,"
he said. "I mean, what are you going to do about nuclear—what are you
going to do about the boat people, what are you going to do about anything? There's nothing you can do."

Echoing the words that he had once commanded Howard Beale to
speak, he added:

> I think the great distrust of the American people led them to
> become, "Look, just leave me alone, let me just have my little
> T.V. and let me take care of my little family and that's all I
> want to do." In that sense, I almost feel like they do. But I
> always wrote what I was. That was the one smart thing I did.
> I never tried to be what was out there, I always wrote the way
> I thought it was. So I maintained at least a working relation
> with reality.

After dismissing much of his career as a television and stage author,
as a hapless screenwriter for hire and a dramatist who could not exert
his will even when he had "every contractual control that you can
legally obtain," Chayefsky said the work of his that pleased him most

was *Network*. The day its editing was completed, he recalled, "Sidney Lumet turned to me and to the producer and to the head cutter, and said, 'I don't know how this is going to be received, but I think it's a goddam good movie.' And that's exactly how we all felt. You never know. After all it's a picture full of ideas, it didn't have much chance, I thought. And we might get by on it, we might get a little hit out of it. And we did."

On Christmas Day 1980, *Altered States* was finally released to a largely positive reception from critics, many of whom felt the film had faithfully executed Chayefsky's intentions. *Time*, in a rave review, said, "This one has everything: sex, violence, comedy, thrills, tenderness. It's an anthology and apotheosis of American pop movies: *Frankenstein*, *Murders in the Rue Morgue*, *The Nutty Professor*, *2001*, *Alien*, *Love Story*. It opens at fever pitch and then starts soaring—into genetic fantasy, into a precognitive dream of delirium and delight. Madness is its subject and substance, style and spirit." The *New York Times* noted that it was "easy to guess why" Chayefsky and Russell "didn't see eye to eye" on the film: "The direction, without being mocking or campy, treats outlandish material so matter-of-factly that it often has a facetious ring. The screenplay, on the other hand, cries out to be taken seriously, as it addresses, with no particular sagacity, the death of God and the origins of man." But if *Altered States* was not "wholly visionary at every juncture," the review observed, "it is at least dependably—even exhilaratingly—bizarre. Its strangeness, which borders cheerfully on the ridiculous, is its most enjoyable feature."

These plaudits were all lost on Chayefsky, who had refused his screenplay credit for the movie and instead attributed the script to a pseudonym: Sidney Aaron, his given first and middle names. The cumbersome attribution, as rendered in the film, reads, "Written for the Screen by Sidney Aaron / From the Novel *Altered States* by Paddy Chayefsky." At a party to celebrate his fifty-eighth birthday in January 1981, his friend Bob Fosse surprised Chayefsky with two cakes: one bearing the name Paddy Chayefsky, the other made out to Sidney Aaron.

Chayefsky had in the preceding months begun exploring a new project he hoped would mark his return to the theater: a historical drama about Alger Hiss, the accused Soviet spy and convicted perjurer, and a fictional young lawyer who fabricates evidence in an attempt to see Hiss vindicated. But that winter, Chayefsky developed a bad cough that worsened into pleurisy, an inflammation of the linings of the lungs and chest. When the ailment returned in February, he went to the hospital for testing and was diagnosed with cancer, the precise nature of which he did not tell even his wife or son. He declined surgery, believing it would surely kill him, but underwent chemotherapy that left him looking gaunt and turned his hair a shocking bone white. (Some friends said this was not his natural hair but a wig that he wore after his chemotherapy began.)

On July 4 he was admitted for treatment at Columbia Presbyterian Hospital in Manhattan. From his hospital bed, he told his family he was "having visions of great beauty." "They weren't delusional or hallucinatory," his son, Dan, recalled. "I thought they were very inspired." But as his condition worsened, he required an emergency tracheotomy to remove fluid that was building up in his lungs, and the surgery robbed him of the ability to speak. Chayefsky's great, angry, unyielding voice, which no occasion or adversary had ever been able to suppress, had been silenced at last.

Before he died at 11:45 A.M. on August 1, 1981, he wrote his last words on a pad to his wife, Susan. They read, "I tried. I really tried."

With the same prescient accuracy that informed so much of his writing, Paddy Chayefsky seemed to sense that he was not destined for old age. As Dan Chayefsky would later recall, "I once read his palm when I was young, and I said, 'You have a long life,'" which was of course not correct, because he died at fifty-eight. And he said, 'Oh, shit.'" As his father neared the end of his life, Dan said, "He almost willed himself to go. There was a lot of pressure on him, that he took on. I think if he had a choice to stay or go, he would go."

The author had seriously contemplated the likelihood of his own demise in the months after his 1977 heart attack, and at that time had drafted a set of instructions for his funeral, as precise and exacting as any script he had written, yet more forgiving and informal than any production he had previously overseen. He wanted the service "to be as easy on those attending as possible," and not to cause his family "unnecessary distress." A eulogy would be nice, the instructions continued, but not from "a rabbi who never met me in his life." "Since I don't know any rabbis that well," Chayefsky added, "I guess that leaves out rabbinical eulogies."

Furthermore, Chayefsky wrote in these directions, "Our family has never taken death all that seriously, and I don't want my death taken all that seriously either. Say what prayers have to be said to maintain my Jewishness; a few kind words about me from people who mean it would be appreciated; as brief and as painless a burial service at the cemetery as possible; and then back to the comfort of somebody's home where I honestly wish everybody a good time."

In keeping with these wishes, Chayefsky's funeral service was held on August 4 at Riverside Memorial Chapel on the Upper West Side, drawing more than five hundred attendees that included family members, friends, and admirers from throughout his career. In a eulogy, the historian Arthur M. Schlesinger Jr. said that the theme of Chayefsky's life's work had been "the corrupt and lunatic energies secreted by our great modern organizations . . . those energies that in time crazily explode through the deceptively rational surface of things." Despite his unsentimental bent, Schlesinger said, Chayefsky was "sardonic, not cynical. . . . For all his relish in human folly, he never abandoned hope in humanity. " Nodding to that first sympathetic television drama that had made Chayefsky's whole career possible, he added that the writer's gift for satire "sprang from love—from his instinctive, sweet understanding of the inarticulate Martys and Claras of the world, bravely living lives of quiet desperation."

Lumet said at the funeral, "Of all the people I worked with, the only one who is irreplaceable is Paddy." Bob Fosse said, "Paddy and I had a deal: If I died first, he'd tell jokes, and if he died first, I'd do a dance"; he began to perform a tap step but broke down crying. "I'm doing it for you, Paddy," he said through tears. "I can't imagine my life without you." Herb Gardner said in his remarks, "Paddy is dead, and when he finds out he's going to be mad as hell."

In one of the last interviews he gave before his death, Paddy Chayefsky offered his typically modest, emblematically skeptical wishes for how he wanted to be preserved by history. "A writer is what he writes," he said, "and I would like to be remembered as a good writer. I would like the stuff I write to be done and read for many generations. I just hope the world lasts that long."

8

IT'S ALL GOING TO HAPPEN

Speaking from his comfortably shabby office at 850 Seventh Avenue in the spring of 1981, Paddy Chayefsky offered his vision for what he expected the network news would look like someday—not as it might be depicted in *Network*, but as he believed it would appear on actual television sets as watched by people across the country. "There will be soothsayers soon," he asserted. *Network*, he said, "wasn't even a satire. I wrote a realistic drama. The industry satirizes itself."

Pointing to the rise of so-called happy news programs on ABC, Chayefsky asked, was this "much different from what I said was going to happen?" Instead of turning its news division over to a made-up figure such as Diana Christensen and her programming department, hadn't this network instead simply placed it under the direction of her real-life equivalent Roone Arledge, its young and innovative head of sports? "What's the difference?" Chayefsky grumbled. "It's all going to happen."

It is not hard to imagine readers in 1981 laughing to themselves at Chayefsky's remarks and the thought of this funny, fussy curmudgeon having fallen down the rabbit hole of his own prophecy. Certainly, *Network* was a passionate and sometimes wildly visionary movie. But it was just a movie. Even its most ardent admirers knew that it was an outrageous, over-the-top send-up of what could happen to television if all the wrong choices were made, not a step-by-step proposal for its eventual undoing. Anyone who was overly troubled by *Network* or who received its twisted wisdom with a straight face was a person not to be trusted entirely—even if that person was its own author.

Paddy Chayefsky lived and died in a world of three monolithic television broadcasters, invincible in their hegemony, transmitting their content to hundreds of millions of American viewers. There was only one way for them to present the news: stoic and serious, and read by a white man; the information offered by each network was generally identical to what the others provided, and its overall accuracy was regarded as unimpeachable. The only widely available means of instantaneous, two-way communication was the telephone, and keyboards were for typewriters, which were used to write letters, or possibly novels or screenplays, if you believed that you inhabited a world of ideas and were strong and single-minded enough to think that your thoughts and feelings could reshape it.

Yet to look at the American media landscape some three decades later is to see an environment that is unmistakably Chayefskyian. It is a realm where the oligarchy of the three networks has been assailed by a fourth rival and by a fifth, and overwhelmed by a hundred-pronged attack from cable, a metastasizing organism perpetually subdividing itself into smaller and narrower niches. Where nationally televised news had been a once-nightly ritual, it has since grown into a twenty-four-hour-a-day habit, available on channels devoted entirely and ceaselessly to its dissemination. The people who dispense these versions of the news seem to take their direction straight from the playbook of Howard Beale: they emote, they inveigh, and they instruct their audiences how to act and how to feel; some of them even cry on camera.

There is no longer one holistic system of news for audiences of every stripe, size, color, and creed: there is news for early-morning risers and news for late-night insomniacs; news for liberals and news for conservatives; sports news for men and feel-good news for women; news delivered in comedic voices and even, for a time, news for viewers who preferred to receive it from a Spanish-speaking puppet. Information is instantaneous and perilously subjective in an era when every man or woman can potentially be his or her own broadcaster. But when this array of apparently endless choice is untangled, and every cable wire and satellite beam is followed back to its source, what is revealed is a decidedly finite roster of media companies with the power to decide what is said and who is saying it: a college of corporations providing all necessities, tranquilizing all anxieties, amusing all boredoms.

Such a world may sound like the wildest dream of the *Network* corporate chief, Arthur Jensen, but it reverberates with the prophetic echoes of Howard Beale, who preached that television was "the ultimate revelation": "This tube is the most awesome goddam force in the whole godless world! And woe is us if it ever falls in the hands of the wrong people." And deeper still, one can hear the voice of Paddy Chayefsky, who warned without irony or tongue in cheek, "It's all going to happen."

In fact, it has already happened. And it is with only the slightest exaggeration that a contemporary screenwriter such as Aaron Sorkin can say, "No predictor of the future—not even Orwell—has ever been as right as Chayefsky was when he wrote *Network*."

So how did it happen?

"Chayefsky's warning was made to people who knew everything he said was true, but they felt powerless to stop it," said Peggy Noonan, the *Wall Street Journal* columnist and former speechwriter to presidents Ronald Reagan and George H. W. Bush, who in the late 1970s was a producer for CBS Radio. "It was as if a young doctor came into a great teaching hospital in nineteenth-century France and announced, 'I've figured it out, if we wash our hands before operating there will be fewer infections!' And the other doctors look at him and say, 'Yes, but we're not going to start washing our hands for a long time.' We're on an irrevocable slide in that department."

To a generation of television news professionals who came of age in the post-*Network* era, the film does not play as a radical comedy so much as a straightforward, that's-the-way-it-is statement of fact. Short of witnessing the assassination of an on-air personality, "I have seen everything in that movie come true, or it's happened to me," said Keith Olbermann, the former anchor of ESPN's *SportsCenter* and MSNBC's *Countdown*. "There have been enough broadcasters killed—it's just that we haven't gotten around to any of them being killed for bad ratings."

To Olbermann and many of his peers, whatever sanctity their industry still possessed was lost only a few years after Chayefsky's death. First came the 1986 maneuvering by the sibling corporate titans Robert Preston Tisch and Laurence A. Tisch that gave their Loews Corporation a substantial stake in CBS—at the time, the nation's second-place network, behind NBC—and helped put Laurence Tisch in charge of a broadcasting company saddled with $1 billion in debt. Next came the dark day in March 1987 when CBS fired 215 employees from its news department, despite an offer by CBS anchor Dan Rather and others to reduce their own salaries if it would save the jobs of some colleagues.

Before that day, the notion that news divisions were supposed to be self-supporting profit centers for their networks was broadcasting heresy. "They lost thirty million dollars a year," said Olbermann, "when thirty million dollars a year was not the price of the highest-paid baseball player—thirty million dollars bought you maybe sixty Walter Cronkites. It was essentially the charitable contribution that those three networks paid to be allowed to dump everything else on TV in the audience's mind." But, he added, "once news got out from under the sacrosanct umbrella of public service, of a commitment that the FCC demanded of the individual stations, it would become part of entertainment."

There is a self-admitted tendency in the news business to remember the broadcast industry's golden age as more pristine and objective than it actually was: even in its formative days, even before television was the dominant medium, Edward R. Murrow was delivering radio broadcasts from the London Blitz that, in their stark factuality, were also meant to encourage American intervention in World War II; later, on TV, he was making his "urbane small talk" with Samuel Goldwyn, Eva Gabor, and Groucho Marx on *Person to Person* while addressing the impact of McCarthyism on *See It Now*. Walter Cronkite wiped his watery eyes as he reported the assassination of John F. Kennedy and cheered the moon landing and editorialized against the Vietnam War, but he jostled privately with colleagues, chased ratings fervently, and made no secret of his liberal leanings. "God Almighty," he declared at a 1988 dinner honoring the Democratic congresswoman Barbara Jordan, "we've got to shout these truths in which we believe from the rooftops, like that scene in the movie *Network*. We've got to throw open our windows and shout these truths to the streets and to the heavens."

But something changed forever in the 1980s, as the networks and their news divisions were absorbed into larger conglomerates and wrung for every penny they could produce; and those journalists who kept their lucrative jobs were left, as *60 Minutes* creator Don Hewitt would later write, "in no position to join the chorus" of criticism against these troubling consolidations. "Why aren't we broadcast journalists hollering about it?" Hewitt asked. "Because we want it both ways. We want the companies we work for to put back the wall the pioneers erected to separate news from entertainment, but we are not above climbing over the rubble each week to take an entertainment-size paycheck for broadcasting news."

In that same era, the Federal Communications Commission in

1987 abolished its long-standing Fairness Doctrine, which was supposed to ensure that broadcasters covered crucial public issues with
impartiality and balance, and rules were relaxed that had prevented
the concentration and cross-ownership of media companies in the
hands of only a few parent corporations. When journalists entered the
industry after this point, they joined up accepting certain fundamental truths that would have horrified previous generations.

"It was everyone's basic understanding—and never necessarily
even spoken of as a problem, just a basic, tacit understanding—that the
information business was a *business*," said Bill Wolff, the vice president
of programming at MSNBC and executive producer of *The Rachel Maddow Show*, who began his career at ESPN in 1989. "You were responsible
to be profitable. It was true in sports in 1989, and it's true across the
board today."

The proliferation of cable television channels, which barely registered a blip in Chayefsky's day, has added hundreds of UBS-style networks to the programming grid, all scrambling to fill their airtime
with content that will deliver maximum returns on minimum investments, including a whole new breed of channels reporting the news for
increasingly narrow slivers of niche viewerships and aiming their coverage at partisan audiences.

"There's a segment of the viewing population which likes to either
have their opinion validated, or watch somebody they disagree with, and
connect with them in that way," said Anderson Cooper, CNN anchor
and *60 Minutes* correspondent.

And where these news channels have found devoted audiences,
there has simultaneously arisen a new category of anchors who see it as
their purpose to articulate their rage for them. "As a viewer, I watch
some people and I think, is that person really angry, or is this just part
of their shtick?" Cooper said. "Is this just what they do? They get their
veins pulsating and they're yelling. I can't imagine they're that angry
all day long. They've got to be gearing themselves up for it and then
putting on a show."

The cable channels and their on-air talent do not necessarily consider themselves as having political biases or identifying with specific ideologies or parties. But the concern and the sense of immediacy they say they feel are real. "As far as I'm concerned," said Bill O'Reilly, the Fox News personality and host of its top-rated show, *The O'Reilly Factor*, "I do my job, and I do it in an authentic way. If I'm mad as hell and not going to take it anymore, I'm going to say that. But it's not because of the movie—it's just because that's the way I feel."

O'Reilly sees himself as a successor to journalists such as John Chancellor, Eric Sevareid, and David Brinkley, who provided televised commentary and editorials but who "did it in a much more traditional, button-down way." "Today," O'Reilly said, "they'd never even get on the air. It's a different society—you have to raise the level of urgency and the level of presentation so that people will watch. There's just simply too many choices."

With this hypercompetitive broadcasting environment, O'Reilly said, comes the mandate not only to inform viewers but also to entertain them, even if it comes at the cost of overlooking important stories of the day. "We think our mission is basically to look out for the folks, to be a watchdog crew, an ombudsman sometimes," he said. "But to put on an entertaining program, it has to be entertaining, no doubt. I think Syria's an important story, but I can't cover it. Nobody's going to watch, and I know that. That's the limitations of my job."

Other contemporary newscasters have made it a virtue to wear their passions and emotions on their sleeve and cite *Network* sincerely as an inspiration for their work. Glenn Beck, the former CNN *Headline News* and Fox News commentator who now oversees his own satellite and Internet TV service, TheBlaze, has claimed Howard Beale as an influence and said that he identifies with the character's alienated, apocalyptic furor. "I think that's the way people feel," he has said. "That's the way I feel."

Popular frustration with events as well as with broadcasting—in both its traditional network mode and its excitable cable incarnations—has created opportunities for jesters such as Jon Stewart, who has become a reliable source of the news even as he mocks it on Comedy Central's *The Daily Show*; and his 2.0 upgrade Stephen Colbert, who, as the host of *The Colbert Report*, has turned news satire into a full-time act of performance art, creating an on-air alter ego who emulates the theatrical style of a partisan cable host while simultaneously illuminating the hypocrisy, dishonesty, and ignorance of such personalities. After hearing Glenn Beck observe that his influences included not only Howard Beale but Jesus, Gandhi, and Martin Luther King Jr., Colbert said, "I thought, wow, none of those stories end well."

The real-life Colbert calls *Network* his favorite movie, though he does not consider the film to be a direct inspiration for his vainglorious Stephen Colbert character. Howard Beale, Colbert said, is "a hopeless character who ultimately does not succeed in what he wants to do, and is killed. He's not a messianic figure."

But having studied his share of modern-day Beales, Colbert said that what *Network* correctly anticipated was an attitude these broadcasters share, which is, he said, "'I will tell you what to think.' That's what it prefigures most of all. 'I will tell you what to think and how to feel.'" When Howard Beale is preaching to his flock, at least he "is doing it in a quasi-benevolent way—'I'm going to remind you that you're being anaesthetized right now.'" What *Network* got right, Colbert said, "is a great bulk of what happens with news now. And not just the nighttime people that I'm sort of a parody of, not just the opinion-making people. But even what is left of straight news, that a long time ago became about how to dramatize the situation."

The fragmentation of the television news marketplace need not be an entirely negative development. One point on which broadcasters such as Bill O'Reilly and Anderson Cooper see eye to eye is that a wider array of choices has allowed more news, and more kinds of news presenters, to get on the air. "Back in Cronkite's day," Cooper said, "it was three white, middle-aged guys saying what the news was, and obviously there was a lot more going on. You didn't see people of color, you didn't see diversity on the screen, you didn't see a great diversity of people and stories. It was not representative of the United States." Today, O'Reilly concurred, "You have so many good options to get information and that's very, very healthy. Whereas twenty, twenty-five years ago, you were being told, hey, this is the way you should think and this is the way we see it—because all the networks pretty much see it the same, even today."

But not all their industry peers agree with the assessment that more avenues of information have created more diversity. "I don't know what diversity there is," said Gwen Ifill, senior correspondent of PBS's *NewsHour* and the moderator and managing editor of *Washington Week*. "You mean, other than me? I think that's where we've actually fallen down."

Ifill added that true diversity in news broadcasting is not necessarily measured on-screen, by "the people reading the news," but has to happen behind the scenes, based upon "who's in the room making the decisions about the news that does and does not get covered." "If you went and took a tour of most newsroom morning meetings, where the decisions are made," she said, "you'd still find mostly white male faces, maybe white female if you're lucky. And the higher you go in the news business, more Ivy League, more people who come from a pretty closed environment and upbringing. I think that's actually one of our great failures, is that we haven't figured out how to incorporate diversity of thinking—thought and experience and background."

She cautioned that trends in cable news did not reflect the state of play at the broadcast networks or on public television. "I don't see any sign that the cable networks are setting the tone," Ifill said. "They're functioning and thriving, to the extent that they thrive at all, on a completely different kind of journalism. To the extent that it is journalism."

Yet even in their decline, the network news broadcasts still command audiences larger than their cable television counterparts. At the end of 2012, each of the three network programs drew between 6.9 million and 9.4 million viewers a night. These are numbers that the cable competition simply cannot touch: in a comparable period, *The O'Reilly Factor* was watched by an average of 3.52 million viewers, while *The Rachel Maddow Show* was seen by 1.69 million, and *Anderson Cooper 360* drew 913,000.

What concerns broadcast journalists on both sides of the divide is that, as surely as the distinctions between the network news and entertainment have gradually eroded, the proverbial firewall between acceptably overheated cable news commentary and genteel network news objectivity will someday be annihilated—most likely when it makes good business sense for these channels' parent companies.

In his tenure at MSNBC, Keith Olbermann—who was known to dress up in the soggy raincoat of Howard Beale and impersonate the character on his show from time to time—said he resisted efforts to make his pointed political commentaries a permanent element of his *Countdown* program, but went along with experiments to air his cable news show on its sibling broadcast network. "We ran *Countdown* several times on NBC, up against *60 Minutes*, to see basically if the universe would melt," he said. "And it didn't."

What such trials inevitably portend, Olbermann said, is the broadcast networks' gradual incorporation of more partisan content and entertainment-style formats first developed in the laboratories of their cable channels. "If you told the heads of ABC, CBS, and NBC News," he said, "that they could prolong the life of these cash cows at six thirty"—that is, their evening news shows—"by adding Keith Olbermann commentary every night or Bill O'Reilly commentary every night or Glenn Beck commentary every night, I don't know what the outcome would be. But eventually one of them would say yes. And certainly there'd be people saying yes right now."

Even without adding politically polarized commentary to its flag-ship evening news show, a network such as NBC already undermines its own integrity by simultaneously operating news shows, hard and soft, neutral and partisan, all under the same corporate banner. "What do you do," Olbermann asked, "when your brand is on so-called pure news, and on something like *The Today Show* and on MSNBC? Can you have that logo represented by Brian Williams, Katie Couric, and Keith Olbermann? It becomes a juggling act."

Bill Wolff of MSNBC said he expected that cable-style news would continue to coexist with its rival media and would not cannibalize tra-ditional print, radio, and network television offerings. But to the extent that such news outlets continue to exist, he said, they validated a blunt Chayefskyian lesson in capitalist economics. "There is still a tremen-dous appetite for straight, sober information," said Wolff. "The reason it's there is that there is demand for it."

It is a lesson that Wolff said applies in his corner of the industry, too. "If no one were watching Rachel Maddow, there wouldn't be a *Rachel Maddow Show*," he said. "But people are, because there's demand for it. She's intellectually rigorous and she's extremely ethical, so she's to the good. And the reason she gets to be on TV is that a big company makes a lot of money because people watch her."

But when such a responsibility is taken away from broadcasters themselves and yielded to the phantom forces of the market, what remains is the reality that it is up to viewers to decide for themselves who is truthful and reliable and who is providing them with informa-tion that is accurate—a conclusion that O'Reilly said is the moral he took away from *Network*.

"The movie, I thought, was about the audience more than the pre-senters," he said. "And that the audience was demanding more and more craziness and stimulation from the news presentation." A careful viewing of *Network*, O'Reilly said, shows that "Chayefsky is chiding the audience more than he is chiding the people like Howard Beale, and that, I think, is a legitimate concern. The audience, in many, many cases, is going for the lowest common denominator."

Still, even broadcast journalists have their guilty viewing pleasures. For Anderson Cooper it is Walter Mercado, the astrologer who gave daily readings on the Univision news show *Primer Impacto*. "He looks like Liberace, in capes and everything, and he would have two cameras," Cooper said. "And he'd look at one camera and he'd be like, '*Tauro*,' and then he'd give the horoscope for Taurus; then he'd do a very dramatic turn on the other camera and be, '*Gemini*,' and then he would give the Gemini forecast for the day."

There won't be soothsayers soon; they are already here.

Network is ultimately just a movie. But it is a movie that accom-plished something truly remarkable and even radical: it used the money and the means of production of the Hollywood motion picture industry to criticize not only a rival medium but the entire field of mass communication, the vast system of corporations nested within corporations that contained it, and a distinctly American way of life that these institutions dictated. The film starred several of the top actors of its era and was made with one of its most celebrated directors at the helm; it was designed to reach the widest possible swath of movie-goers, and it succeeded in selling tickets by the millions, gaining critical acclaim, and winning approbation at the Academy Awards. It did this all while awakening its viewers to ugly and unflattering truths about their lives and the world they inhabited, and it did not communicate its messages in a subtle or soft-spoken manner: it put its most urgent and passionate ideas in the mouth of a man who at times is literally screaming them at his audience, commanding them to go to their windows and scream their dissatisfaction themselves.

These qualities can make *Network* seem like a onetime occurrence: the result of a rare confluence of an author with a mission to make his voice heard, a movie business that cared more about being taken seriously than (or at least as much as) about turning profits, and audiences eager to be engaged by challenging ideas. In an age when all the major broadcast networks are now either owned by or affiliated with a motion picture and entertainment conglomerate, and when their empires have grown to include cable TV channels and home video distribution services that exploit and repurpose the content they create, it is hard to imagine a studio turning its guns on itself in the same way, let alone providing one angry man with the ammunition to satirize them so savagely.

Was Paddy Chayefsky the last member of a class of dramatists who would grab you by the lapels and shout in your face if that was what it took to get you to pay attention? And when he correctly predicted the conditions that would lead to the diminishment of television news and the networks that broadcast it, was he also anticipating the circumstances that would spell the demise of the confrontationally consciousness-raising style of moviemaking he purveyed? Or does his rabble-rousing, mad-as-hell spirit live on in some part of mainstream Hollywood entertainment?

Some filmmakers who hit their stride in the period following Chayefsky's argue that there is a retrospective tendency to romanticize the 1970s as a decade when it was somehow easier to make studio movies with strong points of view. "It's never easy," said Oliver Stone, who became enamored of *The Hospital* soon after he graduated from New York University's film school in 1971. "It wasn't easy back in the seventies, and it's certainly not easy now. People complain about that, but if you do it, you do it. It gets done."

Stone first wrote some of his best-known scripts in the late 1970s, including *Platoon* (which would later win him an Oscar for best director and a nomination for best screenplay), in 1976, the year of *Network*'s release, and *Born on the Fourth of July* (which would eventually earn him another Oscar for best director), in 1979, but both were considered too risky—"too downbeat, too realistic"—to get made at the time, and would remain on hold for at least a decade.

Network, for all of its fire and brimstone, was nonetheless propelled along by the part of Chayefsky that knew how to keep audiences amused even as he was exhorting them. "You've got to make it entertaining enough as a whole," Stone said. "Sometimes you need that soapy advertising line. 'I'm mad as hell and I'm not going to take this anymore'—whoever thought that line would go down? He wrote so many brilliant lines; that's not his best. But that line for some reason caught on."

But what made the difference in getting *Network* produced was Chayefsky's single-minded drive to see it brought to the screen. "He sweated buckets to do what he did," Stone said, "and sometimes I guess you've got to be a little bit tougher, because you're going to get your heart broken."

Even if the modern-day movie studios could countenance a film as volatile as *Network*, Stone said the economics of such a movie would likely make it untenable, with no way to satisfy their needs for mammoth opening-weekend grosses and ongoing franchises. "They had to make bigger and bigger tent poles in order to attract attention," he said. "The occasional blockbuster became the ordinary event. You have to open on a Friday with numbers that are essentially the old blockbuster numbers, and no one can rub the wheel that way and not get ground up at the end of the day."

James L. Brooks, who revisited the scene of the cutthroat television newsroom for his 1987 romantic comedy *Broadcast News*, said he could still envision a category of studio filmmaking that *Network* would fit into today. "It was great," said Brooks. "Could I imagine a great movie getting made today? Yeah. That's the genre. The genre is: great."

Brooks, who was himself a thoroughly accomplished television writer and producer before he turned to writing and directing his own films, knew Chayefsky casually in his career and attended the author's funeral. But while *Broadcast News* explores some of the same issues as *Network* (albeit with a gentler, more humanistic approach)—the moral responsibility of mass communication and the toll it exacts from the people who produce it—Brooks said his film was not inspired by Chayefsky's. Rather, Brooks was looking to tell a story about a certain kind of woman who defined the moment—and not Diana Christensen. At that time in the mid-1980s, Brooks said, "Every picture was a feminist picture, every picture was saying the same thing. And I just felt, really, in my gut, that there was a different kind of woman happening, and to try to find her."

The preliminary research that Brooks, a self-described "news junkie," did for his *Broadcast News* characters at the 1984 Republican and Democratic national conventions revealed attitudes that were far less respectful to the news media than when Chayefsky undertook his own similar investigations a decade prior. Brooks said of one TV journalist (whom he declined to identify), "He had gotten a job because he was a pretty face, and I had this pissy attitude toward him. Then, during the course of the interview, I realized he knew they were laughing at him; he knew they were feeling superior to him." As surely as he saw in this person the recognition that his own viewers regarded him as inadequate, Brooks said he saw the inverse in himself: "feeling like an asshole that I had been one of those smug people."

Broadcast News, which concludes with a wave of firings and corporate restructurings that scrambles the lives of its characters, arrived in theaters only a few months after the industry-altering bloodletting at CBS News. Brooks said he did not require any clairvoyance to see it coming. "I was chasing a movie that was happening in front of me, that's basically it," he said. "Everything about the movie was based on conversations and just really doing the homework."

In spite of his optimism that a provocative film such as *Network* could still find favor in the studio system, Brooks wondered whether the uniquely nonconformist talent required to create it could still navigate contemporary Hollywood without being corrupted. "It's very, very tricky, 'cause everybody's been co-opted—almost everybody," he said. "Somebody comes out here and they write a good screenplay, and all of a sudden they have a lawyer; all of a sudden they have a company name. Every man a salesman."

Even if such a person could bring this idea to bear, Brooks wondered whether a movie studio would still be able to recognize its intrinsic value. "It used to be that the pursuit of excellence was part of the conversation," Brooks said. "I did just have a studio head say to me, 'My prayer is every day, don't let me make something just because I like it'—saying it like it was a badge of honor."

To a new class of filmmakers who idolize the movies of the 1970s—in many cases the decade when they first started going to the movies—features such as *Three Days of the Condor* and *All the President's Men* represent a quintessence of cinematic realism and social consciousness combined with commercial success, yet something about *Network* exceeds them. "The difference between commerce and art is that in art there is a kind of insurgency," said Ben Affleck, the actor and director. "And there's a profound insurgency in *Network*."

Affleck, who stylistically modeled his 2012 Iranian hostage thriller, *Argo*, on the hit dramas and suspense movies of the film's turn-of-the-eighties setting, also included in his film the real-life news footage of a man who quotes Howard Beale's "Mad as hell" speech to express his sense of helplessness about the hostage crisis. For Affleck, this moment was his tip of the hat to the enduring resonance of Chayefsky's words, and how "society was still really informed by that perspective on the world—that sense of being beaten down and the game is rigged."

"In *Network*," Affleck said, "we're straining against the confines of corporatism and complacency, and the other pernicious effects of society are starting to strangle us, and we want to break out of that—even if it's through a kind of madness or illogical behavior. That's a theme, an undercurrent in the era."

If the twenty-first-century equivalents of *Network* seem harder to find on movie studios' release schedules, Affleck said that may be partly the fault of directors preemptively talking themselves out of such projects. "There's been a ghettoization of these kinds of films, and part of that's self-conscious because people go, 'Oh, no one's going to see this, so I'm just going to make it for a few people,'" he said.

But other key dynamics of the entertainment industry, well known to Chayefsky and his peers, have not changed. "The studios then, like they are now, are influenced almost exclusively by the marketplace," Affleck said. "If people are going to see superhero movies in huge numbers, that's what they're going to keep making. Then, it was cool to make interesting movies. *Kramer vs. Kramer* was a blockbuster and made people rich. *Kramer vs. Kramer* wouldn't make people rich today. There's a bunch of those movies that came out then that would now be vying, basically, for a slot at Sundance."

To make a movie like *Argo*—a film that gives nearly equal consideration to Iran's position in the events that precipitated the hostage crisis as it does to America's—Affleck knew that he would have to trade in part on his celebrity and the desire of a studio to want to remain in business with him. But what such projects ultimately come down to is a filmmaker's will. "It can get made, but you have to want to make it," he said. "You've got to believe in that kind of film as something that is relevant and that can work to a broader audience. It's definitely possible."

The public's eroding esteem for the news media, not to mention its progressively diminished expectations for an entertainment industry that can defy its expectations or speak to it intelligently, has not stopped dramatists from continuing to view the television newsroom as a tantalizing crucible of character and human conflict. "People become aware of very dramatic things first," said MSNBC's Bill Wolff. "We know about stuff first. And then there is a lot of drama in the decision making about how to report and what to report." He continued, "Among the non-heroic, non-lifesaving professions, ours is pretty dramatic"— even if, he added, "we're not nearly as important as we think we are."

Nor have the years since *Network*'s release seen any appreciable reduction in the uneasiness we feel about the world around us. While there may be no way to determine if the number of existential threats we face on a daily basis has increased or decreased, we have more media than ever at our disposal to educate us about crises and catastrophes brewing anywhere on the globe, and we have become increasingly accustomed to having this information delivered to us instantly. "In the 1970s," said Wolff, "mass communication was still in its infancy, and it had a greater effect on people's level of anxiety. People are just used to it now. The choice was: become numb to the threats or become paralyzed by fear."

So it was a bittersweet moment in 2011 when Aaron Sorkin took the stage of the Kodak Theatre to accept his Academy Award for the screenplay of *The Social Network*, a motion picture about the dizzying reach of mass media, the responsibility of wielding it, and the enmity it stirs up in the people who do. Sorkin, who in his television series *Sports Night, The West Wing*, and *The Newsroom* offers his own idealized visions of how information is transmitted to the American people, began his Oscar acceptance speech by saying, "It's impossible to describe what it feels like to be handed the same award that was given to Paddy Chayefsky thirty-five years ago, for another movie with *Network* in the title." As Sorkin said later, "The commoditization of the news and the devaluing of the truth are just a part of our way of life now. You wish Chayefsky could come back to life long enough to write *The Internet*."

Paddy Chayefsky was an accidental prophet. For all the iras-cible, after-the-fact certainty he professed about *Network* and the specter of television's future that it predicted, his ambitions in creating it were grander and more wide-reaching. He sought to do more than simply speculate on the fortunes of a medium he alternately regarded as past its prime and eternal, and whose true capacity for decadence would not come into view for many years after his death, in forms that even a wit as uncompromising as his had suggested only as jokes. He

242 MAD AS HELL

shared perhaps a little too much with his greatest creation, Howard Beale, a forecaster attuned to higher truths whose origins he could not pinpoint, and who, in his lifetime, would not see his divinations appreciated for their accuracy.

What Chayefsky understood best of all, better than television and better than the business behind it, was anger: omnipresent in his own life, in his frustrations and his failures as well as his successes, and how it had become an indivisible part of the American character. Rage fueled competition, put wind in sails, and powered that patriotic desire to succeed at all costs; it also offered cover from all the world's unfairness and uncertainty, and protection from the elements that gave rise to what the uninitiated and naïve dismissed as paranoia but that an educated, attentive few knew were worthy and sensible fears. Sometimes it was the only way to get people's attention. Chayefsky saw a country burning from the heat of its thwarted ambitions and the friction of running up against its own limitations, and no matter his life span, he knew that those fires would only grow stronger and hotter in time.

In *Network*, Chayefsky bequeathed to America more than a movie, more than its characters or their lasting speeches, even if it could all be distilled down to those few words that the author himself never gave any special credence. To declare for yourself that you were mad as hell and not going to take it anymore was not just a way to rally fans at sporting events, to protest the loss of your economic security, gun rights, or health care access, or to vent your desire to maintain a vegan diet in a world biased toward carnivores—although it would become the rallying cry in all these scenarios and many more like them. It was an act of acknowledging all the forms of anger that preceded it and the unknown expressions yet to come, a plea for basic dignity and a recognition that in anger there was power and there was community. It said that it was permissible to be angry, and if all you could do was be angry, it was enough.

As his friend the writer-director Joshua Logan said of Chayefsky,

"You can't build for the future with nice, polite people. They're too round. What you need are concrete blocks like Paddy." Thick, sturdy, stubborn, and unrelenting, Chayefsky could be a vessel to contain those flames, but he was also occasionally the great gust of air that stoked them. His only peace was in shouting ever more loudly. Nothing made him madder than voicelessness. And he shouted.

Notes

All citations beginning CP, followed by a box number and a folder number, refer to the Paddy Chayefsky papers (1907–1998, bulk 1952–1981), archived at the Billy Rose Theatre Division of the New York Public Library for the Performing Arts, New York, NY.

1. The Imposter

8   Lee Marvin and Clint Eastwood couldn't "sing for shit": Shaun Considine, *Mad as Hell: The Life and Work of Paddy Chayefsky* (New York: Random House, 1994), p. 249.

8   They were three Jewish show business veterans kibitzing around a table: This story is derived from an author's interview with Howard Gottfried, Mar. 9, 2012, and from Chayefsky's own fictionalized account of the event in the pilot treatment of *The Imposters* (CP, Box 127, Folder 8).

10   "television has been a kind medium": Paddy Chayefsky, *Television Plays* (New York: Simon and Schuster, 1955), pp. ix–xiv.

11   "Are people any wiser than they were a hundred years ago?": Paddy Chayefsky, *The Collected Works of Paddy Chayefsky: The Television Plays* (New York: Applause Books, 1994), p. 79.

12   Chayefsky wandered away from rehearsals and encountered a leftover sign: Tom Stempel, *Storytellers to the Nation: A History of American Television Writing* (New York: Continuum Publishing, 1992), p. 49.

13   "Sooner or later," he declares, "there comes a point in a man's life": Chayefsky, *Television Plays*, p. 154.

13   "You don't like her. My mother don't like her": Ibid., p. 182.

13   "it tried to show love to be a very real emotion": Paddy Chayefsky, "Playwright Turns Self-Critic," *TV Guide*, Oct. 22, 1955.

14   "We thought that 'Marty' was based upon, a lot, on Paddy Chayefsky": Interview for PBS, *The Golden Age of Television*, Aug. 29, 1981.

14   born on January 29, 1923, in the Bronx home of his parents: CP, Box 166, Folder 3.

14   "the rich Bronx—in the Riverdale section—not the Odets Bronx": J. P. Shanley, "Big Decision on a Bronx Gridiron," *New York Times*, Dec. 12, 1954.

14   His bar mitzvah was held at a storefront synagogue on West 234th Street: Considine, *Mad as Hell*, p. 12.

15   "My parents weren't writers but they were great readers": Carol Taylor, "I'm Never a Prima Donna at Work," *World-Telegram and Sun* (New York), June 7, 1958.

15   a machine-gun-wielding infantryman in the army's 104th Division: CP, Box 166, Folder 3. According to his discharge papers, Chayefsky incurred the injury on Nov. 23, 1944.

15   "We were out on patrol": Considine, *Mad as Hell*, p. 22.

16   "Paddy is built like an office safe": Joshua Logan, *Movie Stars, Real People, and Me* (New York: Dell, 1978), p. 116.

16   "I thought I was the sloppiest soldier in the Army": Helen Dudar (with Sally Hammond and Jack Fox), "A Post Portrait: Paddy Chayefsky," *New York Post*, Jan. 4, 1960.

16   "I copied it out word for word": Elliot Norton, "Chayefsky Learned by Copying a Play," *Boston Daily Record*, Mar. 14, 1958.

17   "I stormed and ranted": Philip Minoff, "Chayefsky Churns Ahead," *Cue*, Nov. 28, 1953.

17   "Nobody called me to tell me what night they were putting it on": George Anthony, "Chayefsky's Latest—All Fabricated, All Fiction and All True," *Toronto Sun*, Mar. 14, 1976.

17   "the most perishable item known to man": Rod Serling, *Patterns* (New York: Bantam, 1957), introduction.

17   "He had the gift of melding significance and meaning and humor": Author interview with Carol Serling, May 23, 2012.

18   "My position is nonnegotiable": John Brady, *The Craft of the Screenwriter* (New York: Simon and Schuster, 1981), p. 37.

18   All his demands were accepted: Reg Ovington, "TV's Fair-Haired Boy," *Pictorial TView*, Mar. 27, 1955.

18   "studio story editors better spend more time at home": Ronald Holloway, review of *Marty*, *Variety*, Mar. 22, 1955.

18   "the whole truth and nothing but the truth about the unattached male": "Cinema: The New Pictures," *Time*, Apr. 18, 1955.

19   "The industry has no pride and no culture": Joe Hyams, "Chayefsky Assails TV as Stupid and Doomed," *New York Herald Tribune*, Sept. 2, 1957.

19   "frankly demanding to be relieved of the epithet": Paddy Chayefsky, "Not So Little," *New York Times*, July 15, 1956.

19   "a short, stocky and heavy-shouldered chap": Minoff, "Chayefsky Churns Ahead."

19 "a squarish, hefty young playwright": "People Are Talking About . . . ," *Vogue*, Oct. 15, 1955.

19 "a chunky, Bronx-born, reformed éclair addict": Dudar, "A Post Portrait."

20 "Mr. Chayefsky did not wear a hat": Don Ross, "Chayefsky Is Bearded and Busy," *New York Herald Tribune*, Jan. (possibly Feb.) 22, 1959.

20 "Once they got control, it would be so dehydrated": "Chayefsky Walks Out on Psychiatric Series in Hassle over Control," *Variety*, Oct. 25, 1958.

20 "They did everything possible to divert our attention": Dudar, "A Post Portrait."

20 he was "sick of" Broadway due to "economic futility": "Irked Chayefsky Says He's 'Sick' of Broadway, Will Work Elsewhere," Associated Press, June 3, 1962.

21 "I should never have tried to direct it, too": Frances Herridge, "Chayefsky Says It with Humor," *New York Post*, Nov. 23, 1964.

21 "so rich, deep, comic and pitiable": Clive Barnes, "Theater: 'The Latent Heterosexual,'" *New York Times*, Mar. 22, 1968.

21 "the best platform to express meaningful drama": Kay Gardella, "A Chayefsky Deal with CBS," *Daily News* (New York), Dec. 8, 1967.

22 they struck a deal with CBS in July 1969: Val Adams, "Chayefsky Writing CBS-TV Pilot," *Daily News* (New York), July 15, 1969.

22 a three-part *TV Guide* series he had been reading that summer: Richard Warren Lewis, "The Man on the 34th Floor," *TV Guide*, July 12–18, 1969; July 19–25, 1969; and July 26–Aug. 1, 1969.

23 "We're not in the business of good drama": CP, Box 127, Folder 8.

24 "Well, Charley, what do you feel like doing?": Ibid.

24 "Mike said, 'I'm sorry—we can't do this'": Author interview with Howard Gottfried, Mar. 9, 2012.

25 "the hospital represents American society": CP, Box 127, Folder 3.

25 *The Latent Humanitarian*: A. H. Weiler, "What's Up, Doc? Murder!" *New York Times*, Aug. 2, 1970.

25 "They didn't bother you": Author interview with Howard Gottfried, Mar. 9, 2012.

26 he "just couldn't work" with Ritchie: Considine, *Mad as Hell*, p. 278.

26 "I've lost my raison d'etre, my purpose": Paddy Chayefsky, *The Collected Works of Paddy Chayefsky: The Screenplays Vol. II* (New York: Applause Books, 1994), pp. 53–54.

27 in April 1972, Chayefsky gave a brief acceptance speech: Paddy Chayefsky, Academy Awards acceptance speech, Apr. 10, 1972, aaspeechesdb.oscars.org/link/044-22/.

27 "Those other four guys, they got mothers, too": Ernest Tidyman, Academy Awards acceptance speech, Apr. 10, 1972, http://www.youtube.com/watch?v=uad8qcBIRS4.

27 "someone had asked him to go up to Hefner's": Author interview with Warren Beatty, Nov. 8, 2012.

28 newer and more unconventional treatments, including the drug Elavil: Considine, *Mad as Hell*, p. 289.

28 "She was a perfectionist": Author interview with Dan Chayefsky, Mar. 1, 2013.

28 In one instance she went into a frenzy: Considine, *Mad as Hell*, p. 335.

28 "It almost gave her withdrawal a cause": Author interview with Dan Chayefsky, Mar. 1, 2013.

29 "He was a fortress, my dad": Ibid.

29 Dan remained by himself in the family apartment: Considine, *Mad as Hell*, p. 294.

29 "I was just very self-destructive and very lost": Author interview with Dan Chayefsky, Mar. 1, 2013.

29 "he brought this bonfire to his office": Ibid.

30 he was not some "new-Mobe militant or placard carrier": CP, Box 140, Folder 24.

30 "Six million went up with a snap of the finger": G. Y. Dryansky, "Chayefsky: 'Save the Jews,'" *Women's Wear Daily*, 1971.

31 "I don't know that it's that guy": Author interview with David Steinberg, May 10, 2012.

31 "These Arabs would like you to believe": Display advertisement, *New York Times*, Dec. 17, 1973.

31 a screenplay set in the West Bank about a pair of police officers: CP, Box 123, Folder 3.

32 "There is a Jew dog here!" CP, Box 126, Folder 5.

32 "I'll tell you about your civilized world!": Ibid.

33 "Now, one might say it was in the contract": Author interview with Howard Gottfried, Mar. 9, 2012.

33 "they said they couldn't make it in Jerusalem": Author interview with Maurice Spanbock, June 21, 2012.

34 "they broke up the fee for the whole bundle": Author interview with Howard Gottfried, Mar. 9, 2012.

34 the IRS said *The Goddess* was Columbia's property: "Limit Indies Loan Credits," *Variety*, Feb. 21, 1973.

34 a tax bill of $86,770, plus a $5,248 penalty for late filing: "Chayefskys Are Losers," *Variety*, Feb. 13, 1973.

34 "the main character is a revered and retired old rabbi": CP, Box 137, Folder 10.

35 *Your Place or Mine*: CP, Box 137, Folder 6.

35 "He said he could not master it": Author interview with Dan Chayefsky, Mar. 1, 2013.

2. Strangelove-y as Hell

37 "I'm going to spend the day with you": Author interview with Richard Wald, Feb. 2, 2012.

37 *HUT ratings. Audience flow. The dark weeks*: CP, Box 91, Folder 9.

37 "I expected grunts": Author interview with Richard Wald, Feb. 2, 2012.

38 "it is an indestructible and terrifying giant": CP, Box 93, Folder 4.

39 "the American people are angry and want angry shows": Ibid.

39 Chayefsky recorded the clockwork precision of their schedules: CP, Box 91, Folder 2.

40 a *60 Minutes* segment from March 10, 1974, titled "The Ratings War": CP, Box 91, Folder 3.

41 "Cats, Dogs and Underdogs": Les Brown, "Livelier and Longer TV News Spurs Hunt for Talent," *New York Times*, Apr. 22, 1974.

41 "You win because you have a competitive edge": Pat Polillo, Remarks to National Association of Television Program Executives convention, Los Angeles, Feb. 19, 1974.

42 "The Atlanta trip made it clear that there was nothing": Author interview with Howard Gottfried, Mar. 9, 2012.

42   "the concept of RATINGS UBER ALLES": CP, Box 91, Folder 9.

43   "FAUST + MEPHISTOPHELES today": CP, Box 91, Folder 10.

43   "If you can get in four good hours a day": Brady, *Craft of the Screenwriter*, p. 60.

43   haphazardly furnished with a piano: Ibid., pp. 31, 60.

43   The view his workspace offered: Joan Barthel, "Paddy Chayefsky: 'TV Will Do Anything for a Rating. Anything!'" *New York Times*, Nov. 14, 1976.

44   "BY THE END OF THE PICTURE": CP, Box 92, Folder 2.

44   "a tough, but righteous fellow": CP, Box 91, Folder 1.

45   a nod to the baseball pitcher Harold "Prince Hal" Schumacher: Author interview with Howard Gottfried, Mar. 31, 2012.

45   "His method of doing this is to adopt a tabloid attitude": CP, Box 92, Folder 1.

45   "ten minutes into the news cast he flips out": Ibid.

45   "this time, his flip is not an unruly, profanity-ridden flip out": Ibid.

46   "we put a raging prophet on the air, a prophet in the biblical sense": Ibid.

47   "In keeping with Channel 40's policy": Jon Dietz, "On-Air Shot Kills TV Personality," *Sarasota Herald-Tribune*, July 16, 1974.

47   "like that girl in Florida": CP, Box 95, Folder 5.

47   a set of screenplay notes dated July 16, 1974: CP, Box 93, Folder 1.

47   "tall, willowy and with the best ass ever seen": CP, Box 94, Folder 4.

48   "Howard doesn't need the encouragement. He gets madder and madder": CP, Box 93, Folder 1.

48   "She looks him up and down": Ibid.

48   "Leader of the People guy": CP, Box 92, Folder 6.

48   "the individual human will be just a piston rod in the whole vast machinery": CP, Box 93, Folder 1.

49   Chayefsky wrote year-by-year biographies for his characters: CP, Box 91, Folder 9.

49   *Surgeon's Hospital*, *Pedro and the Putz*, *Celebrity Canasta*: CP, Box 92, Folder 5.

49   a page-long list of synonyms for the verb *corrupt*: CP, Box 92, Folder 10.

49   a separate, three-page list of the increasingly ominous political calamities: CP, Box 93, Folder 1.

50   "the states of human consciousness": CP, Box 62, Folder 3.

50   "If their show is a hit, they already have attention—Ransom?" CP, Box 93, Folder 3.

50   "if he assassinates Beale and takes film of it": Ibid.

51   "We've got to replace Beale": Ibid.

51   "THE SHOW LACKS A POINT OF VIEW": CP, Box 93, Folder 2.

52   "This story is about Howard Beale": CP, Box 92, Folder 6.

53   "She sank into an overstuffed chair": Ibid.

53   "What was this, some kind of demented gag!" CP, Box 92, Folder 8.

54   "He was hoping I'd fall on my face with this Beale show": CP, Box 94, Folder 1.

54   Howard Beale is found by his housekeeper: CP, Box 92, Folder 5.

54   Beale's nineteen-year-old daughter, Celia: CP, Box 92, Folder 9.

54   a psychiatrist, Dr. Sindell: CP, Box 94, Folder 1.

54   "Its propagandist potential hasn't even been touched": Ibid.

54   *The Madame Defarge Show* and something called *Rape of the Week*: CP, Box 95, Folder 1.

55 "You and Ed Murrow and Fred Friendly": CP, Box 92, Folder 7.

55 "If I could stand the taste of liquor I'd be a lush": CP, Box 92, Folder 9.

55 "it was nipple clear that she was bra-less": CP, Box 92, Folder 8.

56 "Sounds like good family entertainment": CP, Box 92, Folder 10.

56 "I'll try to make a home with you": CP, Box 93, Folder 7.

57 "We're born in terror and we live in terror": CP, Box 93, Folder 6.

57 "Wayward husband comes to his senses": Chayefsky, *The Screenplays Vol. II*, p. 216.

57 "We can hear the CLICK of the door being opened": Ibid.

58 "I don't have to tell you things are bad": Ibid., pp. 173–74.

60 "Since that production," the article said, "nothing": Richard Hatch, "Follow-Up on the News: Paddy Chayefsky," *New York Times*, Jan. 12, 1975.

60 "She had the kind of skin that doesn't need powder or makeup": Considine, *Mad as Hell*, p. 334.

61 "I got the wedding; Paddy got the honeymoon": Author interview with Mary Lynn Gottfried, Mar. 31, 2012.

61 Susan offered Paddy her comments, recorded on a memo pad: CP, Box 95, Folder 2.

63 Chayefsky received an offer on June 24: CP, Box 213, Folder 10.

64 "People thought about making good movies to make money": Author interview with Mike Medavoy, Mar. 12, 2012.

64 A deal offered by United Artists for the *Network* screenplay in the fall of 1974: CP, Box 182, Folder 1. As executed, the deal paid Chayefsky in six installments of $50,000: on signing; on delivery of the script; on approval of the film's budget and director; on approval of its principal cast; on completion of principal photography; and the final deferment.

64 the studio gave a substantial 42.5 percent of any net profits from the picture to Chayefsky's Simcha Productions: CP, Box 214, Folder 2. Those profits were then split between Chayefsky and Gottfried, who also received a producer's fee of $110,000 and a further $15,000 for "script supervising services."

64 An internal MGM memo cited "an off-the-record speculation": CP, Box 96, Folder 3.

65 *Network* "is all madness and bullshit philosophy": Considine, *Mad as Hell*, p. 310.

65 "I turned to both of them and I said, 'Are you serious?'": Author interview with Mike Medavoy, Mar. 12, 2012.

65 Summarizing a May 15 meeting with the United Artists executive Dan Rissner: CP, Box 215, Folder 8. Chayefsky was not particularly consistent about the spelling of the name of the Great Ahmed Kahn. In the closing credits of *Network*, his surname is given as "Kahn," while some screenplay drafts and script pages render it as "Khan."

66 "He says, 'Listen, guys, it's a great script'": Author interview with Howard Gottfried, Mar. 9, 2012.

67 "They didn't want to have anything to do with it": Considine, *Mad as Hell*, p. 312.

68 "he made it plain that UA would look like assholes": Author interview with Howard Gottfried, Mar. 9, 2012.

68 *Variety* reported that MGM and United Artists had made a deal: "Chayefsky's 'Network' Via Metro and UA," *Variety*, July 2, 1975.

3. A Great Deal of Bullshit

69 a budget of about $4 million: According to the film's production designer, Philip Rosenberg, the budget for *Network* may have been as little as $3.5 million.

70 One list of candidates compiled by Chayefsky: CP, Box 95, Folder 6.

70 Chayefsky wrote that the directing of *Shampoo* was "blunt and obvious": CP, Box 94, Folder 3.

70 William Bernstein . . . wrote to Chayefsky's lawyer, Maurice Spanbock: CP, Box 96, Folder 3.

71 "We said, 'Here it is. You name the part'": Author interview with Howard Gottfried, March 20, 2012.

72 Van Devere wrote directly to Chayefsky: CP, Box 96, Folder 3.

72 on July 31 he finally wrote to her: Ibid.

73 "I advise all the children who want to go on the stage": "Young Veteran on 'Warpath,'" no publication, no date [probably 1937].

73 "As a Jew, I'm very judgmental": John Lombardi, "Lumet: The City Is His Sound Stage," *New York Times Magazine*, June 6, 1982.

73 A 1953 feature in *Life* magazine: "Director Participation: Sidney Lumet Kisses, Fights, Dies, Running Two Top TV Shows a Week," *Life*, June 8, 1953.

74 "I spent nights puzzling the problem": "Good Men and True and All Angry," *Life*, Apr. 22, 1957.

74 front-page news in the summer of 1963: "Sidney Lumet Takes Overdose," *New York Post*, Aug. 26, 1963.

74 Lumet later joked that what he'd indulged in: "Lumet Did Wed Lena Horne's Girl," *Daily News* (New York), Dec. 21, 1963.

75 finally admitting to their nuptials: Ibid.

75 Lumet was "everybody's second choice": Pauline Kael, "The Making of *The Group*," in *Kiss Kiss Bang Bang* (London: Calder and Boyards, 1970), pp. 70, 82.

75 "I found that I was getting something back": Randolph Hogan, "At Modern, Lumet's Love Affair with New York," *New York Times*, Dec. 31, 1981.

75 "I never left television; it left me": Lumet made remarks to this effect in interviews in the *New York Post*, Dec. 6, 1975; the (Los Angeles) *Herald-Examiner*, Nov. 14, 1976; and the *Christian Science Monitor*, Aug. 13, 1981.

76 Amjen Entertainment, would ultimately receive 12.5 percent of the film's net profits: CP, Box 214, Folder 2.

76 "Paddy is a tough writer and creator": Author interview with Philip Rosenberg, Mar. 23, 2012.

76 "Most of the directors who worked in New York": Author interview with Alan Heim, Apr. 5, 2012.

76 "His cynicism was partly a pose": Sidney Lumet, *Making Movies* (New York: Random House, 1995), p. 42.

77 "I think of Faye Dunaway as an enchanted panther in a poem": "A Panther of an Actress Springs Back to the Top," *People*, Dec. 30, 1974.

77 gossipy newspaper columns and their readers: Hy Gardner, "Where Did Faye Fade To?" Glad You Asked That (column), *Jersey Journal*, Sept. 25, 1970.

78   a poetically apt summation of the actress: Brad Darrach, "A Gauzy Grenade Called Dunaway," *People*, July 29, 1974.

78   "You have, I guarantee, never seen such certifiable proof of craziness": Tom Burke, "The Restoration of Roman Polanski," *Rolling Stone*, July 18, 1974.

78   "The fact is a man can be difficult and people applaud him": Faye Dunaway, *Looking for Gatsby* (New York: Simon and Schuster, 1995), p. 260.

78   a one-room frame house on the Florida farm: Ibid., p. 11.

79   "I would never allow myself to be in the position": Ibid., p. 39.

79   she passed up a Fulbright Scholarship: Ibid., p. 66.

79   "a creature who wanted freedom, and a bra just didn't fit": Ibid., p. 127.

79   "These were women who found out who they were": Ibid., p. 162.

79   she had to give back $25,000 of her $60,000 salary: "Biography: Faye Dunaway," *Movie News*, Mar. 1972.

80   "I couldn't stand how I was—my manners, my gestures": Dunaway, *Looking for Gatsby*, p. 118.

80   "I used men as buffers against the world": Production notes for *Network*, as printed in the novelization of *Network* by Sam Hedrin (New York: Pocket Books, 1976), p. 184.

80   "She wasn't beautiful": Marcello Mastroianni with Oriana Fallaci, "X Ray of a Man," *McCall's*, Sept. 1971.

80   Dunaway married Peter Wolf: *Time*, Aug. 19, 1974.

81   "I could no longer represent her if she didn't do this film": "A List: Art of the Deal," *W*, Feb. 2006.

81   "one of the most important female roles to come along": Dunaway, *Looking for Gatsby*, pp. 293–94.

81   "'Where's her vulnerability? Don't ask it'": Lumet, *Making Movies*, p. 41.

81   Max Schumacher should be played by Robert Mitchum: Dunaway, *Looking for Gatsby*, p. 296.

82   a press release announcing that Dunaway would star: Press release from Metro-Goldwyn-Mayer and United Artists, Sept. 24, 1975.

82   Dunaway's salary of $200,000: *Parade*, Aug. 14, 1977.

82   An item published in *Variety*: "A Spoofing 'Network,'" *Variety*, Sept. 24, 1975.

83   "I was halfway through when I hit a hidden rock headfirst": "William Holden Talks About . . . The Film I'll Never Forget," *National Enquirer*, Jan. 21, 1973.

83   "the hairline is receding, the skin has leathered": Arthur Bell, Bell Tells (column), *Village Voice*, June 12, 1978.

83   "a whisky baritone buried by a coffee-table carton of Carleton cigarettes": Jan Hodenfield, "Holden's Network of Sighs," *New York Post*, Nov. 1976.

83   "A crazy-faced middle aged man": Rex Reed, "Holden: Movies Have Grown Up. So Have I," *Sunday News* (New York), Nov. 21, 1976.

84   a family that claimed George Washington and Warren G. Harding among its relations: Alan Chester, "Game Farm for Holden," CNS News Service, *Newark Sunday News*, Nov. 5, 1967. Holden's mother was a descendant of Martha Bell, mother of George Washington, and his maternal grandfather, Samuel Bell, was a cousin of Warren G. Harding.

84 a fifty-dollar-a-week contract with the studio: William Holden, "The Player," *New Yorker*, Oct. 21, 1961.

84 changed it to Holden: Sidney Skolsky, "Tintypes: William Holden," *New York Post*, Oct. 12, 1974.

84 Rouben Mamoulian chose him from among some three thousand contenders: Chester, "Game Farm for Holden."

84 "I've put up with a lot of asinine suggestions": Holden, "The Player."

85 a contract that paid him $3 million: "Liz's 'Cleo' 10% Mebbe Soon; But Holden Coin Tops," *Variety*, no date [1963?].

85 investments in nearly every part of the globe: Joe Hyams, "'The Wasted Life' of William Holden," *New York Herald Tribune*, Sept. 28, 1960.

85 "I'm living in Switzerland": James Bacon, "American in Alps: Holden Plans Films in Hollywood, Europe," Associated Press, *Newark Evening News*, no date [1960?].

85 1,200 acres of ranch land near Nairobi: Chester, "Game Farm for Holden."

85 played host to the likes of Bing Crosby and Lyndon B. Johnson: "William Holden: The Man," *Palm Springs Life*, Nov. 1975.

85 the couple announced their separation: "William Holden, Wife Separate," Associated Press, Aug. 26, 1963.

85 they briefly reconciled: Dwight Whitney, "To Africa, with Love," *TV Guide*, Mar. 22–28, 1969.

85 finally divorced in 1971: Toni Holt, Column, *Daily Mirror*, July 9, 1971.

85 Holden was involved in a fatal car accident: "William Holden Is Involved in Fatal Car Crash in Italy," Associated Press, *New York Times*, July 23, 1966.

85 ultimately cleared of any wrongdoing in the crash: "Holden Freed in Auto Death," Associated Press, *New York Times*, Oct. 27, 1967.

85 Holden "had sought some solace in the bottle": Whitney, "To Africa, with Love."

86 he had quit drinking altogether: Earl Wilson, "Holden's a Teetotaler Now," It Happened Last Night (column), *New York Post*, Mar. 2, 1976.

86 Holden had recently been seeing the actress Stefanie Powers: Aljean Harmetz, "The Happy Journey of Holden and Powers," *New York Times*, May 12, 1977.

86 "the one real embarrassment, the chief invasion of privacy": William Holden, "Love in a Fishbowl: Movie Clinches Embarrass William Holden," UPI, *Newark Evening News*, Sept. 17, 1962.

86 a generous bonus plan: CP, Box 214, Folder 2. According to the bonus schedule, Holden received $50,000 when the grosses for *Network* reached $2.5 million; Dunaway's Port Bascom production company received $50,000 when the grosses reached $5 million; Holden received another $50,000 when the grosses reached $7.5 million; and so on.

86 "Bill Holden is Bill Holden": Author interview with Howard Gottfried, Mar. 20, 2012.

87 "I'm all excited he returns my call": Author interview with Barry Krost, Mar. 30, 2012.

88 Born Frederick George Peter Ingle-Finch in London in 1916: Elaine Dundy, *Finch, Bloody Finch: A Life of Peter Finch* (New York: Holt, Rinehart and Winston, 1980), p. 29.

88 met George Finch at an officers' dance during World War I: Ibid., p. 28.

88 put him in the care of Buddhist monks: Ibid., p. 37.

88 Peter had his head shaved and was dressed in yellow silk robes: 20th Century–Fox studio

biography of Peter Finch, 1960, Peter Finch file, New York Public Library, Billy Rose Theatre Division.

88 an adventure, "sometimes in thinking and learning": "Actor Apprenticed to Buddhist Monk," *Warner Bros. Rambling Reporter,* June 18, 1959.

88 "it would destroy the British Empire": David Galligan, "Peter Finch: A Lot of Phantasmagoria," *The Advocate,* Mar. 23, 1977.

88 known as "Finch's Follies": 20th Century–Fox studio biography of Peter Finch, 1960.

88 a lunch-hour production of Molière's *The Imaginary Invalid*: Richard Whitehall, "Peter Finch: Britain's Best," Personality of the Month (column), *Films and Filming,* July 1960.

88 After moving to London in 1948: Dundy, *Finch, Bloody Finch,* p. 130.

89 he was also slated to play Julius Caesar in *Cleopatra*: "Man in Waiting," *New York Times,* May 31, 1964.

89 "Errol used to say we were the last ones in London": David Barry, Arts & Pleasures (column), *Women's Wear Daily,* Oct. 11, 1976.

89 "He had a streak of mad anger": Dundy, *Finch, Bloody Finch,* p. 266.

89 An affair that Finch conducted during the 1950s: Richard Brooks, "Olivier Worn Out by Love and Lust of Vivien Leigh," *Sunday Times* (London), Aug. 7, 2005.

89 divorce from his first wife: Dundy, *Finch, Bloody Finch,* p. 213.

89 divorced his second wife: "Peter Finch's Wife Granted Decree," *Daily Mirror,* Dec. 11, 1965.

89 Shirley Bassey was named a corespondent: Dundy, *Finch, Bloody Finch,* p. 280.

89 he himself had been the product of her adulterous liaison: Ibid., p. 259.

89 "Nobody can take away my car or my home or my swimming pool": Roderick Mann, "A Barefoot Life for Peter Finch," *Sunday Express* (London), Apr. 3, 1966.

90 an eleven-acre farm of citrus, banana, allspice, and timber trees: Vernon Scott, "Finch Farms: Raises Crops in Jamaica," UPI, *Newark Evening News,* Sept. 17, 1967.

90 their first encounter was either at a party: "Queen's Cardinal," *New York Post,* Sept. 21, 1974.

90 or at a fence that Finch was climbing: Earl Wilson, "The Women in Peter's (Film) Life," *New York Post,* Nov. 13, 1976.

90 he married Eletha in 1973 at a civil ceremony in Rome: "Peter Finch Weds in Rome," Associated Press, *New York Post,* Nov. 9, 1973.

90 "All women want to nest a little": Enid Nemy, "Peter Finch, A Loner on the Loose," *New York Times,* Sept. 22, 1968.

90 "I hear he has a fondness for black girls": *Parade,* Nov. 21, 1971.

90 "his need for the gutter": Yolande Finch, *Finchy* (New York: Simon and Schuster, 1981), p. 27. The none-too-subtle subtitle that appeared on the book's cover was *A Drunkard, a Womanizer, a Genius.*

91 "The truth is, you try to get actors jobs": Author interview with Barry Krost, Mar. 30, 2012.

91 "Howard said, 'Bingo'—he'd got the part": Ibid.

91 "to be perfectly candid . . . we were pretty ready to shoot the movie": Author interview with Howard Gottfried, Mar. 20, 2012.

92 "'Give me my bloody wallet'": Author interview with Barry Krost, Mar. 30, 2012.

92 "Paddy did run the show": Author interview with Juliet Taylor, Mar. 5, 2012.

93 "He didn't have any of the Western thing going on": Ibid.

93 "a handsome matron of fifty": Chayefsky, *The Screenplays Vol. II*, p. 167.

93 Lumet had had his eye on Candice Bergen: Author interview with Howard Gottfried, Mar. 20, 2012.

93 in a single appointment on the morning of November 10: CP, Box 95, Folder 6.

93 "she had us weeping": Bob Weiner, "A Straight Arrow Pierces the Heart," *Sunday News* (New York), Nov. 14, 1976.

94 "A bobby grabbed my wrist": Author interview with Marlene Warfield, Jan. 16, 2013.

94 Roberts Blossom . . . whom they cast this time as Arthur Jensen: CP, Box 95, Folder 6.

94 who had played Frederick Douglass in a one-man show: "Arthur Burghardt to Dramatize Douglass on ABC," *Jet*, July 8, 1976.

94 "At one point, this character bursts in the front door with a gun": Author interview with Howard Gottfried, Mar. 9, 2012.

94 "I went looking very much like a deposed street punk/gangster": Author interview with Arthur Burghardt, Feb. 11, 2012.

95 "how much of that was Sidney's and Dad's old friendship": Author interview with Kathy Cronkite, Feb. 21, 2012.

95 "The expense of my fee is absolutely inconsequential": Author interview with Philip Rosenberg, Mar. 23, 2012.

96 "the cinematographers were, for the most part, World War II vets": Author interview with Tom Priestley Jr., Feb. 3, 2012.

96 "nobody from our production has had an opportunity to discuss the use of a wig": CP, Box 96, Folder 7.

4. The Daily Parade of Lunacies

98 A Christmastime bombing at LaGuardia Airport in Queens: Peter Kihss, "Bombing Damage Is Put at $750,000," *New York Times*, Jan. 6, 1976.

98 fires raged in South Brooklyn, where a series of fuel-oil tanks had exploded: David Vidal, "A Second Explosion Fans Fuel-Oil Fire in Brooklyn," *New York Times*, Jan. 6, 1976.

98 stripped its streets of more than 4,200 police officers: Francis X. Clines, "994 More Job Cuts Proposed by Police," *New York Times*, Jan. 6, 1976.

98 Zabar's had sold out its supply of a new home appliance: Keith Love, "Store Cuts Cuisinart Price but Can't Replenish Stock," *New York Times*, Jan. 7, 1976.

99 a single-room-occupancy hotel on West Forty-Third Street that had previously served: David W. Dunlap, "An Aging Midtown Hotel That Will Not Go Gently," *New York Times*, Nov. 7, 1993.

99 they found the hall unheated and had to flee: Kay Chapin, diary entry, Jan. 5, 1976.

99 "Bill and Peter took to each other instantly": Dundy, *Finch, Bloody Finch*, p. 325.

99 "I'm a pain in the ass and I know it": Ibid., p. 321.

100 "Sidney knows specifically what he wants and is very adept": Chapin, diary entry, Jan. 6, 1976.

100 The company spent the next few days in the ballroom: Chapin, diary entries, Jan. 7 and 8, 1976.

100 he had given up his own acting career because he realized: Chapin, diary entry, Jan. 8, 1976.

101 "he looked everywhere but directly into her eyes": Lumet, *Making Movies*, p. 66.

101 "I shot it," she said, "and it scared the hell out of me": Author interview with Kathy Cronkite, Feb. 21, 2012.

101 wrapped for the day at 10:00 A.M.: *Network* shooting script, Museum of the Moving Image, New York, NY.

102 "Paddy wants it less theatrical": Chapin, diary entry, Jan. 16, 1976.

102 While playing a scene with Dame Edith Evans: Ibid.

103 In New York, it was simply not practical or affordable: Author interview with Philip Rosenberg, Mar. 23, 2012.

103 Union rules . . . created further financial complications: Author interview with Richard Wald, Feb. 2, 2012.

103 "we couldn't get cooperation from any of the networks": Author interview with Owen Roizman, Jan. 25, 2012.

103 MGM and United Artists executives stated in a January 9 memo: CP, Box 96, Folder 3.

104 "It took a lot of work for the script girl and Sidney": Author interview with Philip Rosenberg, Mar. 23, 2012.

104 the Hotel Toronto on University Avenue: CP, Box 96, Folder 6.

104 "just then, Paddy and Bill Holden came walking by": Author interview with Owen Roizman, Jan. 25, 2012.

104 Principal photography for *Network* began on Monday, January 19: *Network* shooting script.

105 he wanted the visual look of *Network* to proceed in three distinct phases: "Network and How It Was Photographed," *American Cinematographer* 58, no. 4 (Apr. 1977).

105 "The movie was about corruption": Lumet, *Making Movies*, p. 85.

105 "'Cut, print, move on.' That was his slogan": Author interview with Fred Schuler, Jan. 28, 2012.

105 "He was, like, in a frenzy": Author interview with Tom Priestley Jr., Feb. 3, 2012.

105 Lumet as prowling "like a caged tiger": Chapin, diary entry, Jan. 20, 1976.

106 "He wasn't a fusspot when it came to technical things": Author interview with Owen Roizman, Jan. 25, 2012.

107 "they called it the Paddy light": Author interview with Fred Schuler, Jan. 28, 2012.

107 "I told the guard to take in Peter Finch's disheveled state": Lumet, *Making Movies*, p. 43.

107 "In his mind, he wanted to retire": Author interview with Diana Finch-Braley, Aug. 26, 2012.

107 "The physical transformation of Peter on the set was remarkable": Dundy, *Finch, Bloody Finch*, p. 325.

108 "He was what you'd call a Method actor, without ever studying the Method": Author interview with Diana Finch-Braley, Aug. 26, 2012.

108 "Like Daniel and the burning bush": Ibid.

108 Take 3 was halted at the one-minute mark: *Network* shooting script.

108 it was back to "Mad as hell": *Network* shooting script, and CP, Box 95, Folder 6.

109 "I want all of you to get up out of your chairs": Chayefsky, *The Screenplays Vol. II*, pp. 173–74.

110 Lumet attempted it only twice, and Finch completed it only once: *Network* shooting script, and Lumet, *Making Movies*, p. 122.

110 "No reloading . . . No time lost between takes": Lumet, *Making Movies*, p. 122.

110 "he just ran out of gas": Sidney Lumet, *Network* DVD, director's commentary.

110 from the first half of Take 2 and the second half of Take 1: Lumet, *Making Movies*, pp. 122–23.

110 a painted piece of canvas: Author interview with Philip Rosenberg, Mar. 23, 2012.

110 a reporter for the *Toronto Sun* found Chayefsky in the CFTO-TV cafeteria: George Anthony, "Chayefsky's Latest—All Fabricated, All Fiction and All True," *Toronto Sun*, Mar. 14, 1976.

112 "the first known instance of a man": Chayefsky, *The Screenplays Vol. II*, p. 222.

112 "Everybody in the place—everybody in the studio": Author interview with Arthur Burghardt, Feb. 11, 2012.

113 "you'll see that Faye fumbles a few places": Author interview with Alan Heim, Apr. 5, 2012.

113 "he was thinking of replacing Faye": Ibid. Asked whom Lumet planned to replace Dunaway with, Heim politely replied, "I won't tell you that. *He* did, but I won't tell you. Nothing personal."

113 "I said, 'Walter, let the government sue us!'": Chayefsky, *The Screenplays Vol. II*, pp. 190–91.

114 "I could not afford to stumble on a single word": Dunaway, *Looking for Gatsby*, p. 300.

114 "There were long talks about it": Ibid., p. 301.

115 Chayefsky had already deleted a scene: *Network* script, with Dan Melnick notes, dated June 2, 1975, archived at the Margaret Herrick Library of the Academy of Motion Picture Arts and Sciences, Beverly Hills, CA.

115 "She wouldn't budge": Author interview with Howard Gottfried, Mar. 20, 2012.

116 a February 2 letter from Gottfried to Dunaway: CP, Box 96, Folder 4.

117 "some dreadful grief": Chayefsky, *The Screenplays Vol. II*, pp. 192–93.

117 on Wednesday, February 4: *Network* shooting script.

117 the Apthorp building: CP, Box 95, Folder 6. Lumet says on his DVD commentary for *Network* that the scene was filmed in the apartment of "Alfred Maysles." He may have meant the *Grey Gardens* and *Gimme Shelter* documentarian Albert Maysles, but he was more likely referring to his brother and codirector David Maysles, who lived in the building.

117 Scene 127: *Network* shooting script.

117 "This isn't just some convention weekend with your secretary, is it?": Chayefsky, *The Screenplays Vol. II*, pp. 192–93.

118 "'I know more about divorce than you do'": Lumet, *Making Movies*, p. 43.

118 "The word, of course, is *emeritus*": Author interview with Alan Heim, Apr. 5, 2012.

119 there is "no America" and "no democracy": Chayefsky, *The Screenplays Vol. II*, pp. 204–5.

119 "a lot of pressure was put on the president of the Exchange": Author interview with Philip Rosenberg, Mar. 23, 2012.

120 the *Network* cast and crew had overlapped with Robert Altman and his team: In her diary, Kay Chapin records a January 28 visit by Altman, his production manager, and his assistant director to the cafeteria of CFTO-TV, where *Network* was being filmed.

120 "that little guy who smiled every three or four years or so": Author interview with Ned Beatty, Mar. 8, 2012.

121 "'I've got another offer, and it's for more money'": Ibid.

121 Chayefsky described with precision and specificity how the sequence should look: Chayefsky, *The Screenplays Vol. II*, p. 205.

122 "You'd have to put smoke in the room, and backlight the smoke": Author interview with Owen Roizman, Jan. 25, 2012.

123 "He's not just doing any ape": Author interview with Ned Beatty, Mar. 8, 2012.

123 "how perspicacious of you to facilitate this scene": Author interview with Tom Priestley Jr., Feb. 3, 2012.

123 "She flubs a lot and had a hard time getting through a long speech": Chapin, diary entries, Feb. 2–6 and Feb. 9 and 10, 1976.

124 "knee deep in dog shit": Chapin, diary entry, Feb. 19, 1976.

124 Filming there was scheduled for three days: Chapin, diary entry, Feb. 2–6, 1976.

124 He had special nicknames: Chapin, diary entry, Mar. 5, 1976.

125 he seemed either to have trouble remembering his lines: Ibid.

125 "watch somebody get guillotined, hung, electrocuted, gassed": Chayefsky, *The Screenplays Vol. II*, pp. 119–20.

125 "fondling, fingering, noodling and nuzzling": Ibid., p. 147.

126 "lying naked on a maelstrom of sheets": *Network* shooting script.

126 "All of life is reduced to the common rubble of banality": Chayefsky, *The Screenplays Vol. II*, p. 210.

126 "I said, 'Bill, I want you to do just one thing'": Lumet, *Network* DVD, director's commentary.

127 "isn't connected as a woman, doesn't feel like a woman": Dunaway, *Looking for Gatsby*, p. 302.

127 "Something happened in the focusing process": Author interview with Alan Heim, Apr. 5, 2012.

127 The empty upper floors of the tower: Author interview with Philip Rosenberg, Mar. 23, 2012.

128 "He opened up the window and screamed out": Author interview. This person asked not to be identified for attribution, for obvious reasons.

128 "Remember that this was not a set": "Network and How It Was Photographed."

128 "Some of the extras are black. And some of them are women": Author interview with Howard Gottfried, Mar. 20, 2012.

129 "Not to get into any kind of a battle with him": Author interview with Philip Rosenberg, Mar. 23, 2012.

129 a reporter from the *Sunday News* came to visit the *Network* set in early March: Kathleen Carroll, "Hollywood Zaps the Boob Tube," *Sunday News* (New York), Mar. 14, 1976.

131 in his acerbic stage directions, described it as a "shambles": Chayefsky, *The Screenplays Vol. II*, p. 181.

131 the site of a 140-year-old farmhouse: http://www.drdaviesfarm.com/history.htm.

131 the "increasingly desperate, imperialist ruling clique": Chayefsky, *The Screenplays Vol. II*, p. 134.

132 "This scene should come out": *Network* script with Dan Melnick notes, dated June 2, 1975.

132 "a fire-eating militant with a bandolier of cartridges": Chayefsky, *The Screenplays Vol. II*, p. 181.

132 "there was so much challenge to my individuality from Dad": Author interview with Kathy Cronkite, Feb. 21, 2012.

133 "Fugginfascist!": Chayefsky, *The Screenplays Vol. II*, p. 196.

133 "I'm coming down the stairs screaming this line of propaganda": Author interview with Kathy Cronkite, Feb. 21, 2012.

134 actually an office building in Melville, Long Island: "Hollywood on the LIE," *Newsday*, Mar. 14, 1976.

134 "a racist lackey of the imperialist ruling circles": Chayefsky, *The Screenplays Vol. II*, p. 178.

134 "It tasted very good": Author interview with Marlene Warfield, Jan. 16, 2013.

135 The U.S. Supreme court was about to review the case: "Actor Is Released after 28 Months in Draft Evasion," Associated Press, *New York Times*, Feb. 16, 1974. On May 28, 1974, the Supreme Court ruled, in an 8–0 decision, that a writ of mandamus issued by a federal judge in Indiana that prohibited Kunstler from representing Burghardt had been "improvidently granted."

135 "I knew that black people were far more relevant to the world": Author interview with Arthur Burghardt, Feb. 11, 2012.

137 "I'm never at ease in love scenes": Dunaway, *Looking for Gatsby*, p. 301.

137 "We would open with a high shot of the two in bed": Considine, *Mad as Hell*, pp. 324–25.

137 The official filming log from that day is consistent: *Network* shooting script.

138 "it was a very uneventful shoot that day": Author interview with Philip Rosenberg, Mar. 23, 2012.

138 "Bill could not make it through a scene without dissolving into laughter": Dunaway, *Looking for Gatsby*, p. 301.

138 "you have to lie there, faking that you're pumping into her": Lumet, *Network* DVD, director's commentary.

138 "You could have shown a little more": Author interview with Howard Gottfried, Mar. 20, 2012.

139 "She was wearing a sheet for the most part": Author interview with Alan Heim, Apr. 5, 2012.

140 a lion's tooth from Holden and a Gucci checkbook wallet from Finch: Chapin, diary entry, Mar. 5, 1976.

140 "You have to be disciplined": Author interview with Marlene Warfield, Jan. 16, 2013.

140 "Faye Dunaway ducked the 'wrap-up' party of the film": Earl Wilson, It Happened Last Night (column), *New York Post*, Mar. 22, 1976.

140 "the rain-swept streets of the Upper East Side": Chayefsky, *The Screenplays Vol. II*, p. 176.

141 "One day when we were talking about it, Sidney comes in with an idea": Author interview with Howard Gottfried, Mar. 19, 2012.

141 "'You want a crane? Sure, no problem, you got a crane'": Author interview with Fred Schuler, Jan. 28, 2012.

141 three nights of filming, from March 23 through 25: *Network* shooting script.

141 "fire trucks with water hoses to wet down the buildings": "Network and How It Was Photographed."

142 "You are a man of your word and of your words": CP, Box 96, Folder 3.

143 "Sunday night, I got a call from Howard Gottfried": Author interview with Alan Heim, Apr. 5, 2012.

5. A Storm of Humanity

147 the handiwork of Stephen Frankfurt: Leslie Kaufman, "Stephen Frankfurt, Artist on Madison Ave., Dies at 80," *New York Times*, Oct. 3, 2012.

147 "I know I am in for a storm of humanity": CP, Box 96, Folder 6.

147 a marketing campaign budgeted at nearly $3 million: Arthur Unger, "Film Jars TV Industry," *Christian Science Monitor*, Nov. 2, 1976.

148 This compilation of personal biographies, cast and crew rosters: *Network* production notes, Apr. 12, 1976.

148 "DO NOT EVER refer to this film NETWORK as a 'black' comedy": CP, Box 96, Folder 4.

149 "Dear Mr. Chayevsky [sic]": CP, Box 214, Folder 1.

149 "The adaptor must remain entirely outside the telling of the story": CP, Box 96, Folder 7.

150 "What's this shit got to do with anything?": CP, Box 96, Folder 1.

151 "the bitterest attack yet on television": This *Women's Wear Daily* article was attributed to Louise J. Esterhazy, the pseudonym used by John Fairchild, the publisher and editorial director of the newspaper and the grandson of Fairchild Publications founder Edmund Fairchild.

152 "the most controversial movie ever made about television": The original *Newsday* article was written by Bill Kaufman and Joseph Gelmis and published under the titles "'Network' Film Roughs up Television" and "'Network' Zeroes in on the Tube."

153 "you must have some idea of the hysteria attendant on the opening of a film": CP, Box 96, Folder 6.

154 "People in broadcasting," Shales wrote, "are calling it 'preposterous'": Tom Shales, "'Network': Hating TV Can Be Fun," *Washington Post*, Oct. 24, 1976.

155 an outwardly joyous Chayefsky was in the Milton Berle Room: Clarke Taylor, "Paddy May Have a Hit on His Hands," *Los Angeles Times*, Nov. 21, 1976.

156 "a searing but unfair indictment of television morality": Unger, "Film Jars TV Industry."

156 "such an incompetent movie, such a poor job, that any point it tried to make was lost": "How Television Rates 'Network,'" *W*, Nov. 12–19, 1976.

157 a "first revolt against bullshitism": CP, Box 140, Folder 3.

158 "I'm just beginning to get some negative feedback on my movie": CP, Box 96, Folder 6.

158 "Has this caused you any embarrassment or professional discomfort?": Ibid.

159 "I should have had my head examined": Author interview with Barbara Walters, Apr. 12, 2012.

159 the very first sentence of its front-page story: Robert D. McFadden, "Barbara Walters Accepts ABC's Offer," *New York Times*, Apr. 23, 1976.

160 "I went on the night of Yom Kippur": Author interview with Barbara Walters, Apr. 12, 2012.

161 Diana Christensen was the "Great American Bitch": Attributed to Deborah Rosenfelt, as cited in Dunaway, *Looking for Gatsby*, p. 312.

161 "People will think they're getting the inside story, and they're not": Shales, "'Network': Hating TV Can Be Fun."

161 "If people accept the film as reality," she said, "it will be dreadful": Unger, "Film Jars TV Industry."

161 "you had to be tough as nails": Author interview with Barbara Walters, Apr. 12, 2012.

162 "They hated it. Oh my God": Author interview with Richard Wald, Feb. 2, 2012.

163 Chayefsky said he was "upset to hell": Earl Wilson, "Paddy Was Affectionate, Says Paddy," It Happened Last Night (column), *New York Post*, Nov. 9, 1976.

163 "My rage isn't against television": Allan Wolper, "Paddy Chayefsky: TV Goes to the Movies," *SoHo Weekly News*, Nov. 11, 1976.

164 "the look of a satyr who has retired from active duty": Howard Kissel, "Chayefsky and Television: Rating Each Other," *Women's Wear Daily*, Nov. 12, 1976.

164 "Television is democracy at its ugliest": Barthel, "Paddy Chayefsky: 'TV Will Do Anything for a Rating. Anything!'"

164 the principal members of its creative team gathered for a 10:00 A.M. press conference: Ray Loynd, ". . . And the Stars Talk," *Los Angeles Herald-Examiner*, Nov. 14, 1976.

165 "I consider them decent, respectable, sensitive people": Carmie Armata, "Chayefsky on 'Network,'" *Focus on Film*, No. 26, 1977.

166 "It's also brilliantly, cruelly funny, a topical American comedy": Vincent Canby, "Chayefsky's 'Network' Bites Hard as a Film Satire of TV Industry," *New York Times*, Nov. 15, 1976.

166 "a ruthless exploration of the 'aesthetics' and 'art' of television": Judith Crist, "The Day TV Went Mad," *Saturday Review*, Nov. 13, 1976.

166 The *Daily News* gave it two thumbs-up as well: Considine, *Mad as Hell*, p. 328.

167 "a satiric send-up of commercial television": Vincent Canby, "'A Surreal Attack on American Life,'" *New York Times*, Nov. 28, 1976.

167 *Network* "inherits the Glib Piety Award direct from the hands of *The Front*": John Simon, "Vicious Video," *New York*, Nov. 22, 1976.

168 "So this is a slashing comment on network television": Robert Hatch, Films (column), *The Nation*, Dec. 4, 1976.

168 "drastically out of control—dramatically, cinematically and intellectually": Frank Rich, "'Network' Caught in Its Own Web," *New York Post*, Nov. 1976.

169 "Paddy Chayefsky blitzes you with one idea after another": Pauline Kael, "Hot Air," The Current Cinema (column), *New Yorker*, Dec. 6, 1976.

170 "As satire or as serious comment, the movie seemed oddly pious and heavy-handed": Michael J. Arlen, "What We Do in the Dark," The Air (column), *New Yorker*, Dec. 6, 1976.

170 An item in *New York* magazine straightforwardly declared: "The 'Network' Guessing Game: Who's Who?" *New York*, Nov. 29, 1976.

171 Lin Bolen, who had spoken briefly by phone with Dunaway: Vernon Scott, "Producer Lin Bolen Denies She's 'Network' Character," UPI, *Milwaukee Sentinel*, July 31, 1978.

171 *Time* magazine published its own battlefield update: "The Movie TV Hates and Loves," *Time*, Dec. 13, 1976.

172 "P.S. I'm quitting my job": CP, Box 96, Folder 6.

6. Primal Forces and Phantasmagoria

174 a *New York Times* essay proclaiming the arrival of the new "cynical cinema": Vincent Canby, "Cynical Cinema Is Chic," *New York Times*, Nov. 21, 1976.

174 grossing more than $20 million in its original theatrical release: CP, Box 214, Folders 8 and 9. According to quarterly statements from United Artists, *Network* had grossed $7,255,587.60 by Mar. 26, 1977; $11,841,862.53 by June 25, 1977; $16,859,744.68 by Sept. 24, 1977; and $20,868,133.31 by Dec. 30, 1978, at which point it had been in theatrical release for more than two years.

175 "footage showing the tragedy of Danang, with the blood of civilians flowing": Guy Flatley, At the Movies (column), *New York Times*, Nov. 12, 1976.

175 the "ever so slight a suggestion of a harrumph": Jan Hodenfield, "Holden's Network of Sighs," *New York Post*, Nov. 1976.

175 a joint interview with Holden in the upscale pages of *W* magazine: Christopher Sharp, "Dunaway and Holden: A 'Network,'" *W*, Nov. 26–Dec. 3, 1976.

175 "If you blink, you miss it, but it is a lucky break": Bob Weiner, "A Straight Arrow Pierces the Heart," *Sunday News* (New York), Nov. 14, 1976.

176 they lived in an apartment on West Hollywood's Sunset Strip: Barbara Wilkins, "Peter Finch Used to Grow Them, but Now He Is Going Bananas in 'Network,'" *People*, Dec. 6, 1976.

176 "This is the place where all the deals are made": David Barry, Arts & Pleasures (column), *Women's Wear Daily*, Oct. 11, 1976.

176 a lead role as Yitzhak Rabin: *New York Post*, Jan. 15, 1977.

176 "We're all so dreadfully egocentric in this business:" Considine, *Mad as Hell*, p. 330.

176 "Peter wanted to win that Oscar": Dundy, *Finch, Bloody Finch*, p. 334.

177 "He would turn to my mom and he would say": Author interview with Diana Finch-Braley, Aug. 26, 2012.

177 preferred to walk four or five miles a day: Wilkins, "Peter Finch Used to Grow Them."

177 "He always knew somebody—because he was Peter Finch—would buy him breakfast": Author interview with Barry Krost, Mar. 30, 2012.

177 "The problems and the potential power of TV exist everywhere": David Sterritt, "Peter Finch Won't Accept Superviolent Roles," *Christian Science Monitor*, Dec. 10, 1976.

177 "There had to be a suggestion that he was eminently sane": David Galligan, "Peter Finch: A Lot of Phantasmagoria," *Advocate*, Mar. 23, 1977.

177 a book about his experiences, which he planned to call *Chutzpah*: Production notes for *Network*, as cited in *Network* novelization by Sam Hedrin, p. 188.

177 "There is a lot of phantasmagoria in my life": Galligan, "Peter Finch: A Lot of Phantasmagoria."

178 Chayefsky . . . had gone to the hospital to visit Fosse: Richard Eder, "Lumet Discovers Marvels and Puzzles in Shooting 'Equus,'" At the Movies (column), *New York Times*, Dec. 31, 1976.

178 the New York Film Critics Circle named Chayefsky the author of the year's best screen-play: *Daily News* (New York), Jan. 4, 1977.

178 The Los Angeles Film Critics Association also chose *Network*: http://www.lafca.net/years/1976.html.

178 "Paddy Chayefsky, when he gets his dander up on something": *The Tonight Show Starring Johnny Carson*, Jan. 13, 1977, archived at the Paley Center for Media, New York, NY.

180 "Peter talked about death": Dundy, *Finch, Bloody Finch*, p. 338.

180 "I was walking down the staircase toward him": Considine, *Mad as Hell*, p. 330.

181 There, he was pronounced dead of a heart attack: Murray Illson, "Peter Finch Is Dead on Coast at 60; British Actor on Stage and Screen," *New York Times*, Jan. 15, 1977.

181 "I had four phone lines at home": Author interview with Barry Krost, Mar. 30, 2012.

181 "The sudden and untimely passing of Peter Finch has come as a blow": Illson, "Peter Finch Is Dead on Coast at 60; British Actor on Stage and Screen."

181 assembled at the Palm restaurant to pay an impromptu tribute to Finch: Considine, *Mad as Hell*, p. 330.

182 "If the film industry told the truth, it would admit that deceased 60-year-old actors": Russell Davies, *Guardian*, Jan. 16, 1977.

182 An official memorial service for Finch: "Finch Eulogized at Funeral for Professionalism in Film Roles," *New York Times*, Jan. 19, 1977.

183 "a black-and-white painting with pen and ink, of this man": Author interview with Diana Finch-Braley, Aug. 26, 2012.

184 "a two-hour meat parade": Tom O'Neil, "1970 Flashback: George C. Scott Slaps Oscar," *Los Angeles Times*, Feb. 23, 2011.

184 "the treatment of American Indians today by the film industry": Sacheen Littlefeather, Academy Awards speech, Mar. 27, 1973, http://www.youtube.com/watch?v=2QUacU0I4yU.

184 "I don't want any nonsense on my show": Author interview with Howard Gottfried, Mar. 20, 2012.

185 a dislike of "sentimentality": Liz Smith (column), *Daily News* (New York), Apr. 5, 1977.

185 "It was made by the board of governors of the Academy": William Friedkin, "IAmA Hollywood film director (Killer Joe, The Exorcist, French Connection). I'm William Friedkin. AMA," http://www.reddit.com/r/IAmA/comments/u2y5r/iama_hollywood_film_director_killer_joe_the/c4sac3g.

186 "I knew that she had a reputation as a bit of a loose cannon": Author interview with Alan Heim, Apr. 5, 2012.

186 "People were going to change, and they just didn't know it": Author interview with Marlene Warfield, Jan. 16, 2013.

186 "We agreed that I would tell Friedkin": Author interview with Howard Gottfried, Mar. 20, 2012.

186 "Eletha, will attend Oscar ceremonies in case her late husband wins": *New York Post*, Mar. 17, 1977.

187 Box 13, Row F, Seat 46: CP, Box 96, Folder 6.

187 *People* published a cover story on Dunaway: Brad Darrach, "Will She Win the Big O?" *People,* Mar. 28, 1977.

188 "They gave the best supporting actor thing right off the bat": Author interview with Ned Beatty, Mar. 8, 2012.

188 "It's very heavy" . . . "and I'm the dark horse": Beatrice Straight, Academy Awards speech, Mar. 28, 1977, http://www.youtube.com/watch?v=o3g7kclmm0I.

188 Chayefsky was going to confess his dislike of "modest acceptance speeches": CP, Box 140, Folder 1.

189 "it's time that I acknowledge two people whom I can never really thank": Paddy Chayefsky, Academy Awards speech, Mar. 28, 1977, http://collections.oscars.org/ics-wpd/exec/icswppro.dll?AC=qbe_query&TN=AAtrans&RF=WebReportOscars&MF=oscarsmsg.ini&NP=255&BU=http://aaspeechesdb.oscars.org/index.asp&QY=find+acceptorlink+%3d049-21.

189 "I didn't expect this to happen quite yet": Faye Dunaway, Academy Awards speech, Mar. 28, 1977, http://www.youtube.com/watch?v=ePkEsHmwCZE.

190 "She was panic-struck": Author interview with Barry Krost, Mar. 30, 2012.

190 250 million people watching the ceremony around the world: Jon Nordheimer, "'Rocky' Gets Oscar as Top Film; Finch, Dunaway Win for Acting," *New York Times,* Mar. 29, 1977.

190 "I want to say thanks to members of the Academy": Eletha Finch, Academy Awards speech, Mar. 28, 1977, http://www.youtube.com/watch?v=FnL3uE-TzFw.

191 "We were sitting with a bunch of executives—accountants, really": Author interview with Alan Heim, Apr. 5, 2012.

192 "'I've got this idea for a picture that I wanted to do'": Author interview with Terry O'Neill, Aug. 15, 2012.

193 "as Peggy Lee sang, 'Is that all there is?'": Dunaway, *Looking for Gatsby,* p. 319.

193 the Beverly Hills Hotel sent a note to the room: CP, Box 96, Folder 6.

193 in the possession of Howard and Mary Lynn Gottfried: Author interview with Howard Gottfried, Mar. 31, 2012.

7. Corrupt and Lunatic Energies

196 news clippings that all . . . referenced Howard Beale's combustible catchphrase: CP, Box 96, Folder 7.

196 the story of Anthony Kiritsis, a failed businessman: *Time,* Feb. 21, 1977.

196 a *Mad* magazine parody of the movie: Mort Drucker and Stan Hart, "Nutwork," *Mad,* no. 192, July 1977.

197 "They shouldn't have appropriated my idea": J. A. Trachtenberg, "How Suite It Is," *Women's Wear Daily,* Dec. 20, 1978.

197 "I just made it up": Brady, *Craft of the Screenwriter,* pp. 69, 70, 78.

197 "It's the world that's gone nuts": Paddy Chayefsky, interview with Dinah Shore, *Dinah!,* recorded Jan. 19, 1977, http://www.youtube.com/watch?v=nNa019FaNW0.

197 a $500,000 offer to write a screenplay about the Israel Defense Forces': CP, Box 182, Folder 5.

197 "the subject was simply too painful for me to write about": Brady, *Craft of the Screenwriter,* pp. 64–65.

198 "The assassination, of course, was a fraud": Ray Bradbury, "Second Coming of 'Network,'" *Los Angeles Times*, Feb. 2, 1977.

198 "Among other things, it gives us a chance for NETWORK two": CP, Box 11, Folder 15.

199 "I was mooching on his opinion": Author interview with Warren Beatty, Nov. 8, 2012.

199 "We've got a guy who falls in love with his role in history": CP, Box 135, Folder 7.

199 "an associate professor in behavioral psychology": CP, Box 94, Folder 2.

199 "bipedal, protohuman creature": Lois Gould, "Special Effects," *New York Times*, June 18, 1978.

199 "Paddy decided he wanted a million bucks": Author interview with Howard Gottfried, July 6, 2012.

200 traveling to hospitals and universities and meeting with scientific experts: Paddy Chayefsky, *Altered States: A Novel* (New York: Harper and Row, 1978), pp. ix–x.

200 "a warm return to your mother's womb": Considine, *Mad as Hell*, p. 354.

200 a short, incomplete treatment of his proposed film: CP, Box 185, Folder 2.

200 "We reached the point where Paddy really has nothing else to say": Author interview with Howard Gottfried, July 6, 2012.

201 Chayefsky nonetheless had his million-dollar deal: CP, Box 182, Folder 7.

201 "At least this proves I'm mortal": Considine, *Mad as Hell*, pp. 356–57.

201 "I've got two children to raise": "Eletha Acts," Page Six (column), *New York Post*, Apr. 6, 1977.

201 The value of that estate . . . was placed at $115,000: "Finch's Widow Hits Will," *Daily News* (New York), May 16, 1977; "Finch Progeny Challenge 2d Wife," *Variety*, July 27, 1977.

201 split from her husband, Peter Wolf, by that summer: Page Six (column), *New York Post*, Aug. 16, 1977.

202 an affair with Terry O'Neill, the photographer: Page Six (column), *New York Post*, Feb. 3, 1978.

202 $1 million to star in Irvin Kershner's thriller *Eyes of Laura Mars*: *Parade*, Aug. 14, 1977.

202 $750,000 to appear . . . in a remake of the boxing drama *The Champ*: "Champ to Star Faye Dunaway and Jon Voight," *New York Times*, Apr. 29, 1978.

202 "She just didn't like me" . . . "and I didn't like her": "A List: Art of the Deal," *W*, Feb. 2006.

202 the portrait of Dunaway that ran on its cover: "New Mag's Cover Girl Unmasked," *New York*, Feb. 27, 1978.

202 "I have been an actor for 38 years": Harmetz, "Happy Journey of Holden and Powers."

203 The couple sent Christmas cards to Chayefsky: CP, Box 9, Folder 7.

203 had been told to avoid caffeine, tobacco, and salt and to exercise more: Considine, *Mad as Hell*, p. 357.

203 "the P.L.O. says Israel has no right to exist": Display advertisement, *New York Times*, Sept. 21, 1977.

203 "the only comment you keep hearing is 'Kill the enemy'": Richard F. Shepard, "Redgrave Film on P.L.O. Stirs a Controversy," *New York Times*, Nov. 10, 1977.

204 "I believe the Palestinian people have been denied the right to be heard": "Redgrave Defends P.L.O. Film," *New York Times*, Nov. 11, 1977.

204 members of the Jewish Defense League from turning out at the 1978 Oscars: Aljean Harmetz, " 'Annie Hall' Wins 4 Academy Awards," *New York Times*, Apr. 4, 1978.

204 a role that Faye Dunaway had turned down: Dunaway, *Looking for Gatsby*, p. 320.

204 "the threats of a small bunch of Zionist hoodlums": Vanessa Redgrave, Academy Awards speech, Apr. 3, 1978, archived at the Paley Center for Media, New York, NY.

205 "Paddy just went nuts after her speech": Author interview with Mike Medavoy, Mar. 12, 2012.

205 "everybody ran to Paddy and wanted to say something": Author interview with Sherry Lansing, Mar. 14, 2012.

205 "Before I get onto the writing awards, there's a little matter I'd like to tidy up": Paddy Chayefsky, Academy Awards speech, Apr. 3, 1978, archived at the Paley Center for Media, New York, NY.

207 "Arthur didn't speak to me for five years": Author interview with Shirley MacLaine, Nov. 16, 2012.

207 numerous appreciative letters and correspondence that applauded him: CP, Box 19, Folder 17.

207 "My husband would be proud of you": CP, Box 96, Folder 7.

207 "You damned near made me cry with your gutsy but courteous put-down": CP, Box 19, Folder 17.

207 "Miss Redgrave's acceptance speech did not appear as a grandstand play at all": Ibid.

208 "the fustian fancies later delivered by Paddy Chayefsky": Vincent Canby, "In the Afterglow of the Oscars," *New York Times*, Apr. 16, 1978.

208 Columbia Pictures tested the project with such names as *The Atavist*: CP, Box 60, Folder 6. Among the titles that were field-tested by Columbia Pictures, *Altered States* was deemed to possess a "critical weakness," according to a studio memo: "This title conjured up the greatest variety of interpretations—almost all of them bearing no relation to the proposed movie. Brain-washing, war between the states, witchcraft. . . . A number of people perceived that it would be a movie dealing with drugs, but in the illicit sense rather than the experimental sense. The lack of a clear message produced the lowest degree of interest."

208 "all the electronic-spin resonance tests": Gould, "Special Effects."

208 "a few passages of spectacularly bad writing": Alan Harrington, "Madness in the Deep," *Saturday Review*, July 1978.

208 a medical expert who had helped him with the novel was suing him: CP, Box 62, Folder 2.

209 his lawsuit said was "a substantial contribution" to the screenplay: "St. Vincent M.D. Sues Chayefsky," *Variety*, May 31, 1978.

209 requiring Chayefsky to exhaustively inventory every document, draft, and discarded page: As thoroughly catalogued in CP. The case was settled in 1982 after a two-week jury trial, with Lieberman receiving a payment of $40,000.

209 Melnick had risen to the studio's presidency: Aljean Harmetz, "Melnick Named President of Columbia Pictures," *New York Times*, June 2, 1978.

209 STUNNING, BRILLIANT, BREATHTAKING—BUT WE CAN FIX IT: CP, Box 19, Folder 17.

209 "I think you know how sad I am that 'Altered States' did not work out": CP, Box 11, Folder 15.

211 a "flaming cloud of gasses, hydrogen and helium": Chayefsky, *The Screenplays Vol. II*, pp. 256–57.

211 "He was sort of waiting for *us* to do something": "The Filming of Altered States," *Cinefantastique* 11, no. 2 (Fall 1981).

211 "He had the power to veto everything": Considine, *Mad as Hell*, p. 363.

212 CBS, which paid $5 million for three showings: *Variety*, June 1, 1977.

212 once contemplated the idea of replacing "bullshit" with "bullsoup": Val Adams, "Television Hopes to Go 'Network,'" *Daily News* (New York), Dec. 23, 1976.

212 "The use of BS is a focal point of the movie": "Taking Bed and Bawdy out of 'Network,'" *New York Daily Metro*, Sept. 26, 1978.

212 Principal photography for *Altered States* began on March 23, 1979: CP, Box 182, Folder 9.

212 "I was the 27th person they offered it to": "The Filming of Altered States."

213 Melnick helped get *Altered States* reinstated at Warner Bros.: Aljean Harmetz, "Melnick Production Unit Leaves Columbia for Fox," *New York Times*, Jan. 23, 1980.

213 "eight voluble academics gabble away": Chayefsky, *The Screenplays Vol. II*, pp. 248–49.

213 Almost immediately, Chayefsky and Russell disagreed: "The Filming of Altered States."

214 "the point where we have teetered into non-salvageable": CP, Box 60, Folder 5.

214 "you will be able to forestall a crisis": CP, Box 60, Folder 4.

215 "Paddy said to me, 'Howard, I can't work with him'": Author interview with Howard Gottfried, July 6, 2012.

215 "the marriage took Hollywood by surprise": "Actor Peter Finch's Widow, 41, Weds Young Hollywood Actor, Age 21," *Jet*, Oct. 18, 1979.

216 "eventually I fought my way back": "A New Start," *Parade*, Nov. 18, 1979.

216 Chayefsky attempted to send a check for $200 to the Gordonstoun school: CP, Box 96, Folder 7.

217 "Bill did more in his life, on and off the screen": Stefanie Powers, *One from the Hart* (New York: Gallery Books, 2010), p. 190; also Linda Charlton, "William Holden Dead at 63; Won Oscar for 'Stalag 17,'" *New York Times*, Nov. 17, 1981; and Andrew M. Brown, "When Alcoholics Drink Themselves to Death," *Telegraph* (London), Apr. 7, 2011.

217 "Faye Dunaway is doing the 'I want to be alone' bit": Page Six (column), *New York Post*, July 20, 1979.

217 the actress had been dropped from an upcoming cover of *Los Angeles* magazine: Jack Martin, "Faye's 'Too Fat' to Be Magazine's Cover-girl," *New York Post*, Aug. 22, 1979.

217 the closure of a troubled clothing store and antiques emporium: Jack Martin, "Pity Poor Old Faye: Nobody Wants to Buy Her Antiques," *New York Post*, Sept. 21, 1979.

218 "I really like things to be done right . . . I'm like Joan in that way": Peter Lester, "Faye Dunaway Surfaces with Sympathy for Joan Crawford Despite a Harrowing Movie Portrayal," *People*, Oct. 5, 1981.

218 "Dunaway starts neatly at each corner of the set in every scene": *Variety* review of *Mommie Dearest*, http://www.variety.com/review/VE1117793196?refcatid=31&printerfriendly=true.

218 "These scenes have been in the finished motion picture since it was released": CP, Box 96, Folder 4.

219 "I feel almost totally alienated from what's going on today": Ronald L. Davis, "Interview

with Paddy Chayefsky," Ronald L. Davis Oral History Collection, DeGolyer Library, Southern Methodist University, Dallas, TX.

220 "This one has everything: sex, violence, comedy, thrills, tenderness": Richard Corliss, "Cinema: Invasion of the Mind Snatcher," *Time*, Dec. 29, 1980.

220 "it is at least dependably—even exhilaratingly—bizarre": Janet Maslin, "Screen: Ken Russell's 'Altered States,'" *New York Times*, Dec. 25, 1980.

221 a historical drama about Alger Hiss: CP, Box 182, Folder 11. The drama would not have included Hiss, who was still alive at the time, due to concerns about defamation of character and invasion of privacy. But Whittaker Chambers would have appeared in the play, as would a fictional lover of Chambers's, called "Mr. X."

221 Some friends said this was not his natural hair: Considine, *Mad as Hell*, pp. 393–95.

221 On July 4 he was admitted for treatment: CP, Box 166, Folder 12.

221 "They weren't delusional or hallucinatory": Author interview with Dan Chayefsky. Mar. 1, 2013.

221 "I tried. I really tried": Considine, *Mad as Hell*, p. 396.

221 "I once read his palm when I was young": Author interview with Dan Chayefsky, Mar. 1, 2013.

222 "Our family has never taken death all that seriously": CP, Box 182, Folder 8.

222 Chayefsky's funeral service was held on August 4: Herbert Mitgang, "Chayefsky Praised for Passion in Exposing Life's Injustices," *New York Times,* Aug. 5, 1981.

223 "Paddy and I had a deal": Author interview with James L. Brooks, Nov. 9, 2012; and Martin Gottfried, *All His Jazz: The Life and Death of Bob Fosse* (New York: Bantam Books, 1990), pp. 405–6.

223 "I just hope the world lasts that long": John Brady, "We Were Writing for Criers, Not for Laughers," *American Film*, Dec. 1981.

8. It's All Going to Happen

224 "There will be soothsayers soon": Brady, *Craft of the Screenwriter*, p. 69.

226 "This tube is the most awesome goddam force in the whole godless world!": Chayefsky, *The Screenplays Vol. II*, p. 183.

226 "No predictor of the future—not even Orwell": Author interview with Aaron Sorkin, May 2, 2011.

226 "Chayefsky's warning was made to people who knew everything he said was true": Author interview with Peggy Noonan, Mar. 12, 2013.

227 "I have seen everything in that movie come true": Author interview with Keith Olbermann, Nov. 8, 2012.

227 First came the 1986 maneuvering by the sibling corporate titans: "Business People: Corporate Newsmakers of 1986; Tisch's Regimen Built Trimmer CBS," *New York Times*, Dec. 26, 1986.

227 when CBS fired 215 employees from its news department: Peter J. Boyer, "CBS's Tisch Responds," *New York Times*, Mar. 10, 1987.

227 "thirty million dollars bought you maybe sixty Walter Cronkites": Author interview with Keith Olbermann, Nov. 8, 2012.

228 his "urbane small talk" with Samuel Goldwyn, Eva Gabor, and Groucho Marx on *Per-*

son to Person: "Edward R. Murrow, Broadcaster and Ex-Chief of U.S.I.A., Dies," *New York Times*, Apr. 28, 1965.

228 "we've got to shout these truths in which we believe from the rooftops": Chris Matthews, "And That's the Way It Was: 'Cronkite,' a Biography by Douglas Brinkley," *New York Times*, July 6, 2012.

228 "we are not above climbing over the rubble each week to take an entertainment-size paycheck": Don Hewitt, *Tell Me a Story: Fifty Years and 60 Minutes in Television* (New York. PublicAffairs, 2001), p. 168.

229 abolished its long-standing Fairness Doctrine: Robert D. Hershey Jr., "F.C.C. Votes Down Fairness Doctrine in a 4–0 Decision," *New York Times*, Aug. 5, 1987.

229 "It was everyone's basic understanding . . . that the information business was a *business*": Author interview with Bill Wolff, Dec. 27, 2012.

229 "There's a segment of the viewing population which likes to either have their opinion validated": Author interview with Anderson Cooper, Nov. 13, 2012. Among broadcast journalists, Anderson Cooper has unique connections to *Network*: his mother, Gloria Vanderbilt, was married to Sidney Lumet from 1956 to 1963; the couple dated again briefly after the death of Wyatt Emory Cooper, Anderson Cooper's father, in 1978. Vanderbilt and Cooper are also cousins of Beatrice Straight.

230 "If I'm mad as hell and not going to take it anymore, I'm going to say that": Author interview with Bill O'Reilly, Dec. 12, 2012.

230 Glenn Beck . . . has claimed Howard Beale as an influence: Brian Stelter and Bill Carter, "Fox News's Mad, Apocalyptic, Tearful Rising Star," *New York Times*, Mar. 29, 2009.

231 "I thought, wow, none of those stories end well": Author interview with Stephen Colbert, May 12, 2011.

231 "it was three white, middle-aged guys saying what the news was": Author interview with Anderson Cooper, Nov. 13, 2012.

232 "I don't know what diversity there is": Author interview with Gwen Ifill, Dec. 18, 2012.

233 At the end of 2012, each of the three network programs: http://tvbythenumbers.zap2it .com/2012/12/04/world-news-slashes-total-viewing-gap-by-with-nbc-nightly-news-by -double-digits/160248/.

233 numbers that the cable competition simply cannot touch: http://www.mediabistro.com /tvnewser/the-top-cable-news-programs-in-november-2012-were_b156891.

233 "We ran *Countdown* several times on NBC": Author interview with Keith Olbermann, Nov. 8, 2012.

234 "There is still a tremendous appetite for straight, sober information": Author interview with Bill Wolff, Dec. 27, 2012.

234 "Chayefsky is chiding the audience": Author interview with Bill O'Reilly, Dec. 12, 2012.

235 "He looks like Liberace, in capes and everything": Author interview with Anderson Cooper, Nov. 13, 2012.

236 "It wasn't easy back in the seventies, and it's certainly not easy now": Author interview with Oliver Stone, Nov. 19, 2012.

237 "Could I imagine a great movie getting made today? Yeah": Author interview with James L. Brooks, Nov. 9, 2012.

239 "society was still really informed by that perspective on the world": Author interview with Ben Affleck, Jan. 21, 2013.
240 "we're not nearly as important as we think we are": Author interview with Bill Wolff, Dec. 27, 2012.
241 "the same award that was given to Paddy Chayefsky thirty-five years ago": Aaron Sorkin, Academy Awards speech, Feb. 27, 2011, http://www.youtube.com/watch?v=0VP5mFHl_lY.
241 "You wish Chayefsky could come back to life long enough to write *The Internet*": Author interview with Aaron Sorkin, May 2, 2011.
243 "You can't build for the future with nice, polite people": Logan, *Movie Stars, Real People, and Me*, p. 125.

Acknowledgments

Television, as someone once observed, may be a goddamned amusement park, but book publishing is serious business, and telling this remarkable story required the assistance of many people, to whom I am most grateful.

Jonathan Pace introduced me to the Paddy Chayefsky papers at the Billy Rose Theatre Division of the New York Public Library for the Performing Arts, and launched me on a cinematic and literary journey that continues after three years and counting. Kit Messick and Brad Campbell performed the invaluable service of cataloguing and processing the Chayefsky papers, and offered essential guidance at the outset of my research. Karen Nickeson, Annemarie van Roessel, Jeremy Megraw, and the staff of the New York Public Library for the Performing Arts consistently went above and beyond to facilitate my access to the Chayefsky papers and other archival materials.

Of everyone who shared their personal recollections with me, I am particularly indebted to Dan Chayefsky and Howard Gottfried, who were unfailingly generous with their time and their candor.

Owen Roizman bravely agreed to speak to me before I'd conducted any other interviews, and was crucial in connecting me to many more of his *Network* colleagues.

I am doubly obliged to Kay Chapin, who allowed me to review her *Network* production diary, and who taught me how to read a shooting script.

For offering their memories of Paddy Chayefsky, the making of *Network*, its era, and its aftermath, I thank: Ned Beatty, Warren Beatty, Arthur Burghardt, Jordan Charney, Francis Ford Coppola, Kathy Cronkite, Diana Finch-Braley, Mary Lynn Gottfried, Alan Heim, Barry Krost, Sherry Lansing, Shirley MacLaine, Mike Medavoy, Terry O'Neill, Tom Priestley Jr., Philip Rosenberg, Fred Schuler, Carol Serling, Maurice Spanbock, David Steinberg, Juliet Taylor, Richard Wald, Barbara Walters, and Marlene Warfield.

Michael Ginsburg added further dimensions of emotion and humanity to this story with his extraordinary photographs from the *Network* set.

Keith Olbermann was an especially energetic source of insights about the television news business and the prophetic genius of Paddy Chayefsky. I also suspect he knows the entire *Network* screenplay by heart.

For sharing their thoughts about the enduring influence of *Network*, I thank: Ben Affleck, James L. Brooks, Stephen Colbert, Anderson Cooper, Gwen Ifill, Peggy Noonan, Bill O'Reilly, Aaron Sorkin, Oliver Stone, and Bill Wolff.

For arranging interviews, connecting me to sources, and sharing ideas, materials, and conspiracy theories, thank you also: Susie Arons, Michael Barker, Anne Bell, Cindi Berger, Peter Biskind, Carrie Byalick, Leslee Dart, Patrick Farrell, Joy Fehily, Leslie Gimbel, Bill Hader, Simon Halls, Sean Howe, Lilith Jacobs, Melody Korenbrot, Matt Mayes, Deborah Miller, Stan Rosenfield, Shawn Sachs, Betsy Sharkey,

Shimrit Sheetrit, Lauren Skowronski, Jonathan Wald, Makeda Wubneh, Nicole Yavasile, and Mark Scott Zicree.

Tomoko Kawamoto, Barbara Miller, and the Museum of the Moving Image; Carrie Oman and the Paley Center for Media; and Jenny Romero and the Margaret Herrick Library of the Academy of Motion Picture Arts and Sciences were instrumental in providing documents and other resources.

Stephen Rubin turned a vague pitch about a collection of papers into the story of a man who made a movie that defined an era. Paul Golob, my extraordinary editor, worked with me every day to push me past my boundaries, and helped me accomplish something I didn't believe I was capable of achieving. Their colleagues at Times Books have been deeply supportive, especially Emi Ikkanda, Ellis Levine, Jenna Dolan, and Christopher O'Connell.

Daniel Greenberg, my tireless agent, encouraged all my ideas, no matter how far-fetched, then seized upon a genuinely good one. He and his staff at Levine Greenberg have never let anyone fuck with my distribution costs.

I cannot sufficiently convey my gratitude to Jonathan Landman, Sia Michel, Scott Veale, Alex Ward, and all my colleagues at the holy goddamn *New York Times*, who first gave me the opportunity to write about Paddy Chayefsky and *Network* in the pages of the world's greatest newspaper, and then allowed me to pursue this project to its fullest extent.

My wife and my family have all my love for teaching me that there is more to life than a 30 share and a 20 rating.

Index

About the Author

DAVE ITZKOFF is a culture reporter at *The New York Times*, where he writes regularly about film, television, theater, music, and popular culture. He has previously worked at *Spin*, *Maxim*, and *Details*, and his work has appeared in *GQ*, *Vanity Fair*, *Wired*, and other publications. He is the author of two previous books, *Cocaine's Son* and *Lads*. He lives in New York City.